10/29/9

D1234910

CATALOGUING

CATALOGUING

Eric J. Hunter MA FLA AMIET MIInfSc

and

K. G. B. Bakewell MA FLA MBIM MIInfSc

Third edition
revised and expanded by
Eric J. Hunter

LIBRARY ASSOCIATION PUBLISHING
LONDON
(A CLIVE BINGLEY BOOK)

Published by
Library Association Publishing Ltd
7 Ridgmount Street
London WC1E 7AE

First published 1979
Second edition 1983
This third revised edition 1991

British Library Cataloguing in Publication Data

Hunter, E. J.
    Cataloguing. — 3rd ed.
    I. Title   II. Bakewell, K. G. B.
    025.3

    ISBN 0-85157-467-X

Typeset in 11/12pt Times by Library Association Publishing Ltd
Printed and made in Great Britain by Billing & Sons Ltd, Worcester

Contents

Acknowledgements

This work could not have been written without the assistance and cooperation of a number of organizations, institutions and individuals.

I am grateful to the following for their help, advice and/or permission to reproduce material. A few of these acknowledgements are carried forward from the second edition but most relate to this new, third edition: Aurora High School, Ontario, Canada; Bibliothèque Nationale, France; Bibliotekstjänsts AB, Sweden; BLCMP Library Services Ltd, UK; British Library National Bibliographic Services; Cheshire Libraries, UK; CL Systems Inc, US; Clwyd Library Service, UK; DIALOG Information Services, US; Fretwell Downing, UK; H. W. Wilson Co, US; Learned Information, UK; Leicester Polytechnic Library, UK; Library of Congress; LIBRIS, Sweden; Liverpool Polytechnic Library; National Diet Library, Japan; National Library of Scotland; OCLC Online Computer Library Center Inc, US/UK; PICA, Netherlands; SLS (Information Systems) Ltd, UK; St Helens College Library, UK; University College of Wales Library; University of California Division of Library Automation; University of Hull Library, UK; University of Newcastle-upon-Tyne Library, UK; University of Stirling Library, UK; UTLAS International, Canada; WLN, US.

The individuals who have given valuable assistance include: Rushton Brandis (WLN); Alastair Bruce (Original Design); Rob Caley (Liverpool Polytechnic); Steve Cropper (St Helens College); Stewart Ede (British Library National Bibliographic Service); Laine Farley (University of California); Bernard Gallivan (National Library of Scotland); Peter Hilton (Fretwell Downing); Alan Jeffreys (University of Newcastle-upon-Tyne); Cynthia McKinley (British Library National Bibliographic Service); Ian Mowat (University of Hull); Carol Raper (Liverpool Polytechnic); Lawrence Rawsthorne (Clwyd Library Service); Glyn Rowland (Liverpool Polytechnic); Bruce Royan (University of Stirling); Audrey Taylor (Aurora High School); Keith Trickey (Liverpool Polytechnic); Ben Tucker (Library of Congress); Tina van Zellar (OCLC); Terry Willan (BLCMP). Other people, some of whom are connected with the organizations and institutions noted in the second paragraph above, helped in a variety of ways and my thanks are also due to them although it is impractical to mention all by name.

Author's note

Developments in cataloguing are taking place at such speed that, inevitably, any work dealing with the subject is dated in some respects as soon as it is written. For example, libraries and other cataloguing agencies may well have teams of programmers constantly improving their software and therefore the computer screen displays associated with the various cataloguing systems are continually changing. Apologies are offered, in advance, for any omissions or errors but it is hoped that this will not detract from the work's general aim of providing an introductory overview of the current cataloguing scene. It is stressed that examples cited in the text are intended merely as illustrations of a wide range of activity. It should also be noted that reproductions of screen formats are not necessarily to scale, although display layouts do conform to the originals.

Because textbooks cannot possibly keep pace with progress, it is essential to read professional journals. A select list of some of the periodicals consulted whilst this work was being prepared is given below. It will be seen that this list includes not only dedicated cataloguing journals but also publications which relate to automation and more general periodicals which often contain news and information which is of relevance to the cataloguer.

American libraries   American Library Association. Monthly/Bi-monthly.
Aslib proceedings   Monthly.
BLAISE-LINE newsletter   British Library National Bibliographic Service.
   6 times a year.
Cataloging and classification quarterly   Haworth.
Catalogue and index   Library Association Cataloguing and Indexing Group.
   Quarterly.
CD-ROM librarian   Meckler. Monthly except Jul/Aug.
Electronic library   Learned information. 6 times a year.
The indexer   Society of Indexers and the affiliated American, Australian
   and Canadian Societies. Twice a year.

Information bulletin Library of Congress. Bi-weekly.

Information processing and management Pergamon. Bi-monthly.

Information retrieval and library automation Lomond Systems Inc. Monthly.

Information technology and libraries Library and Information Technology Association, a division of the American Library Association. Quarterly.

International cataloguing and bibliographic control IFLA UBCIM Programme. Quarterly.

Library journal Bowker. 21 times a year.

Library resources and technical services Association for Library Collections and Technical Services, a division of the American Library Association. Quarterly.

Library technology reports American Library Association. 6 times a year.

Program Aslib. Quarterly.

Select: National Bibliographic Service newsletter British Library National Bibliographic Service. 3 times a year.

Technical services quarterly Haworth.

VINE: a Very Informal NEwsletter of library automation Library and Information Technology Centre, Polytechnic of Central London. At least 4 times a year.

Wilson library bulletin H. W. Wilson. Monthly except Jul/Aug.

Abbreviations and acronyms used

AA 1908	Anglo-American cataloguing code 1908
AACR	Anglo-American cataloguing rules
AACR 2	Anglo-American cataloguing rules 2nd ed. 1988 revision
ABN	Australian Bibliographic Network
AKWIC	Author and KeyWord In Context
ALA	American Library Association
ANB	Australian National Bibliography
APIF	Automated Process Information File
ASCII	American Standard Code for Information Interchange
ASI	Articulated Subject Index
ASSASSIN	Agricultural System for Storage And Subsequent Selection of INformation
AUSMARC	AUStralian MARC
AVMARC	Audio-Visual MARC
BALLOTS	Bibliographic Automation of Large Library Operations using a Time-sharing System
BEDIS	Book Trade Electronic Data Interchange Standards
BL	British Library
BLAISE	British Library Automated Information SErvice
BLCMP	formerly Birmingham Libraries Cooperative Mechanization Project
BLDSC	British Library Document Supply Centre
BLISS	British Library Information Sciences Service
BLMARC	British Library MARC, ie UKMARC
BLNBS	British Library National Bibliographic Service
BNB	British National Bibliography
BNBMARC	British National Bibliography MARC, ie UKMARC
BOSS	BLCMP Online Support Service
BUMS	Bibliotekstjänsts Utlanings-och Mediakontroll System

CAG	Cooperative Automation Group
CANMARC	CANadian MARC
CATSS	CATalog Support System of UTLAS
CBI	Cumulative Book Index
CD-I	Compact Disc-Interactive
CD-ROM	Compact Disc-Read Only Memory
CIFC	Centre for InterFilm Comparison
CIG	Cataloguing and Indexing Group of the Library Association
CIP	Cataloguing-in-Publication
CLAIM	Centre for Library and Information Management
CLR	Council on Library Resources
CLRU	Cambridge Language Research Unit
COM	Computer Output Microform
COMARC	COoperative MARC
COMPASS	COMPuter Aided Subject System
COMPENDEX	COMPuterized ENgineering inDEX
CONSER	Cooperative ONline SERials
COPOL	Council Of POlytechnic Libraries
CPM	Critical Path Method
DALNET	Detroit Area Library NETwork
DATASTAR	DATA STorage And Retrieval
DBMS	DataBase Management System
DC	[Dewey] Decimal Classification
DIANE	Direct Information Access Network for Europe
EARN	European Academic Research Network
EEC	European Economic Community
EMMA	Extra MARC MAterial
EPSILON	Evaluation of Printed Subject Indexes by Laboratory investigatiON
ERIC	Educational Resources Information Centre
ESA-IRS	European Space Agency-Information Retrieval System
ESTC	Eighteenth century Short Title Catalogue
EURONET	EUROpean NETwork system
GLIS	Geac Library Information Systems
GMD	General Material Designation
HMSO	Her Majesty's Stationery Office
IBM PC	IBM (International Business Machines) Personal Computer
ICCP	International Conference on Cataloguing Principles
IFLA	International Federation of Library Associations and institutions
IPSS	International Packet Switching Service
ISBD(G)	International Standard Bibliographic Description (General) − *also*

	ISBD(A)	Antiquarian books
	ISBD(CF)	Computer Files
	ISBD(CM)	Cartographic Materials
	ISBD(M)	Monographs
	ISBD(NBM)	Non-Book Materials
	ISBD(PM)	Printed Music
	ISBD(S)	Serials
ISBN	International Standard Book Number	
ISI	Institute for Scientific Information	
ISO	International Organisation for Standardization	
ISSN	International Standard Serial Number	
ISTC	Incunable Short Title Catalogue	
J-BISC	Japan MARC on disc	
JANET	Joint Academic NETwork	
JSC	Joint Steering Committee [for revision of AACR]	
KWAC	KeyWord And Context	
KWOC	KeyWord Out-of Context	
LA	Library Association	
LASER	London And South Eastern Region	
LC	Library of Congress	
LCSH	Library of Congress Subject Headings	
LIBRIS	LIBRary Information Service	
LOCAS	LOcal CAtaloguing Service	
LSP	Linked Systems Project	
MARC	MAchine Readable Catalogue	
MBO	Management By Objectives	
MEDLARS	MEDical Literature Analysis and Retrieval System	
MEDLINE	MEDlars onLINE	
MeSH	MEdical Subject Headings	
MOPSI	Manual On Printed Subject Indexes	
MRAP	Management Review and Analysis Program	
MUG	MARC Users Group	
MUMS	Multiple Use MARC System	
NACO	Name Authority COoperative	
NACSIS	National Center for Science Information Systems	
NAF	Name Authority File	
NAFS	Name Authority File Service	
NCLIS	National Commission on Libraries and Information Science	
NEPHIS	NEsted PHase Indexing System	
NLM	National Library of Medicine	
NOTIS	Northwestern Online Totally Integrated System	
NSDC	National Serials Data Centre	
NTIS	National Technical Information Service	
NUC	National Union Catalog	

OCLC	formerly Ohio College Library Center (now Online Computer Library Center Inc)
OPAC	Online Public Access Catalogue
OSI	Open Systems Interconnection
OSTI	Office for Scientific and Technical Information
PAC	Public Access Catalogue
PERT	Program Evaluation and Review Technique
PICA	Project for Integrated Cataloguing Automation
POPSI	POstulate-based Permuted Subject Indexing
PSS	Packet Switching Service
PRECIS	PREserved Context Index System
REMARC	REtrospective MARC
RLG	Research Libraries Group
RLIN	Research Libraries Information Network
ROM	Read Only Memory
RTSD	Resources and Technical Services Division of ALA
SCOLCAP	SCOttish Libraries Cooperative Automation Project (now defunct)
SCONUL	Standing Conference On National and University Libraries
SCORPIO	Subject Content Oriented Retriever for Processing Information Online
SDC	System Development Corporation
SLIC	Selective Listing In Combination
SNI	Standard Network Interconnection
SOLINET	SOuth eastern LIbrary NETwork
SWALCAP	South Western Academic Libraries Cooperative Automation Project (now SLS)
UBC	Universal Bibliographic Control
UBCIM	Universal Bibliographic Control and International MARC
UDC	Universal Decimal Classification
UKLDS	United Kingdom Library Database System
UKMARC	United Kingdom MARC
UKOP	United Kingdom Official Publications [CD-ROM]
UNESCO	United Nations Educational, Scientific and Cultural Organisation
UNIMARC	UNIversal MARC format
USBC	Universal Standard Bibliographic Code
UTLAS	formerly University of Toronto Library Automation System
VDU	Visual Display Unit
VISCOUNT	Viewdata and Inter-library Systems COmmUnication NETwork
VTLS	Virginia Tech Library System

WADEX	Word and Author inDEX
WLN	formerly Washington Library Network and then Western Library Network
WORM	Write Once Read Many Times [optical disc]

Glossary

In this glossary are defined selected terms which are also explained in the text and some other terms which are not referred to in the text but for which the cataloguer may at some time require an explanation. The glossary is not intended to be exhaustive.

Access point: a term under which an item is likely to be sought in a catalogue or bibliography.

Access time: the time taken by a computer system to retrieve requested data or information.

Accession number: a sequential number allocated to an item when it is added to stock.

Acronymic key: *See* Derived key

Added entry: any entry in a catalogue other than the main entry.

Alphabtico-classed catalogue: a subject catalogue consisting of alphabetically arranged broad subject headings with alphabetically arranged subdivisions.

Alternative headings: a system of cataloguing whereby each heading is added in turn above the description and the entries are regarded as of equal status rather than one being designated 'main entry' and the others 'added entries'.

Analog: the representation of data by measurements, e.g. voltages. Sound was usually encoded in this way before the advent of the digital (q.v.) disc.

Analysis: 'the process of preparing a bibliographic record which describes a part or parts of a larger item' (AACR 2).

Analytical entry: an entry in a catalogue or bibliography for part of an item for which a comprehensive entry has been made.

Anonymous: of unknown authorship.

Area of description: a section of the description of an item dealing with a particular category such as 'title and statement of responsibility' or 'publication, distribution, etc.'

Artificial language: a set of items (e.g. subject headings lists, thesauri) or letters/digits (e.g. classification notation) specially compiled to represent the subject content of items in a catalogue or index, as opposed to the *natural language* which a user might be expected to use in everyday speech.

ASCII: in order that text, e.g. catalogue entries, may be processed by a computer, each character or other symbol must be represented by a number. ASCII, or the American Standard Code for Information Interchange, is a common method of ranking characters in a numeric order of value.

Author: the person chiefly responsible for the creation of the intellectual or artistic content of a work.

Authority control: connects the various forms of names or subject terms within a catalogue. *See also* Authority file.

Authority file: a file which indicates the accepted form of an access point (q.v.). When, in a particular catalogue, it is established that Beethoven, Ludwig van is always entered in that way and never as Van Beethoven, Ludwig, an *authority file* is being established. In such a file, the references which should be made from alternative forms of the name should also be indicated.

Backup: to make a reserve copy of data or a file held in machine-readable (q.v.) form.

Batch processing: jobs held back until there are sufficient to process in a group or batch. *See also* Offline.

Baud: a measurement of the speed at which data can be transmitted by a terminal (q.v.). Slow terminals operate at speeds up to 300 baud, faster terminals at 1,200 baud or even more. A baud can be roughly equated to one bit per second which means that 300 baud is approximately 30 characters per second.

Bibliographic utility: an agency which assumes responsibility for the production of cataloguing data which is then made available, together with other services, e.g. retrospective conversion, etc., to any library willing to pay the related subscription(s) or other costs. Such utilities may be profit or non-profit making.

Bibliography: a list of documents and other materials.

Binary system: a numbering system with a base of two which when written appears as a series of 0's and 1's. The computer can only 'recognize' two states 'on' or 'off', i.e. a 'pulse' or 'no pulse', a 'hole' or 'no hole'. The binary system therefore forms the basis of computer operation. A **binary digit** is one of the characters from the set 0 and 1. A binary digit is also known as a **bit**.

Bit: a binary digit. *See under* Binary system.

Book number: similar to call number (q.v.).

Boolean logic: an information retrieval, the use of the Boolean operators AND, OR or NOT to combine search terms in order to produce a more precise statement of the search requirement.

Boot: to start up a computer system.

Byte: the number of bits (q.v.) needed to store a single character (usually eight). Computer storage capacity is often presented in terms of bytes, e.g. 640K = 640,000 bytes (K being roughly equal to one thousand). A 30 megabyte disc will hold 30 million bytes or characters. A CD-ROM will hold 550 megabytes.

Call number: a unique identifier for a particular item, which usually comprises the classification number together with an alphabetical code identifying the responsible person/body (or the title for works entered in that way).

Catalogue: a list of documents and other materials in a collection or collections.

Cataloguing-in-publication: the provision of cataloguing information within a published document. CIP data may also appear in machine-readable form to give early warning of the document's publication, e.g. in an online database.

Character string: a sequence of characters, e.g.: 'computer', or 'comput', or 'PR5647', or '823.91'.

Citation: a bibliographical reference.

Classified catalogue: a subject catalogue arranged in systematic order, normally that of the classification scheme used for the shelf arrangement of a library.

Command mode: a method in which the user interacts with a computer system by entering appropriate commands, e.g. FIND or DISPLAY.

Communication format: *See* Exchange format.

Compact disc: Compact Disc-Read Only Memory (CD-ROM) is a small, digital, optical disc (*See* Optical disc system) which can store enormous amounts of datas (550 megabytes on one 4¾ inch diameter disc). It is primarily used as a publishing medium for the distribution of machine-readable reference works, databases, cataloguing data, etc. The 'read only' feature is a disadvantage but other types of compact disc, e.g. WORM (Write Once Read Many times) and eraseable re-writable discs are now available. A further evolution of CD-ROM is CD-I (Compact Disc-Interactive), which provides a complete format for the interactive handling of music and sound, speech, computer data and programs, graphics, still and animated pictures.

Component part: any document that for the purpose of bibliographic identification or access requires reference to a host document of which it forms a part. Examples of component parts include articles in journals, individual papers in conference proceedings or symposia, and music scores issued with sound recordings.

Computer: an electronic machine capable of receiving, storing, processing and presenting data such as entries in a catalogue.

Connect time: the amount of time that elapses whilst a user is connected online (q.v.) to a computer system.

Control number: a unique number used to identify an item, e.g. the ISBN (q.v.), or an LC (Library of Congress) or BNB (British National Bibliography) number.

Corporate body: 'an organization or group of persons that is identified by a particular name and that acts, or may act, as an entity. Typical examples of corporate bodies are associations, institutions, business firms, non-profit enterprises, governments, government agencies, religious bodies, local churches and conferences' (AACR 2).

Cost-benefit analysis: a consideration of the *cost* of an activity in relation to the value or *benefit* of that activity.

Critical path: in network analysis (q.v.) the *critical path* refers to the critical jobs or activities which control the completion date of an overall project.

Data: the information to be processed by the computer.

Database: a collection of records (q.v.) is referred to as a file (q.v.) and a database consists of one or more files.

Dedicated line: a telephone line which is reserved for the connection of a terminal directly to a computer.

Default: a predetermined value or option automatically assumed by the machine when none has been supplied by the operator.

Derived key: a search key formed from the characters in a particular field in a record, e.g. HUNT,ERI,J could be a coded '4,3,1' key for HUNTER, ERIC J. derived from an author field.

Descriptor: an index term used to 'describe' the subject content of a document.

Diagnostic: printout from the computer for checking.

Dictionary catalogue: a catalogue in which entries under authors, titles and subjects are arranged in one alphabetical sequence. When subject entries are separated from other entries then the result is referred to as a 'divided' catalogue.

Digital: the representation of data by digital numbers, usually binary digits, i.e. 0 or 1.

Display format: the format in which a record is displayed on the computer screen or printed out in hard copy.

Distributed catalogue: a system in which the catalogue is made available at numerous remote locations, thus placing the data nearer to the user. The online (q.v.) catalogue offers great potential in this area, with access being possible even from the comfort of one's own home. CD-ROM also facilitates the placing of catalogues in various locations.

Divided catalogue: *See under* Dictionary catalogue.

Down: a computer is said to be 'down' when it ceases to function for some reason.

Download: to capture data online from a remote host computer and transfer it to the store of an in-house stand-alone system, e.g. a microcomputer, for processing. This can save connect and telecommunication costs. The reverse is to **upload**.

Dumb terminal: opposite of intelligent terminal (q.v.)

Entry:details relating to an item entered in a catalogue. *See also* Record.

Ergonomics:the relationship between the worker, his environment, and the equipment he uses.

Exchange format: a standard format which can be used by different cataloguing agencies for the exchange of records. Usually relates to a machine-readable format.

Exhaustivity: the extent to which the subject content of a document is analysed by the indexer.

Expert system: a computer system which acts in a similar way to a human expert in a particular subject field.

Extent: the part of the physical description area of a catalogue entry relating to the number of pages or parts, dimensions, etc.

Extra-MARC material: records created by outside agencies input to MARC databases.

Field: a subdivision of a record, e.g. the title of an item in a cataloguing record.

File: a collection of related and usually similar constructed records treated as a unit, e.g. the catalogue of a library. A database (q.v.) may consist of one or more files.

Fixed field: a field of a specified length, i.e. limited to a certain number of characters.

Form: (1) a printed form with blank areas to be filled in by the user. (2) a computer screen laid out and completed in a similar way.

Format: the arrangement or presentation of data in a machine-readable record. In a more general sense, any physical presentation of an item.

Free text searching: searching a field or entire record not by the full content of a field but by significant character strings or terms. For example, the search term might be found in a field containing an abstract of an item.

Full text database: a database which contains the full text of a document or documents rather than bibliographic citations.

General material designation: the indication in a catalogue entry of the broad class of material to which an item belongs.

Hard copy: eye-readable output on paper, card, etc.

Hard disc: a rigid disc fixed permanently into a disc drive. An efficient method of storing large amounts of programs and data.

Hardware: the physical components of a computer system.

Heading: a name or word or (in a classified catalogue) notation placed at the head of an entry in a catalogue or bibliography to provide an access point.

Hit: the finding of a record which matches a search request.

Host: a main computer, being accessed via terminals (q.v.) and/or mini/micro-computers.

Host document: a document containing component parts (q.v.) which require individual description.

Housekeeping: looking after a particular system.

Human engineering: *See* Ergonomics.

Hypertext: a method of presentation of information which reflects the manner in which the user of the information system might wish to browse rather than the more usual linear pattern of searching. For example, choosing a particular bird from a database of birds could provide the user with a picture of a bird and its habitat and a soundtrack of its song. Another option would let the user see a map of its range or an animation of its flight pattern.

Input: the data to be read into a computer system *or* the process of reading the data into the system.

Intelligent terminal: a terminal (q.v.) equipped with a separate data processing capability.

Inter-library comparisons: comparison of cost and other data in libraries with a view to assessing and improving efficiency.

Interactive: a mode of online (q.v.) interaction between the user and a computer system.

Interface: the connection between two systems or two parts of the same system.

International standard book number: a unique number allocated to each *book* published so that computerization in the book trade is facilitated.

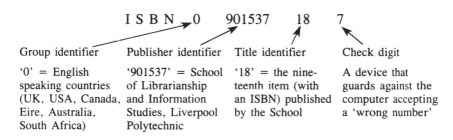

Group identifier	Publisher identifier	Title identifier	Check digit
'0' = English speaking countries (UK, USA, Canada, Eire, Australia, South Africa)	'901537' = School of Librarianship and Information Studies, Liverpool Polytechnic	'18' = the nineteenth item (with an ISBN) published by the School	A device that guards against the computer accepting a 'wrong number'

International standard serial number: a unique number allocated to a serial.

Inverted file: a sequential, e.g. alphabetical, index of some or all of the various fields in the records of a file, e.g. an alphabetical author index.

Key title: a unique name assigned to a serial by the International Serials Data System.

Keyword: similar to character string (q.v.) but usually comprises a complete word, e.g.: 'computers' is a keyword in the title *Using computers*.

Known item search: a search for an item of which the bibliographic details are known.

Limited cataloguing: a generic term covering selective cataloguing (q.v.) and simplified cataloguing (q.v.)

Logical operators: *See under* Boolean logic.

Logon/Logoff: the procedure for gaining access to or leaving a host computer system.

Machine-readable: a record capable of being read by a machine, normally a computer.

Main entry: the principal entry in a catalogue, containing the fullest information.

Management by exception: a management technique whereby only exceptional issues are referred to higher management and others are dealt with according to precise instructions or general principles in accordance with an organization's objectives.

Management by objectives: a management technique which involves formulating objectives, setting realistic targets to allow these objectives to be met, and identifying and removing any obstacles to the achievement of these targets. The objectives should be regularly and systematically reviewed.

Material (or type of publication) specific details area: in AACR 2, a special area of the description which is only used for cartographic materials, computer files, music and serials. In the case of computer files, for example, it is a file designation area, e.g.: 'Computer data (1 file : 150,000 records)'.

Menu: a system of operation in which the user is offered a series of options, i.e. a 'menu'.

Mixed responsibility: a work is said to be of mixed responsibility when different persons or corporate bodies have made different kinds of intellectual contribution, e.g. a work containing text and illustrations or words and music.

Modem: the linking device between a terminal and a telephone line; the signal transmitted over the line is converted into a form suitable for the terminal and vice versa. 'Modem' is a contraction of 'modulator-demodulator'.

Mouse: a device which facilitates movement of a cursor over a computer screen and which provides control over certain operations. Moving the mouse over the desktop also moves the cursor and pressing buttons on the mouse will activate system functions.

Multi-access: access provided to more than one user at the same time.

Name catalogue: a catalogue which contains entries for works by and about persons and/or corporate bodies and/or places.

Natural language: the opposite of Artificial language (q.v.).

Network: in library and information science a group of libraries and/or information service points connected together for the purpose of satisfying specified requirements. This might include the derivation or exchange of cataloguing information. Also refers to a system of inter-connected computers and other devices.

Network analysis: a generic term referring to a group of related techniques for use in the planning and control of complex projects. The best known of the many network analysis techniques are critical path method (CPM) and program evaluation and review technique (PERT). These techniques may be used in library management for such projects as recataloguing and reclassification.

Offline: relates to 'batch mode', operating without direct and continuous communication with the main computer system. *See also* Online.

Online: a system in which there is direct communication with the processing unit of a computer, allowing a user to interact with the computer and receive an almost immediate response to a message or instruction. Online is to offline as the telephone is to the postal service. *See also* Offline.

Operating system: the set of internal programs which make up the control system of the computer. Only when an operating system is loaded does the computer become 'alive' and usable by other packages such as word processors, database management systems, etc.

Optical character recognition: a method by which printed characters can be 'read' by a computer; a light-sensitive machine converts the print into electrical impulses which can be stored in machine-readable form.

Optical disc system: a system which uses discs which are written or read by a laser beam, the narrowest form of read/write head currently available.

Other title information: any title other than a title proper or parallel title, including a subtitle and any phrase used with a title to convey an item's character, contents or purpose.

Output: the data transferred from the computer system to the user *or* the process of transferring the data.

Packet switching: the transmission of messages through a communication network.

Parallel title: the title proper of an item in another language or script.

Peripherals: input and output devices, backing store, etc. of a computer system.

Physical description area: an area of the description containing such information as number of pages or parts, specific material designation, running time and dimensions.

Post-coordinate indexing: a system of indexing in which a compound subject is analysed into its basic concepts by the indexer but these concepts are not combined until the search stage.

Pre-coordinate indexing: a system of indexing in which a compound subject is analysed into its basic elements by the indexer, who then combines these elements in a predetermined order. Examples are entries in conventional classified and alphabetical subject catalogues.

Precision: a measure of the relative efficiency of a system by a comparison of the number of *relevant* documents retrieved with the *total* number of documents, relevant or irrelevant, produced by the search.

Principal author: the main author in a work of shared responsibility.

Program: a sequence of instructions to enable the computer to carry out a particular task.

Pseudonym: an assumed name used by an author.

Query language: a specific method of formulating searches in a computer system.

Real time: computer operations keeping pace with the process. For example, in the process of landing an aircraft 'blind', conditions constantly change and it must be possible for the necessary changes in the aircraft controls to be computed and a correction applied in time for this to be of value.

Recall: the number of documents produced in answer to an enquiry which are relevant to the user's requirements.

Record: the complete set of information relating to a particular item in a file. Each record consists of one or more fields.

Reference: a direction from a heading which is not used in a catalogue or index to one which is used ('see' reference) or from a heading which is used to a related heading ('see also' reference).

Related work: a work which has some relationship to another work, such as an index or a concordance.

Relational database: a type of database in which data manipulation commands relate records in different files on the basis of data values.

Relational operator: a symbol representing 'greater than', 'less than', or 'equal to', i.e. >, <, or =.

Remote access: access to a computer by means of a terminal which may be located some distance away.

Report format: *See* Display format.

Response time: the time taken by the system to respond to the user.

Scope note: an explanatory note indicating the way in which a term is used in a thesaurus.

Selective cataloguing: the omission of catalogue entries for certain items or the use of simplified cataloguing (q.v.) for some material.

Shared responsibility: a work of shared responsibility is one in which two or more persons or corporate bodies have collaborated to perform the same kind of activity.

Simplified cataloguing: overall simplification of catalogue entries within a library system, e.g. by using initials instead of full names of personal authors of by omitting parts of the physical description area.

Software: the programs used to instruct the computer and the other associated documentation.

Specific material designation: a term indicating the precise class of material to which an item belongs. For example 'sound cartridge' and 'sound disc' are specific material designations within the general material designation 'sound recording'.

Specificity: the degree to which an information system allows the exact subject to be specified.

Standard number: a number which uniquely identifies an item, such as an International Standard Book Number (ISBN) or International Standard Serial Number (ISSN).

Statement of responsibility: the statement of person(s) responsible for the intellectual content of an item, corporate body(ies) from which the item emanates or person(s) or body(ies) responsible for the performance of an item.

Tag: a symbol used to identify a particular field or other element in a record.

Terminal: a device used to communicate with a computer system.

Terms of availability: details of the price or hire terms of an item or other information regarding its availability.

Thesaurus: a list of terms for use in an indexing system.

Title proper: the chief title of an item.

Tracing: an indication of the headings under which details relating to an item are entered in a catalogue.

Truncation: use of part of a word or phrase when searching. For example, a search for 'comput' would retrieve 'computers', or 'computing', or 'computerization', etc. (right or back truncation) or a search for 'liott' would retrieve 'Elliott', or 'Eliott' (left or front truncation).

Turnkey package: a complete computer system comprising hardware and software (q.v.) together with service and support.

Uniform title: a title by which an item which has appeared under varying titles is identified for cataloguing purposes. Also, a collective title used to collocate complete works, selections, etc., of an author or composer.

Unit entry: an entry for a document which, with or without the addition of an appropriate heading, may be used for entries under all access points. *See also* Alternative headings.

Universal Standard Bibliographic Code (USBC): a short, fixed length code which provides a unique identifier for a record. It is derived from the *content* of the record, i.e. date, title, volume/edition, and pagination, and is related to the MARC format, athough the principle could be applied to any sort of record provided the fields are tagged.

User-friendliness: the ability of a computer to allow interaction with a user without difficulty for the user.

Variable length field: a field which may contain a varying number of characters; its beginning and end must be indicated by specified tags.

Visual display unit: a unit used to display data from a computer on to a screen.

Word processor: a computer used to facilitate the setting up, manipulation, editing and correcting of text, where this text may be an article, report, letter, etc. or possibly a series of catalogue entries.

Chapter 1
Catalogues and bibliographies

Definitions and purpose

A *catalogue* is a list of, and index to, a collection of books and/or other materials. It enables the user to discover:

what material is present in the collection

where this material may be found.

The 'collection' may relate to one or a number of libraries or information service points. In the latter case, the catalogue is termed a *union catalogue*.

The catalogue has much in common with the *bibliography*, which is also a list of books and/or other material. The same principles are applied to their compilation and they are used interchangeably. For example, the British Museum *General catalogue of printed books* or the various Library of Congress catalogues also act as important bibliographies. The latter represent the most comprehensive current bibliographic service in the world to English-speaking countries but they are still the catalogues of a specific collection. The pure bibliography is not an index to a specific collection but simply a list of books and/or other materials within some restricted field, since it would clearly be impossible to list *all* materials from *all* countries and *all* periods on *all* subjects. Examples of the restriction or limitation are *geographical* (e.g. *The British national bibliography* aims to cover all books with a British imprint); *language* (e.g. *The cumulative book index* tries to list all books in the English language); *subject* (e.g. *Bibliography of cricket*) and *physical form* (e.g. *The British national film and video catalogue*).

To illustrate the affiity between catalogues and bibliographies, shown below is a catalogue entry for a piece of printed music:

> ADLER, Samuel
>   Canto VII : tuba solo / Samuel Adler. —
> New York : Boosey & Hawkes, c1974.
>   11 p. of music ; 30 cm.
>   M97

1

Finding this entry will inform the catalogue user immediately that the particular item is present in the collection indexed and it will at the same time also reveal a great deal about the item, e.g. the title, the composer, the publisher, the date, the number of pages and the size. Not only this but it will reveal the location of the item on the shelves, i.e. the number at which it is classified: M97.

This entry could also be used, without amendment, in a bibliography, although there might not be any need to include the classification number and, on the other hand, further detail such as the price of the item might be required. Nevertheless the close relationship between the entry as used in a catalogue and the entry as used in a bibliography is obvious.

The art (or perhaps it should be the science) of *cataloguing* therefore relates to both catalogues and bibliographies. It is the art of describing and listing material in such a way as to make it as easy as possible to discover the nature and extent of what is available and, if appropriate, where this material may be located or obtained.

The cataloguing process and the role of technology

Contemporary society has experienced an extraordinary explosion in knowledge: this has resulted in a corresponding increase in the publication of books and other materials which act as information carriers. In general terms, without the aid of technology it is now impractical, if not impossible, to ascertain what material exists and where it may be obtained. Production of the *British national bibliography*, for instance, has been computerized for many years. More specifically, in the case of a particular library or information service, technology can be of considerable help in aiding and improving cataloguing techniques and efficiency.

The cataloguing process basically consists of two operations: first, the creation of the appropriate entry relating to a particular item and, second, the subsequent manipulation of this and other entries to form the actual catalogue.

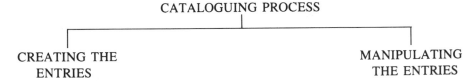

CATALOGUING PROCESS

CREATING THE
ENTRIES

MANIPULATING
THE ENTRIES

The computer cannot replace the first of these, that intellectual element which only a human being can, at present, supply. The creation of a catalogue entry involves the answering of questions such as: What is the title of the item? Which person or body is responsible for its content? Who published it? When was it published? and so on. Questions such as these cannot be answered by a machine, which could not, for instance, distinguish between an author, e.g. Charles Dickens, and a title, e.g. David Copperfield.

However, the computer *is* capable of performing the various clerical functions involved in the manipulation of entries. For example, the computer can quickly *sort* catalogue entries into any desired order, or *search* for entries which conform to a particular search profile. And the search facility that can be provided is a much more powerful one than would be possible in a manual index.

Because the computer can rearrange entries into any desired order, it may be used as a means of producing a catalogue or bibliography in 'hard' copy, i.e. 'printed' onto paper or film. However, it is becoming far more common to use 'online' access, i.e. the catalogue entries are stored within the machine and searched for and displayed as necessitated by the requirements of a user.

Functions of a catalogue

Cutter[1] defined the functions of a library catalogue more than 100 years ago; he said that it should:

1 enable a person to find a book of which either:
    the author ⎫
    the title ⎬ is known
    the subject ⎭
2 show what the library has:
    by a given author
    on a given subject
    in a given kind of literature
3 assist in the choice of a book:
    as to its edition
    as to its character (literary or topical).

These objectives still hold good today, but the word 'book' should be replaced by 'item' or 'document' and the word 'author' should be replaced by 'responsible person or body'. This is because librarians are now concerned with far more than the printed word, e.g. audio and video recordings, microforms, computer files, etc. One British library service, that of the Inner London Education Authority,[2] used the word 'materiography' rather than 'bibliography' for the subject lists which it made available to school libraries.

Further, it should be noted that today's computerized catalogues and bibliographies can offer a far more flexible search facility than Cutter could ever have envisaged. For example, the user may need to know only part of an author, or part of a title, in order to find a particular entry.

The place of cataloguing in the library

Cataloguing must not be considered a self-contained unit; the relationship

---

[1] *Rules for a dictionary catalog* / Charles A. Cutter. — 4th ed. — Washington : GPO, 1904.
[2] ILEA no longer exists; responsibility has reverted to the individual local authorities.

with bibliographies has already been stressed for example. There are also obvious links between cataloguing and classification; the same mental process must take place when deciding on the subject of an item, whether this is described in alphabetical terms or by a classification number. In addition, the catalogue can form the basis of an integrated system with ordering, acquisition and circulation control modules. Indeed, when the computerization of the cataloguing process is being planned, it should not be considered in isolation but as part of a larger entity.

Is the catalogue indispensable?

Not everyone regards the catalogue as an essential tool. D. J. Urquhart showed, for instance, how effectively the National Lending Library for Science and Technology (now the British Library Document Supply Centre) in its early days could be administered without a catalogue. It is seen by some people as a sacred cow and, in the 1960s, Grose and Line[1] referred to it as a white elephant!

Certainly there are many more keys to unlock the doors of knowledge in the form of bibliographies, indexes and databases, and library users can find out very quickly via a computer terminal what is available, in global terms, in any subject field. But what they so often want to know is whether a particular item is available in their particular library, whether it be public, academic or special. Most readers want subject arrangement in the library, so that they can browse, and this means that a catalogue is desirable to show not only what is available but also where it is shelved. The descriptive part of the catalogue entry will help the user to decide whether an item not immediately available is likely to be relevant.

There are other reasons for maintaining a library catalogue. It can provide *analytical entries* for parts of an item (see Chapter 8) and it can record *all* items in a library's stock, acting as a valuable supplement to published bibliographic tools. At present, bibliographical control of English and American books and periodical articles is excellent but this is by no means true of, for instance, report literature, semi-published material and the many forms of non-book media.

---

[1] On the construction and care of white elephants / M. W. Grose and M. B. Line, *Library Association record* 70 (1) Jan. 1968 2−5.

Chapter 2
History

The history of cataloguing can be a fascinating study. One early catalogue, that of a collection of books given by Gregory the Great to the Church of St Clement in Rome in the eighth century AD, was written in the form of a prayer; another, Alcuin's metrical catalogue produced for the monastic library at York, is the only catalogue known to have been written in verse! Unfortunately, Alcuin's catalogue did not possess the major virtue of accuracy, since it claimed for York books which it did not possess.

When looking at early catalogues we can see evidence of their compilers groping towards a 'system'. The need to give locations of books was not appreciated until the fourteenth century and the use of alphabetical order did not become common until the sixteenth century. Compilers of early catalogues (like some modern cataloguers) were not always sure how to deal with such problems as collections, anonymous and pseudonymous works, and translations.

In the early centuries it was the monasteries, cathedrals and, later, the universities which had great collections of books and therefore provided catalogues. Entries tended to be brief, and the main object of the catalogues was to provide inventories of stock rather than finding lists or bibliographical tools. There were, however, some attempts at systematization of cataloguing methods, such as the cataloguing rules of Conrad Gesner (1548), Florianus Treflerus (1560), Andrew Maunsell (1595) and John Durie (1650). Maunsell, a London bookseller, introduced entry under surname, entry of anonymous works under title or subject or both, and entry of translations under original author (when known) as well as under translator and subject.

The first national cataloguing code was the French code of 1791, an outcome of the French Revolution. This made author entry compulsory, specified the form of catalogue (card), and also included rules for accessioning and guiding.

However, it is the events of the nineteenth century onwards, when modern cataloguing practice was shaped and patterned, that are of most interest to present-day students. This period may be viewed from a number of different standpoints: there are the librarians who have contributed towards improved methods by their example and published works; there is the influence wielded by the great institutions such as the Library of Congress and the British Museum Library (now incorporated in the British Library); there are the organizations which have banded librarians together and the conferences which have enabled cataloguers to meet, discuss problems and exchange views; there are the codes produced in an attempt to standardize cataloguing practice; and there are the many examples of outstanding catalogues and catalogue services. The following chart attempts to crystallize the history of cataloguing within these categories whilst, at the same time, illustrating the interplay which exists between them. It is not, of course, exhaustive.

A careful study of this chart shows the interdependence of various movements in cataloguing and the need to take account of methods of the past if improvements are to be made. Without Panizzi's 91 rules there could have been no Anglo-American code of 1908 or ALA codes of 1941 and 1949; with all their faults, these paved the way for the work of Osborn, Lubetzky and the Paris Conference of 1961, leading to the Anglo-American cataloguing rules of 1967, 1978 and 1988. Cutter's work on subject headings led to refinements by Kaiser, Coates and Austin; the desirability of cooperative catalogues was seen by Jewett in the United States and the Kenyon Committee in Britain, but did not become a practical proposition (especially on an international scale) until the development of automated methods following the King report; MARC would not have been possible without the international acceptance of a standard code of cataloguing rules – AACR. Many of these developments owed something to ideas expressed by the great Indian librarian, Ranganathan.

In recent times it has been technological innovation that has made the headlines and advances in computer applications have meant that the last decade has witnessed a major revolution in cataloguing – the introduction of the online public access catalogue (OPAC) – an event of such significance that cataloguing will never be the same again. And, as if this were not enough, there was hardly time for cataloguers to draw breath before CD-ROM arrived, and with it a movement away from record supply and towards system supply, providing the exciting possibility of sending a complete catalogue, catalogue support system or database through the postal service.

CHRONOLOGICAL HISTORY
OF CATALOGUING DEVELOPMENT

1787–1991

Year	People	Reports and publications	Institutions	Organizations	Conferences
1787					
1841	Panizzi		British Museum		
1852	Jewett	*On the construction of catalogs*			
1856	Crestadoro	*The art of making catalogs*			
1864		Manchester Public Library			
1876	Cutter				
1881					
1897					
1899					
1899-1901	Putnam		Library of Congress		
1908				Library Association/ American Library Association	
1911	Kaiser	*Systematic indexing*			
1914			Library of Congress		
1923	Sears				

8

Codes and standards	Cataloguing and cataloguing services	Comment
	First British Museum printed catalogues	
Rules for compiling the catalogue of printed books, maps and music in the British Museum (Rev.ed. 1936)		The first of the modern codes. Great influence
		First American rules for author entry, with suggested supplementary subject list. Also advocated centralized/ cooperative cataloguing
		Advocated detailed main entries beginning with author. Accession number arrangement with indexes of names and subjects. Applied to Manchester Public Library catalogue in 1864
	Catalogue constructed according to Crestadoro's principles (1856) — First KWIC index	
Rules for a dictionary catalog (4th ed. 1904)		Tremendous influence. Basis of American practice. Includes rules for author and subject entries and also filing rules
	First Library of Congress general card catalogue begun	
	Volume one of Biblio-thèque Nationale catalogue published	Only now nearing completion!
Prussian instructions		Rules widely adopted in Germany and many other European countries. Unusual ideas on corporate authorship and anonymous works
	Library of Congress adopts dictionary catalog and begins distribution of catalogue cards	The Library of Congress has since held a central position in US cataloguing
AA code (the 'Joint' code)		Intended to bring uniformity to the cataloguing practice of English-speaking countries
		Significant contribution to the theory of subject headings
Subject headings used in the dictionary catalogs of the Library of Congress		US practice is still largely based upon these working tools which reflect Cutter's rules
Sears' List of subject headings which was based on Library of Congress list		

9

Year	People	Reports and publications	Institutions	Organizations	Conferences
1927		Kenyon Report (Public Libraries Committee Report on public libraries in England and Wales; Cmd 2868)			
1931			Vatican Library		
1934	Cranshaw	Cutting cataloguing costs 50% (In *Library world* 39 1934 179-184)			
1934	Ranganathan				
1941	Osborn	The crisis in cataloguing (In *Library quarterly* 11(4) 1941 393-411)			
1942			American Library Association		
1942-1946			Library of Congress		
1945	Ranganathan				
1949			Library of Congress	American Library Association	
1950			British National Bibliography		
1951			Library of Congress		
1951				British Standards Institution	
1953	Lubetzky	*Cataloging rules and principles*			

Codes and standards	Cataloguing and cataloguing services	Comment
		Plea for local cooperation
Vatican code		Includes rules for alphabetical subject entries and filing rules. Has been described as 'the best statement of American cataloging practice
		Anticipated Osborn and Lubetzky with his ideas on simplification
Classified catalogue code (6th ed 1964)		The only code of rules specifically for the classified catalogue
		Voiced the dissatisfaction felt by many cataloguers with existing codes, especially the preliminary edition of ALA 1949
ALA Rules for filing catalog cards. First edition (2nd ed. 1968; rewritten 1980)		
	First Library of Congress printed catalogs published (167 volumes)	
Dictionary catalogue code		
ALA rules *and* the *Library of Congress rules for descriptive cataloguing*		The ALA rules were heavily criticized for 'enumerating' cases and for being too detailed
	The *British national bibliography* begins publication. A classified arrangement using chain procedure for subject indexing	Influence of Ranganathan
	Introduced 'limited cataloguing' policy. Ceased 1964	
BS 1749: *Specification for alphabetical arrangement and the filing order of numerals and symbols* (revised 1969 and 1984)		
		Very important. Argues for rules based upon principles — 'conditions' rather than 'cases'

Year	People	Reports and publications	Institutions	Organizations	Conferences
1954				IFLA Working Group on the Co-ordination of Cataloguing Principles	
1955	Ranganathan	*Headings and canons*			
1956			British National Bibliography		
1956			Library of Congress		
1956			Library of Congress		
1957				Society of Indexers, UK, founded	
1958-1959			Library of Congress		
1959-1966			British Museum		
1960	Coates	*Subject catalogues: headings and structure*			
1960	Lubetzky	*Code of cataloging rules* ... an unfinished draft			
1961					
1961					ICCP (International Conference on Cataloguing Principles) – Paris
1963		King report on automation and the Library of Congress			
1965					

Codes and standards	Cataloguing and cataloguing services	Comment
		The International Federation of Library Associations has played, and is playing, a vital role in international cataloguing. ICCP was to blossom from this working party
		An important comparative study of five codes of cataloguing rules
	First printed cards from BNB	
	National Union Catalog begins	
Filing rules for the dictionary catalogs of the Library of Congress (rewritten 1980)		Originally issued in loose-leaf form, as *Filing manual*, for LC staff only
	CIS (Cataloguing In Source) experiment	Now CIP (Cataloguing In Publication)
	BM General catalogue published in photo litho edition (263 volumes)	
		Analyses approach of Cutter and Kaiser and develops his own theories, put into practice in *British technology index*
		Incomplete but showed what could be achieved with a drastic reduction in the number of rules
	First automated production of catalogue cards	The Douglas Aircraft Co introduces the first *cataloguing* application of computers, although computers had been used with post-coordinate indexing since 1950s
		A 'statement of principles' based upon Lubetzky's work was adopted at this Conference which has had an enormous effect on cataloguing and cataloguing rules throughout the world
		Led to the MARC project
	The Library of Congress National Program for Acquisition and Cataloging (NPAC) otherwise known as the 'Shared Cataloging Program' begun	

Year	People	Reports and publications	Institutions	Organizations	Conferences
1965					
1966					Brasenose conference on the automation of libraries
1966			Library of Congress		
1967			Library of Congress	Library Association/ American Library Association/ Canadian Library Association	
1967					
1967					
1967			British National Bibliography		
1967			Ohio College Library Center		
1968			Library of Congress		
1969			BLCMP		
1970					
1970					
1971				IFLA	
1971	Austin				
1973				Library Association/ National Council for Educational Technology (now Council for Educational Technology for the UK)	

Codes and standards	Cataloguing and cataloguing services	Comment
	First computerization of catalogues in the UK (the public libraries of Camden and Barnet)	
		Put forward the argument that the computer can produce a 'reactive catalogue', that it can generate from a common bibliographic store a *system* of catalogues that are all mutually compatible
	Project MARC begun	
Anglo-American cataloguing rules		Based upon 'conditions of authorship' and not types of publication
	Introduction of the SBN (Standard Book Number − now ISBN)	
	Attention first focused upon possibility of microform catalogues	At the Lockheed Missiles and Space Co
	UKMARC begun	
	OCLC network set up	
	National union catalog pre-1956 imprints began publication	
	First UK network	
	Introduction of ISSN (International Standard Serial Number)	
Canadian rules for non-book materials		
	Introduction of ISBD (International Standard Bibliographic Description)	
	PRECIS first used in *BNB*	
LANCET rules for non-book materials		

Year	People	Reports and publications	Institutions	Organizations	Conferences
1973					
1974				IFLA	
1975			British Library formed		
Mid-1970s					
1977			British Library		
1977			Library of Congress	Network Advisory Group	
1977					
1978			Library of Congress/ British Library	Library Association/ American Library Association/ Canadian Committee on Cataloguing	
Late 1970s					
1980				American Library Association	
1980			British Library		
1980			Library of Congress		
1980					
1980				CAG (Cooperative Automation Group) formed in UK	
1980					
1981			British Library/Library of Congress/ national libraries of Canada and Australia		
1981			Library of Congress		
1981	Gorman				

Codes and standards	Cataloguing and cataloguing services	Comment
	Books in English first published	An ultra-microfiche bibliography based upon MARC
ISBD(M)		First of the International Standard Bibliographic Descriptions (Monographs)
	Turnkey minicomputer systems and availability of machine-readable cataloguing data brings library automation within reach of smaller libraries	
	BLAISE goes live	
		Recommendations for a US national information and library service
	UK Centre for Catalogue Research (now Centre for Bibliographic Management) established	
AACR 2nd ed. published		Emphasizes integrated approach to cataloguing different library materials
	First online public access catalogues (OPACs) in US	Offshoot of online real-time circulation systems
ALA filing rules		New version of 1968 rules
BLAISE filing rules		
Filing rules		New version of 1956 rules
	Second generation of OPACs offering some keyword post-coordinate facilities	
		Group decides to focus attention on UKLDS (United Kingdom Library Database System)
		Linked Systems Project initiated in US
		Adopted AACR 2
		Policy of 'superimposition', whereby new rules are only used if they do not lead to conflict with existing headings, to be abandoned. Replaced by 'compatible headings'
Concise AACR 2		

Year	People	Reports and publications	Institutions	Organizations	Conferences
1981		*Root thesaurus*	British Standards Institution		
1981			University of Hull		
1982					
1982					
1982 (+1984, 1986)					
1982				IFLA	
1983		*Using online catalogs: a national survey*			
1984		New edition of *PRECIS manual*			
1984					
1984					
1984			British Standards Institution		
1985					
1985			British Library		
1985		*Examining documents, determining their subjects and selecting indexing terms*	British Standards Institution		
1985			Library of Congress/British Library		

18

Codes and standards	Cataloguing and cataloguing services	Comment
	Online public-access catalogue	Probably first UK library to install an OPAC
	BLAISE separated to form BLAISE-LINK and BLAISE-LINE	
		Microcomputer applications in libraries for cataloguing and indexing becoming more widespread
Revisions to AACR 2 published		
Five-year review of ISBD(M), ISBD(S), ISBD(CM) and ISBD(NBM) implemented (first published 1977–8)		
	UKLDS (see 1980) concluded to be no longer a realistic objective	
	Signs that the two developmental paths, i.e. commercial systems and cooperative networks, are beginning to converge	
Alphabetical arrangement and the filing order of numbers and symbols (rev. ed.)		
	First CD-ROM discs available. Bibliofile containing over 3 million records from Library of Congress MARC databases provides support for cataloguers	
	CIP records to form basis of definitive UK 'national bibliographic record'	
		Agreement re MARC. UKMARC database to be distributed in US in USMARC format

19

Year	People	Reports and publications	Institutions	Organizations	Conferences
1986			British Library		
1986					
1987				Committee of Ministers of Council of Europe	
1988			Library of Congress/British Library	Library Association/ American Library Association/ Australian Committee on Cataloguing/Canadian Committee on Cataloguing	
1988				LASER	
1988			British Library		
1989			UK Office for Library Networking established		
1989			The six copyright libraries of the UK		
1990			British Library and the national libraries of Denmark, France, Fed. Rep. of Germany, Italy, Netherlands and Portugal		

Codes and standards	Cataloguing and cataloguing services	Comment
	Licencing of UKMARC records within the EEC begins	
	CD-ROM databases and cataloguing support services begin to make a real impact	
	Adopted recommendations for the guidance of member countries on exchange of data, interconnection and data transfer, etc.	Major implications for cooperation among libraries
AACR 2 1988 revision published		
	VISCOUNT project becomes operational, providing an online search, retrieval, location find and messaging facility	
	Bibliographic Services Division reorganized to form three Directorates: National Bibliographic Services; Computing and Telecommunications; and Acquisitions, Processing and Cataloguing	
	Pilot project commenced after agreement to proceed with a shared cataloguing programme	
	Consortium formed to co-operate on a two-year project to develop common approaches to enable libraries to exchange bibliographic records on CD-ROM	

Year	People	Reports and publications	Institutions	Organizations	Conferences
1990 (Nov)			British Library		
1991			British Library		
1991			British Library		

22

Codes and standards	Cataloguing and cataloguing services	Comment
	Direct online data entry implemented for cataloguing	
	New subject indexing system (COMPASS) introduced	
	Creation of CIP records from advance information supplied by publishers to cease. As an interim arrangement, CIP records to be bought in from Book Data Ltd	

23

Chapter 3
Standardization and the road to AACR 2

The requirements of cooperative and centralized systems ('networks' as they are now known — see p.191) make the acceptance of standards of vital importance. Such standardization might relate to the classification scheme used to arrange the stock of a library, to the alphabetical subject indexing methodology, or to the content and arrangement of the catalogue entry. It is the latter with which this chapter is primarily concerned.

The manner in which a catalogue entry is organized with regard to the amount of detail to be included will depend upon the requirements of the particular cataloguing agency. A reasonably short entry such as that shown on p.1 might be sufficient for some library systems but, on the other hand, a national library, with a commitment to a sophisticated bibliographic service, would find such brevity unacceptable.

Despite differences in the amount of detail required, it is clearly advantageous for various cataloguing agencies to agree to work to the one standard, i.e. a set of rules, to be used by all. The standard would prescribe how the content of the entry was to be organized and how the headings, or access points, under which an item was to be entered should be selected and presented. Whilst entries could be simple, because all elements advocated by the standard need not necessarily be included, briefer entries would still be compatible with those containing more detail because both had been produced using the same standard.

In the United States, standardization of author-title cataloguing has been a way of life in libraries, especially since 1901 when the Library of Congress took over the printed catalogue card service begun by the Library Bureau in 1893.

In Britain, progress towards standardization was much slower — perhaps due to the natural independence of British librarians, or perhaps because Britain's national library did not attempt to take a central role in British librarianship until the 1970s; or possibly simply because no library was willing to accept the Anglo-American code of 1908 without considerable amendment.

Even when the *British national bibliography* began to be published in 1950, using a much amended version of the 1908 code as the basis of its cataloguing, many libraries preferred to continue their own cataloguing practices.

When the *BNB* started to issue printed catalogue cards in 1956 its cataloguing achieved greater acceptance, but there were still libraries which resisted, partly because they had reservations about the *BNB's* use of the Dewey decimal classification. What such libraries fail to appreciate is that standardization does *not* mean accepting without question all of the data provided by a central cataloguing agency; rather it means using common practices as far as possible and allowing the agency to do work which cannot be done better locally.

Even though Americans accepted AA1908 and later the ALA revisions of 1941 and 1949, many of them were not happy with these rules. Their dissatisfaction was voiced by Andrew Osborn in 1941 [1] and, most notably, by Seymour Lubetzky in 1953. Lubetzky's *Cataloging rules and principles* [2] of that year came out strongly against the codification of catalogue rules via the elaborate and complex enumeration of innumerable 'cases' and pointed the way towards the possible formulation of a less complex set of rules based upon well defined principles recognizing more generalized 'conditions'. An encyclopaedia, for example, would not be regarded as a particular 'case', or type of publication, but would be treated in a similar manner to all other works, i.e. according to the particular 'conditions' of authorship or responsibility pertaining to it.

Lubetzky's ideas were widely welcomed and helped pave the way for the International Conference on Cataloguing Principles held in Paris in 1961. A draft statement of principles based upon Lubetzky's *Code of cataloging rules: author and title entry: an unfinished draft* (ALA 1960) was submitted to this conference for discussion along with working papers on the various problems of rules prepared by delegates. A final version of the 'Statement of principles' was adopted and participants agreed to work in their separate countries for revised rules which would be in agreement with these accepted principles.

The Anglo-American cataloguing rules of 1967 (AACR 1) was one of several codes reflecting the 'Paris Principles'; though, unfortunately, it had to be published in two texts (British and North American) because there was not complete unanimity between the two countries' committees, particularly in the areas of description and corporate headings.

AACR 1 was immediately accepted as a standard by the *BNB* and by several British libraries, but certainly not by all of them. In the United States its

[1] The crisis in cataloging / Andrew Osborn, *Library quarterly* (11) 1941 393–411; reprinted in *Library assistant* (35) 1942 54–62, 69–75, and in *Readings in library cataloguing* / edited by R. K. Olding. — London : Crosby Lockwood, 1966, 225–41.

[2] *Cataloging rules and principles* / Seymour Lubetzky. — Washington : LC, 1953.

complete acceptance was hampered by the fact that the Library of Congress, one of the bodies responsible for the rules, adopted a superimposition or 'no conflict' policy – headings from AACR 1 were accepted only if they did not conflict with headings already in the catalogue.

The development of automated cataloguing methods, particularly the MARC (MAchine-Readable Cataloguing) Project (see p.136) made the acceptance of an international standard more urgent, but already AACR 1 was being overtaken by events. Apart from the considerable influence of the computer, there were three factors which were of particular significance.

First, there were the rules being produced by a number of different countries throughout the world. Although these were also based upon the Paris Principles, there were some differences of opinion. European libraries, for instance, had never been happy with editors and compilers of collections being given the status of authors, preferring to enter collections under title, and so this rule was revised by the British and Americans in the interests of international cooperation. Corporate responsibility was another problematic area where unanimity was (and still is) difficult to achieve.

Second, there were the rules developed specifically for non-book materials, an area which was undergoing rapid expansion and for which AACR 1 was not considered satisfactory. In Britain there was *Non-book materials cataloguing rules*, produced by the Library Association's Media Cataloguing Rules Committee, published by the National Council for Educational Technology in 1973, and known as LANCET (the initials of its two sponsoring organizations); in Canada there was *Non-book materials: the organization of integrated collections* by Jean Riddle Weihs, Shirley Lewis and Janet Macdonald, published by the Canadian Library Association in 1973; and in the United States there was *Standards for cataloging nonprint materials: an interpretation and practical application* by Alma Tillin and William J. Quinly, the fourth edition of which was published by the Association for Educational Communications and Technology (Washington) in 1976.

Third, there was the continuous work being undertaken by the International Federation of Library Associations (now the International Federation of Library Associations and Institutions). A Working Group on the Co-ordination of Cataloguing Principles was set up by IFLA as early as 1954 and in 1957 the IFLA General Council adopted a proposal to hold a world-wide conference on basic cataloguing principles. The International Conference on Cataloguing Principles of 1961 was thus IFLA inspired, the necessary financial assistance being forthcoming from the Council on Library Resources in America. The ICCP achieved international agreement on the principles to be adopted for choice of headings but for the international exchange of bibliographic (or materiographic) information, whether in written or machine-readable form, it is obviously also necessary to have a generally accepted standard which lists:

1   the *elements* to be included in the descriptive part of an entry
2   the *order* in which the elements are to be cited
3   the *punctuation* which is to be used to separate the elements.

An IFLA International Meeting of Cataloguing Experts in Copenhagen in 1969 set up a Working Party to study the possibilities for an International Standard Bibliographic Description for monographs. Such a standard, ISBD(M), was subsequently drawn up and was officially adopted by the IFLA Committee on Cataloguing at its meeting in Liverpool in 1971. The publication of this standard necessitated the amendment of the relevant sections of AACR 1, in order to achieve conformity. These amendments included the introduction of a new area to accommodate the recently introduced International Standard Book Number (ISBN) as a unique identifier. Later, the International Standard Serial Number (ISSN) also had to be catered for.

ISBD(M) was to be followed by similar standards for other media such as ISBD(S) for serials and ISBD(NBM) for non-book materials. Almost inevitably, because a different committee was responsible for each standard, certain discrepancies became apparent and, to counteract this, a 'general' framework for description was produced, ISBD(G).

The above brief historical account clearly illustrates that there was a strong case for revision of AACR 1. There was a need to incorporate the ISBD(G) framework and to take account of other international developments. There was a need to examine the expansion in the media industry and the cataloguing rules that had been produced to cater for this expansion. There was also the very important need for one unified Anglo-American text, which would incorporate all amendments issued since 1967. In addition, there was the need to consider other proposals for changes and the effects of library automation. The latter was particularly difficult because these effects are on-going and 'have yet to be completely assessed and understood'.[1]

The Council on Library Resources agreed to fund the revision, with certain conditions, the major one being that royalties from sales should be placed in a common fund for future activities associated with AACR. A Joint Steering Committee for AACR meeting in 1974 confirmed the participation of five bodies as 'authors' (ALA, LC, LA, BL, and the Canadian Committee on Cataloguing). It was agreed to set up national committees to consider issues and proposals for revision. The new rules, the result of collaboration between the national libraries and professional associations of three countries, were published in 1978. The main objectives were to a great extent achieved and not the least part of this remarkable achievement was the fact that any institution, organization or individual with a point of view was given ample opportunity to express it during the process of revision.

Adoption of AACR 2

The publication of AACR 2 was not welcomed by all librarians but, as Peter Lewis, late Director-General of the British Library Bibliographic Services

---

[1] The Anglo-American cataloguing rules, Second edition / Michael Gorman, *Library resources and technical services* 22 (3) Summer 1978 209–25.

Division, and former Chairman of the Joint Steering Committee for AACR, stated: 'for every powerful voice speaking against AACR 2, there is an equally powerful one calling for full implementation without delay'.[1]

The major criticisms levelled against AACR 2 are that with the fast-developing state of automation it is irrelevant, and its implementation increases library costs without increasing benefits.

Despite objections, four national libraries (the British Library, the Library of Congress, the National Library of Australia and the National Library of Canada) adopted AACR 2 from January 1981. Initially, the Library of Congress decided to retain certain pre-AACR headings for economic reasons but it reconsidered its position and decided to abandon this 'compatible headings' policy from 1982. Thus all of the national libraries were then agreed that the adoption of the rules 'as they stood' would bring long-term cost and user benefits.

Whether an individual library decides to use AACR 2 will depend upon factors such as the use made of centralized services and the staff support available to amend existing catalogues. Cataloguing agencies which have adopted AACR 2 are using what is, in effect, an international standard.

Continuing work on AACR

Work on the rules did not cease with the publication of AACR 2 in 1978. Indeed, rather was the reverse the case in that a whole series of related activities was generated. These activities included the implementation of training programmes, and the production of adoption aids, interpretative manuals, illustrative examples and translations. AACR 2 has spread its influence into a number of non-English-speaking countries, and translations have been made into languages such as Arabic, Finnish, French, Japanese, Norwegian, Portuguese, and Spanish.

In 1981 the first edition of Gorman's *The concise AACR 2*, a rewritten and simplified version of the rules, was published. This was intended to provide a readily comprehensible summary of AACR 2 practice for librarians and cataloguers in a number of different situations, such as librarianship students, persons working in small libraries, especially 'one-person' libraries, and cataloguers working in a non-English-language environment.

AACR 2 has also encouraged research. For example, cataloguing rules for choice of access points involve conditional decisions; i.e. if a certain condition applies then take a particular decision. A computerized expert system functions in a similar way using a knowledge base expressed as a set of rules. Because of this similarity, several researchers have investigated the feasibility of creating an expert system for cataloguing (see p.272).

---

[1] *Library Association record* 82 (4) Apr 1980 176.

The international Joint Steering Committee for Revision of AACR continued to meet regularly, as did the various national committees, and in 1981 it was agreed to add an Australian representative to JSC. The revision process also continued and three sets of revisions were prepared and published in 1982, 1984 and 1986. Many of these revisions have formed part of a general 'tidying-up' and correction process, whilst others have been of a more significant nature.

A major decision was taken by the Joint Steering Committee in 1985, when it was resolved to recommend that a consolidated version of AACR 2 be published in 1988. This consolidation was to incorporate all rule revisions passed, and typographical errors found, to that date. If possible, it was also intended to include revised rules for computer files, taking note of work that had already been done in this area such as that by Templeton[1] and by Dodd,[2] and for recently introduced media such as compact discs. This consolidation, including a new chapter for computer files and revised rules for recent media, was published as *Anglo-American cataloguing rules* Second edition 1988 revision.[3]

A survey of AACR 2 users taken in 1985 revealed that 98% favoured a loose-leaf format, and the new revision is available in three versions: softback, hardback and loose-leaf. A new version of *The concise AACR 2* has also been published.[4]

The period in which AACR 2 has developed has been a time when applications of the computer in cataloguing have also been developing at a tremendous rate. Therefore there are bound to be questions posed by library automation which have not been answered by the rules, even though some new concepts have sprung from, or been precipitated by, advances in automation. Gorman, the editor of AACR 2, considers that the fact that AACR 2 has not been able to take library automation fully into account is not really the fault of those responsible for AACR but rather is due to the fact that the effect of library automation on catalogues, as indicated on p.27, has yet to be completely assessed and understood.

---

[1] *Study of cataloguing computer software : applying AACR 2 to microcomputer programs* / Ray Templeton and Anita Witten. — London : British Library, c.1984.

[2] *Guidelines for using AACR 2 Chapter 9 for cataloging microcomputer software* / Committee on Cataloging: Description and Access, Cataloging and Classification Section, American Library Association. — Chicago : ALA, 1984.

[3] *Anglo-American cataloguing rules.* — 2nd ed., 1988 revision / prepared under the direction of the Joint Steering Committee for Revision of AACR, a committee of the American Library Association ... [et al.] ; edited by Michael Gorman and Paul W. Winkler. — Ottawa ; London ; Chicago : Canadian Library Association ; Library Association ; American Library Association, 1988.

[4] *The concise AACR 2 1988 revision* / prepared by Michael Gorman. — Chicago ; Ottawa ; London : American Library Association ; Canadian Library Association ; Library Association, 1989.

For these reasons, Gorman predicts that there will never be an AACR 3 but a new type of code which will deal with the creation of machine-readable records for use in national and international networks.[1] However, in the meantime, revisions to AACR 2 will continue to be made; cataloguing cannot stand still, and the fact that the new revision is available in loose-leaf format reinforces this point.

Continuing work on the ISBDs

An ISBD Review Committee was formed by IFLA in 1981 to implement a five-year review of the ISBDs for monographs, serials, cartographic materials and non-book materials, ISBD(M), ISBD(S), ISBD(CM) and ISBD(NBM), with the intention of publishing revisions in 1987.[2] The Joint Steering Committee for AACR became concerned that ISBD(G), for which, as previously noted, the Joint Steering Committee was jointly responsible, might be effected by this review. Draft texts were circulated for comment in 1983−4; JSC AACR was one of the recipients of these drafts and was therefore given the opportunity to contribute to the review. ISBD(PM) − Printed Music − was also being reviewed and work proceeded on analytical cataloguing (see p.104).

Special attention has also been given to computer files; a Working Group met for the first time in 1986 and the final version of ISBD(CF) was published in 1990.[3] The influence of AACR can be plainly seen in the latter publication with the ISBD adopting the AACR solution for differentiating between the type of file and the physical carrier (see also p.50). A revised draft of the ISBD for rare, antiquarian books, ISBD(A), was circulated for study by appropriate persons in 1988.

The main-entry principle

Although rules for standardizing a bibliographic description (as the ISBDs and AACR 2) and for selecting and formulating access points (as AACR 2) may be necessary, one other aspect of AACR 2 is completely redundant in the machine-readable context, namely the concept of *main entry*.

---

[1] Technical services, 1984−2001 (and before) / Michael Gorman, *Technical services quarterly*, 1 (1/2) Fall/Winter 1983.

[2] *ISBD(M) : International Standard Bibliographic Description for monographic publications* / International Federation of Library Associations and Institutions. — Rev. ed. — London : IFLA UBCIM, 1987. Following the publication of ISBD(M), revised edition of ISBD (CM) and ISBD(NBM) were published in the same year and the revised edition of ISBD(S) was published in 1988.

[3] *ISBD(CF) : International Standard Bibliographic Description for computer files* / International Federation of Library Associations and Institutions. — London : IFLA UBCIM, 1990.

AACR 2 considers 'the concept of main entry to be useful in assigning uniform title and in promoting the standardization of bibliographic citation'.[1] Some cataloguers defend AACR 2 on the ground that, although a number of online catalogues have appeared, the majority of present catalogues are still card catalogues. Other cataloguers would take issue with this defence. In Japan, for instance, cataloguers used codes based upon the main-entry principle under the influence of AACR 2 and the Paris Principles until 1977, when a new code of *Nippon cataloguing rules* (NCR) was compiled.[2] These rules abandon main entry not only because of progress in automation but also because, in non-automated systems, it is seen to be less useful than the unit entry, which is now easy to produce and which ensures that each entry in the catalogue has an equal value.[3]

The Japanese rules also differ from AACR 2 in another respect in that an attempt is made to define an item or unit more clearly. It is claimed that this leads to greater consistency where the cataloguing of multivolume sets and multipart items are concerned.

---

[1] *Anglo-American cataloguing rules.* — 2nd ed. 1988 revision *op. cit.* 2.

[2] *Nippon cataloguing rules.* — Prelim. new ed. / prepared by the Cataloging Committee, Japan Library Association. — Tokyo : Japan Library Association, 1977.

[3] The no-main-entry principle : the historical background of the Nippon cataloging rules / Tadayoshi Takawashi, Tsutomu Shihota, Zensei Oshiro, *Cataloging and classification quarterly* 9 (4) 1989 67−77.

Chapter 4
A brief guide to AACR 2 1988 revision

AACR 2 reverses the pattern of all previous codes of cataloguing rules[1] by placing the rules for description *before* the rules for choice of headings, because it is believed that this is the pattern followed in most libraries and bibliographic agencies. It also accepts the desirability of integrating bibliographic records of books and other kinds of materials. The way in which AACR 2 may be used is illustrated by the work flowchart shown on p.33.

Description
AACR 2 Part One — Description — is based upon the framework of ISBD(G). It begins with a general chapter containing rules which apply to all library materials. Each of the succeeding chapters in Part One, except for chapter 13, is concerned with more detailed rules for specific media, e.g.: chapter 2 Printed monographs; chapter 5 Music; chapter 6 Sound recordings; chapter 9 Computer files; chapter 12 Serials. More than one chapter, apart from the general chapter, may need to be consulted; a serial, for instance, may also be a sound recording. When this sort of situation occurs, AACR 2 states that the description of an item should be based in the first instance on the chapter dealing with the class of materials to which the item belongs. For example, a printed monograph in microform should be described as a microform.

---

[1] It is not the intention of this work to deal with rules which have been superseded by AACR 2. Various earlier codes, such as the British Museum *Rules*, Cutter's *Rules*, etc., are shown in their historical sequence in the chart on pp.8−23. Those requiring further information are referred to works such as

Cataloguing : a guidebook / Eric J. Hunter. — London : Bingley, 1974,

A manual of cataloguing practice / K. G. B. Bakewell. — Oxford : Pergamon, 1972.

Each description is divided into areas, always cited in the same order. These areas are:

Title and Statement of responsibility	1
Edition	2
Material (or type of publication) specific details	3
Publication, distribution, etc.	4
Physical description	5
Series	6
Note(s)	7
Standard number and terms of availability	8

DESCRIBE THE ITEM
Ch 1 — General rules for all materials
Ch 2 – 12 — More detailed rules for specific materials
Ch 13 — Analysis

CHOOSE THE ACCESS POINTS
THE HEADINGS UNDER WHICH THE ITEM
IS TO BE ENTERED
Ch 21 — Headings for main and added entries
(Rules 21.29 and 21.30 — General rules for added entries)

DECIDE UPON THE FORM THAT EACH HEADING WILL TAKE

Persons	Geographic names	Corporate bodies
Ch 22	Ch 23	Ch 24

CONSIDER NECESSITY FOR UNIFORM TITLES
A 'uniform title' being the particular title by which a work that has appeared under varying titles is to be identified for cataloguing purposes
Ch 25

FORMULATE REFERENCES
FROM ALTERNATIVE FORMS OF HEADINGS OR TITLES
Mentioned throughout Ch 22 – 25
Specifically covered in Ch 26

Work flowchart for AACR 2, a copy of the original which appears in An introduction to AACR 2 : a programmed guide to the second edition of Anglo-American cataloguing rules 1988 revision / Eric J. Hunter. — London : Bingley, 1989

The cataloguer brought up on earlier codes, which were concerned almost exclusively with printed material, must now, therefore, become familiar with some new terminology: 'publication, distribution, etc., area' instead of 'imprint'; 'physical description area' instead of 'collation'; and terms such as 'statement of responsibility', 'other title information' and 'statement of extent'. These new terms are largely a reflection of the integrated nature of the rules: 'statement of responsibility' includes the author of a book and the creator of a work of art; 'statement of extent' includes the pagination of a printed monograph or the playing time of a sound recording.

It is not necessary for all of the areas to be present in every case. An item may not, for instance, be included in a series, or have a standard number. Similar a note may not always be required. One area, the 'material (or type of publication) specific details' area, is, in fact, used only for maps, music, computer files and serials.

The number given on the right is the relevant rule number for that particular area. These numbers are used logically and mnemonically so that rule 1.1 will deal with the recording of the title in general terms, rule 2.1 will deal more specifically with the recording of the title of a printed monograph, rule 6.1 with the recording of the title of a sound recording, and so on.

Each area may be further divided into constituent elements, for example the 'publication, distribution, etc.' area could include such elements as the place of publication, publisher and date. These elements are separated by a prescribed punctuation.

The rules provide for the optional inclusion of a General material designation (GMD) in the description to indicate the broad class of material to which the item being catalogued belongs. When used, the GMD follows the title proper within square brackets:

Making human resources productive [videorecording]

A specific material designation, indicating the precise class of material to which an item belongs, is included in the physical description area. For example, the rules state that one of the following specific material designations should be used for sound recordings: sound cartridge; sound cassette; sound disc; sound tape reel; sound track film.

An important provision is made in rule 1.0D, which specifies three possible levels of description, thus allowing simultaneously *flexibility* (in that each library can decide upon the amount of detail it requires in its entries) and *standardization/uniformity* (in that entries are presented in accordance with bibliographical standards). The information specified in these levels is as follows:

First level	Title proper / first statement of responsibility if different from main entry heading in form or number or if there is no main entry heading. — Edition statement. — Material

	(or type of publication) specific details. — First publisher, etc, date of publication, etc; — Extent of item. — Note(s). — Standard number.

Second level   Title proper [general material designation] = Parallel title : other title information / first statement of responsibility. — Edition statement / first statement of responsibility relating to the edition. — Material (or type of publication) specific details. — First place of publication, etc. : first publisher, etc, date of publication, etc — Extent of item : other physical details ; dimensions. — (Title proper of series / statement of responsibility relating to series, ISSN of series ; numbering within the series. Title of subseries ; ISSN of subseries ; numbering within subseries). — Note(s). — Standard number.

Third level   All the elements set out in the rules that are applicable to the item being described.

An important element in this bibliographic standardization is the punctuation pattern shown above, which facilitates recognition of the various parts of the entry regardless of the language or script of the description. Thus, a statement of responsibility is always introduced by a space, slash, space (/), and the areas of description are separated from each other by a full stop, space, dash and space (. —). Alternatively each area of description may begin in a new paragraph.

Notes are intended to amplify and/or clarify the more formal elements of the description. They may take many forms, e.g.:

Bibliography: p. 203-215

Previous ed.: Harmondsworth : Penguin, 1950

Based on the life of Florence Nightingale

For children aged 9-12

Issued also in 16 mm. format

Contents: Rusty bugles / Sumner Locke Elliott — We find the bunyip / Ray Mathew — The well / Jack McKinney

Summary: Pictures the highlights of the play 'Julius Caesar' using photographs of an actual production.

In general, notes should be as brief as possible (see rule 1.7A3 of AACR 2) and should not repeat information given in the body of the entry.

Notes are particularly important where media which cannot be 'browsed' is concerned and they should be freely used. A summary of the content and scope of an item is often essential.

Some writers attempt to differentiate, perhaps unnecessarily, between 'notes' and 'annotation'. The former is said to come within the realms of orthodox descriptive cataloguing, as indicated above, and may include additional information concerning title, edition, publication, content, etc. The latter is said to embody any further information relating to the intellectual content of the work, whether purely informative, or critical and evaluative. This type of 'annotation' may be extremely useful for bibliographies and booklists but subjective opinions should be avoided in a catalogue.

Chapter 13, concerned with analysis, is the final chapter of Part One of the rules (see p.103).

Headings and references

The mnemonic rule numbering is carried on in Part Two, which deals with headings and references. The six chapters of Part Two are numbered 21 – 26, there being no chapters 14 – 19. Chapter 20 is an explanation of the rules in Part Two.

Chapter 21 covers the choice of access points, or the entries which are required to ensure that an item is located by the library user, and each rule specifies that one of these access points should be designated the main entry (or principal entry) heading. The question of the use of the *alternative-heading* principle, whereby all entries are of equal status instead of one being designated 'main entry' and the others 'added entries', was discussed by the Joint Steering Committee for Revision of AACR but not embodied in the rules. It is recognized, however, that many libraries do not distinguish between the main entry and other entries and it is recommended that such libraries use chapter 21 as guidance in determining all the entries required in particular instances. It is, of course, also necessary for all libraries to distinguish the main entry from others when making a single entry listing or making a single citation for a work. In addition, the concept of main entry was considered to be useful in assigning uniform titles and in promoting the standardization of bibiographical citation (see also p.31).

The principle of providing rules for bibliographic conditions rather than types of work, enunciated by Lubetzky and developed at the International Conference on Cataloguing Principles and in AACR 1, is further developed in AACR 2. Thus, there are rules in chapter 21 for works for which a single person or corporate body is responsible; works of unknown or uncertain authorship; works of shared responsibility; works produced under editorial direction; and so on.

As in AACR 1, the rules in AACR 2 proceed from general to special, each chapter beginning with a basic rule which is followed by amplifications or exceptions to meet particular circumstances. Thus rule 21.1 is the basic rule for choice of access points:

– *Entry under personal author* (the person chiefly responsible for the creation of the intellectual or artistic content of a work, such as the writer of a book, the composer of a piece of music, the compiler of a bibliography, or the creator of a work of art): Enter a work under the heading for the personal author, the principal personal author or the probable personal author when one can be determined.

– *Entry under corporate body* (an organization or a group of persons that is identified by a name and that acts, or may act, as an entity, e.g. associations, governments, religious bodies, local churches, conferences): Enter a work emanating from one or more corporate bodies under the heading for the appropriate corporate body if it falls into one or more of the following categories:

1 works of an administrative nature dealing with the corporate body itself
2 some legal and government works (e.g. laws, decrees of the chief executive, treaties, court decisions)
3 works that record the collective thought of the body (e.g. reports of committees)
4 works that report the collective activity of a conference, expedition or event which is prominently named in the item being catalogued
5 sound recordings, films and videorecordings resulting from the collective activity of a performing group as a whole
6 cartographic materials emanating from a corporate body other than a body which is merely responsible for the publication or distribution of the materials.

In case of doubt about whether a work falls into one or more of these categories, treat it as if it did not.

It should be noted that although works which fall into the above categories are entered under corporate body, corporate *authorship* is no longer recognized as a concept.

If responsibility is shared between two or three persons or bodies and principal responsibility is not attributed to any of them by either wording or layout, then entry is under the one named first.

– *Entry under title:* Enter a work under its title when:

1 the personal authorship is unknown and the work does not emanate from a corporate body
2 responsibility is shared amongst more than three persons or corporate bodies, and principal responsibility is not attributed to any one, two or three of them
3 it is a collection or work produced under editorial direction
4 it emanates from a corporate body but does not fall into one of the six categories listed above and is not of personal authorship
6 it is accepted as sacred scripture by a religious group.

Additional rules are required for certain conditions not covered by the basic rule and for certain media:

– *Works of mixed responsibility* (a work of mixed responsibility is one to

37

which different persons or bodies make intellectual or artistic contributions by performing different kinds of activity, e.g. writing, adapting, illustrating, editing, arranging, translating). There are two broad categories:

1 Works that are modifications of other works − A work that is a modification of another work is usually entered under the heading appropriate to the new work if the nature and content of the original have been substantially changed or if the medium of expression is different. If, however, the modification is merely an updating, abridgement, revision, arrangement etc., enter under the heading appropriate to the original.

Example i	Enter a dramatization of a novel under the playwright
Example ii	Enter an engraving from an original painting under the engraver
Example iii	Enter a translation under the heading for the original work
Example iv	Enter a revision under the heading for the original unless the wording of the chief source of information indicates that the person or body responsible for the original is no longer considered to be so; entry is then under the heading for the revision.

2 Mixed responsibility in new works (examples of mixed responsibility in new works include: collaboration between artist and writer; reports of interviews, etc.) − Enter a work which is, or appears to be, a work of collaboration between two or more people under the heading for the one who is named first in the chief source of information (e.g. the title page of a book, or the label of a sound disc) unless the other's name is given greater prominence by the wording or layout.

− *A related work*, such as a continuation, sequel, index, supplement, concordance, or libretto, which is to be catalogued *independently*, is entered under its own heading.

There are still some special rules for certain kinds of publication such as laws, or sacred scriptures:

Example i	Enter laws governing one jurisdiction under the heading for that jurisdiction
Example ii	Enter a work accepted as sacred scripture by a religious group under title.

However, as indicated earlier, there are no rules for such works as encyclopaedias, directories, etc., because these may represent any one of a number of conditions. In AACR 1 there was a rule for another kind of work − serials − but this has been removed from AACR 2 since the problem of choice of heading for serials is covered by the basic rule. There are specific provisions in this rule to cater for special problems, e.g. changes of title proper and changes of persons or bodies responsible for a work.

— *Added entries* supplement the main entry. Added entries should be made under any persons or corporate bodies associated with a publication if it is believed that catalogue users might consult the catalogue under these headings. Added entries are also made under titles and series when necessary.

Headings for persons

Chapter 22 deals with headings for persons — beginning, as usual, with a general rule (22.1), which states that the basis of the heading for a person should be the name by which he or she is commonly known, whether this be the person's real name, pseudonym, title of nobility, nickname or other appellation, e.g.:

Spike Milligan   *not*   Terence Alan Milligan

There are two major problems:
1   Choice between different names, e.g.:

Bachelor Knight   *or*   W. Gilmore Simms

2   Choice between different forms of the same name, e.g.:

Confucius   *or*   K'ung-tzu

In general, the basic rule continues to apply and the name chosen should be that by which the person is clearly most commonly known.

A further problem is, of course, that of choice of entry element. It may, for instance, be necessary to invert the name in order to bring that part of the name under which the heading is to be filed to the lead position, e.g.:

MILLIGAN, Spike

Guidance will also be required for compound names, certain 'foreign' names, entry under phrase, and other difficulties which may be encountered. Examples of rules which cater for these instances are:

Hyphenated surnames   If the elements of the surname are hyphenated, either regularly or occasionally, enter under the first element, e.g.:
KAYE-SMITH, Sheila
Phrases   Enter in direct order a name that consists of a phrase or other appellation that does not contain a forename, e.g.:
FATHER TIME
Thai names   In general, enter a Thai name under the first element, e.g.:
PRAYUT SITTHIPHAN

When names are identical, they should be distinguished by adding dates of birth or death, or some other distinguishing terms, e.g.:

SCOTT, Tom, 1816-1875
SCOTT, Tom, 1925-

When a person is known by surname and initials, or surname, forename(s), and initial(s), the forenames in spelled out form are added and enclosed in parentheses to distinguish between names which are otherwise identical, e.g.:

STEVENSON, D.E. (Donald Edward)
STEVENSON, D.E. (Dorothy Emily)

Note that the name still files under the *common* form, i.e. Stevenson, D.E.

Optionally, such additions as those noted above may be made even if they are not needed to distinguish between headings.

Headings for corporate bodies

The basic rule in chapter 24 (Headings for corporate bodies) states that, in general, entry is made under the name by which the body is commonly identified, as determined from items issued by the body in its language, e.g.:

ALDER HEY CHILDREN'S HOSPITAL
ASLIB

The only exceptions are:
1 Subordinate bodies which may need to be entered under the name of a higher body, e.g.:

LIVERPOOL POLYTECHNIC. *School of Information Science and Technology*

2 A body which may need to be entered under the name of a government, e.g.:

LIVERPOOL. *Public Relations Office*

Problems include such difficulties as changes of name and variant name forms. When the name of a body changes, a new heading is established for items appearing under the new name. This means that various items by the one body may appear under different headings, e.g.:

GREAT BRITAIN. *Ministry of Labour*
GREAT BRITAIN. *Department of Employment and Productivity*

When variant name forms are encountered, e.g.:

NASA *and* National Aeronautics and Space Administration
Canadian Library Association *and* Association Canadienne des Bibliothèques

usually the form used is that given in the item with which the body is concerned. If variant forms are found in the item itself, then the name should be used as it appears in the chief source of information.

There is always a preference for conventional name, e.g.:

Westminster Abbey *not* Collegiate Church of St Peter in Westminster

Some names may need qualification. For instance, if a name does not convey the idea of a corporate body, a general description should be added in brackets and italicized, e.g.:

BEATLES (*Musical group*)

Similarly, it may be necessary to add a place-name to the name of a corporate body, in order to distinguish it from others of the same name, e.g.:

REPUBLICAN PARTY (*Ill.*)
REPUBLICAN PARTY (*Mo.*)

Note that conferences are corporate bodies. The major problem here is one of name but if a conference, congress or other meeting has a name then entry is directly under it. The name should be followed by number, date and place as appropriate, e.g.:

CONFERENCE ON TECHNICAL INFORMATION CENTER
ADMINISTRATION (*3rd : 1966 : Philadelphia, Pa.*)

Geographic names
In between chapters 22 and 24, there is a separate chapter (23) dealing with geographic names. This is presumably placed here, before the rules for corporate headings, because geographic names are frequently used to distinguish between corporate bodies with the same name, as in the additions to the name 'Republican Party' shown above, and as headings in their own right (for governments).

Uniform titles
Chapter 25 deals with uniform titles, a concept introduced in AACR 1 to enable all the catalogue entries for a work to be brought together even though the work may be identified by various titles through different versions or translations. If the work is entered under a person or corporate body, the uniform title is placed in square brackets before the title proper of the item being described:

LEHAR, Franz
[Der Graf von Luxemburg. English]
The Count of Luxembourg ...

but if the main entry is under title, the uniform title may be given as the heading without square brackets.

As in AACR 1, the rules for uniform titles in AACR 2 are not mandatory, but depend on the policy of the particular cataloguing agency or library with regard to the use of uniform titles. The basic rule (25.2) states that a uniform title should be used, for instance, if an item bears a different title proper from the uniform title or if the addition of another element, such as the name of the language of the item, is needed to organize the file. This is followed by rules for individual titles, stating that, in general, the title in the original language should be used as the uniform title, and rules for collective titles, legal materials, sacred scriptures, music, and other works.

The rules for collective titles are valuable because they allow selected or complete works of a prolific author to file together regardless of the title proper of the particular item. For example, various complete editions or recordings of the works of T S Eliot can be given the uniform title [Works] whether the title proper of the item being catalogued is *T S Eliot's works*, *The complete works of T S Eliot* or *Eliot's complete works*; similarly, his complete plays can be given the uniform title [Plays] whether called *Eliot's plays* or *The murder in the cathedral and other plays*.

The usefulness of the uniform title when handling materials other than books, e.g. films, manuscripts, or music, should also be noted. Films, for example, are frequently released in different countries with different titles.

References

Chapter 26 collects together the various rules for references. Apart from the basic rule, there are rules for personal names, names of corporate bodies and geographic names, and uniform titles. Each main section is divided into *see* references, e.g.:

MILLIGAN, Terence Alan
 see MILLIGAN, Spike

see also references, e.g.:

MARKHAM, Robert
 see also AMIS, Kingsley

and explanatory references, which are used when adequate direction cannot be given by simple *see* or *see also* references, e.g.:

GREAT BRITAIN. *Office of Population Censuses and Surveys*
 The name of the General Register Office was changed in 1970 to the Office of Population Censuses and Surveys.

 Works by this body are entered in accordance with the name used at the time of publication.

A new concept is the 'name-title reference', used when a *see* or *see also* reference is made from a title entered under a person or corporate body, thus:

ASHE, Gordon
 The croaker
  see
 CREASEY, John

In this instance, the title page of the work reads 'by John Creasey as Gordon Ashe'.

References may also be used in lieu of added entries where appropriate. For example, where there are many editions of a work, a great deal of economy can be achieved, in the catalogue, by replacing a number of added entries by one reference, e.g.:

GREAT expectations
    For editions of this work, *see*
DICKENS, Charles
    Great expectations

The rules are completed by four appendices (A: Capitalization; B: Abbreviations; C: Numerals; D: Glossary) and a detailed index.

Chapter 5

Examples illustrating AACR 2 1988 revision[1]

The examples on the following pages illustrate the way in which AACR 2 may be applied. For ease of reference, relevant rule numbers from AACR 2 have been given where this is deemed appropriate.

Example 1 A multimedia item
            2 Printed monograph — simple entry under personal author
            3 Printed monograph — entry under title
            4 Printed monograph — entry under name of conference
            5 Printed monograph — entry under government
            6 Music score
            7 Sound cassette
            8 Computer file
            9 Game
         10 Serial

For comparative purposes, and to illustrate the close relationship between AACR 2 and the International Standard Bibliographic Descriptions, example number 8 is also shown catalogued according to ISBD(CF) and a note concerning ISBD(M) follows example number 2.

---

[1] For further examples illustrating the rules, reference should be made to:

Examples illustrating AACR 2 1988 revision / Eric J. Hunter. — London : Library Association, 1989.

An explanation and illustration of the rules can be found in:

Handbook for AACR 2 1988 revision / Margaret Maxwell. — Chicago : American Library Association, 1989.

For self-learning, a programmed guide is available:

Introduction to AACR 2 / Eric J. Hunter. — London : Bingley, 1989

The philosophy and methodology of AACR 2 is discussed in:

The cataloguer's way through AACR 2 from document receipt to document retrieval / Mary Piggott. — London : Library Association, 1990.

Example 1

The FLOOR is yours [multimedia]. — Peterborough :
Guild Sound & Vision, 1973.
1 film reel (26 min.) : sd., col. ; 16 mm.
1 sound disc (16 min.) : analog, 33⅓ rpm, mono. ; 7 in.
1 booklet (64 p.) ; 24 cm.
Guide to public speaking.

Comment: A multimedia item. The GMD (General Material Designation) follows the title proper − this would be [kit] in North American libraries. In accordance with rule 1.10C2(b) the three component parts of the item are described, using chapter 7 for the film reel, chapter 6 for the sound disc and chapter 2 for the booklet, each physical description being given on a separate line. An annotation is provided (rule 1.7B17 to amplify the title).

Example 2

HUNTER, Eric J.
Computerized cataloguing / Eric J. Hunter. — London :
Bingley, 1985. — xxiv, 215 p. : ill. ; 22 cm. — ISBN
0-85157-377-0.

1. Ti

Comment: Uncomplicated entry for a printed monograph described in accordance with chapter 1 and chapter 2. The optional general material designation [text] following the title proper has been omitted.

Work is entered under the single personal author (21.1A and 21.4A).

At the foot of the entry is a *tracing* or indication of any heading or headings under which added entries should be made.

According to rule 1.0C, areas present in an entry may be separated by a full stop, space, dash, space (i.e. . —) or paragraphing may be used. The former method is adopted in the examples given here but this first example is shown below as it would appear if paragraphing were employed for the physical description and subsequent areas:

HUNTER, Eric J.
Computerized cataloguing / Eric J. Hunter. — London :
Bingley, 1985.
xxiv, 215 p. : ill. ; 22 cm.
ISBN 0-85157-377-0.

1. Ti

Whatever layout is adopted, it is important that the library or cataloguing agency uses it consistently.

The above entries for *Computerized cataloguing* would be exactly the same if formulated according to ISBD(M), the International Standard Bibliographic Description (Monographs) – rev. ed. 1987. As with AACR, ISBDs permit paragraphing to be used for the separation of areas as an alternative to the point, space, dash, space (. —).

Example 3

> COMING to London / by William Plomer . . . [et al.]. —
> London : Phoenix House, 1957. — 176 p. ; 19 cm. —
> Reminiscences by 14 distinguished writers on their first
> contact with London, preceded by an introductory note by
> John Lehmann, editor of the volume.
>
> 1. PLOMER, William
> 2. LEHMANN, John

Comment: Fourteen contributors named on the title page, so only the first named in the description followed by marks of omission (. . .) and et al. within square brackets. Annotation in accordance with rule 2.7B17 (summary of content of item) because the title does not give a clear indication of content.

Main entry under title (rule 21.7B collections and works produced under editorial direction with collective title). Headings under which added entries should be made: Plomer as first named of four or more collaborators (rule 21.30B) and Lehmann as editor. Rule 21.30D states that added entries should only be made for *prominently named* editors and Lehmann is not named at all on the title page, so may not justify an added entry. However, he has contributed an introductory note of seven pages and could be regarded as a possible access point, so an added entry is suggested.

Example 4

> INTERNATIONAL CONFERENCE ON ALCOHOLISM AND
> DRUG ABUSE (*1973 : San Juan, Puerto Rico*)
> Proceedings of the International Conference on Alcoholism
> and Drug Abuse = Trabajos presentados en ocasión de la
> Conferencia Internacional sobre Alcoholismo y Abuse de
> Drogas / edited by Eva Tongue, Richard T. Lambo, Brenda
> Blair. — [Lausanne : International Council on Alcohol and
> Addictions, 1974]. — 450 p. ; 21 cm. — Papers are in English,
> Spanish or French. — Conference organised by ICAA in co-
> operation with the Department of Services Against Addiction
> of the Commonwealth of Puerto Rico and the Inter-Caribbean
> Association Against Drug Abuse and Narcotic Addiction.

1. TONGUE, Eva
2. LAMBO, Richard T.
3. BLAIR, Brenda
4. INTERNATIONAL COUNCIL ON ALCOHOL AND ADDICTIONS
5. PUERTO RICO. *Department of Services Against Addiction*
6. INTER-CARIBBEAN ASSOCIATION AGAINST DRUG ABUSE
AND NARCOTIC ADDICTION

Comment: The description is fairly straightforward. Note (1) the parallel title in Spanish; (2) the inclusion of all the publication details within square brackets because they are not found in the document; (3) the provision of notes on language (rule 2.7B2) and statements of responsibility not named in the title and statement of responsibility area (2.7B6).

The heading for the main entry is clearly the name of the corporate body responsible (i.e. the conference) since it is prominently named in the item being catalogued (21.1B2(d)). The heading has been formulated using rule 24.7. In addition to the six added entries, it will be necessary to provide a reference from the Spanish name of the conference:

CONFERENCIA INTERNACIONAL SOBRE ALCOHOLISMO
& ABUSO DE DROGAS
see
INTERNATIONAL CONFERENCE ON ALCOHOLISM AND
DRUG ABUSE

Example 5

UNITED KINGDOM. *Parliament. House of Commons.*
Select Committee on the Telephone Service.
Reports from Select Committee on the Telephone Service
with proceedings, minutes of evidence, appendices and
indices, 1895-98. — Shannon : Irish University Press, 1971. —
1089 p. ; 35 cm. — (British parliamentary papers. Transport
and communications, posts and telegraphs ; 8). — Facsim. of:
1st eds. London : H.M.S.O., 1895 & 1898. Also includes
original pagings. — Quarter leather binding. — ISBN
0-7165-1244-0.

1. Series

Comment: This work clearly falls into one of the categories requiring entry under corporate body, being reports of a committee of the House of Commons. The real problem lies in the choice of heading: the committee must be entered as a subheading of the House of Commons (rule 24.18, type 2); the House of Commons, being one chamber of the British legislature, must be entered as a subheading of the legislature (24.21A); and the legislative body (Parliament) must be entered as a subheading of the government (24.18, type 6).

Note that the heading for the British government, according to the examples in AACR 2, is now UNITED KINGDOM but many libraries, including the Library of Congress and the British Library, are continuing to use GREAT BRITAIN, mainly for economic reasons. An added entry is required under the series (rule 21.30L) and a number of references are called for:

PARLIAMENT (*United Kingdom*)
> *see*

UNITED KINGDOM. *Parliament*

HOUSE OF COMMONS
> *see*

UNITED KINGDOM. *Parliament. House of Commons*

SELECT COMMITTEE ON THE TELEPHONE SERVICE
> *see*

UNITED KINGDOM. *Parliament. House of Commons. Select Committee on the Telephone Service*

UNITED KINGDOM. *House of Commons*
> *see*

UNITED KINGDOM. *Parliament. House of Commons*

UNITED KINGDOM. *Parliament. Select Committee on the Telephone Service*
> *see*

UNITED KINGDOM. *Parliament. House of Commons. Select Committee on the Telephone Service*

UNITED KINGDOM. *Select Committee on the Telephone Service*
> *see*

UNITED KINGDOM. *Parliament. House of Commons. Select Committee on the Telephone Service.*

GREAT BRITAIN
> *see*

UNITED KINGDOM

Example 6

STAINER, J.
The Crucifixion [music] : a meditation on the Sacred Passion of the Holy Redeemer : for two solo voices (tenor and bass) and chorus, and interspersed with hymns to be sung by the congregation / the words selected and written by J. Sparrow-Simpson ; the music by J. Stainer. — Rev. ed. — London : Novello, [19 –]. — 1 score (58 p.) ; 25 cm.

1. SPARROW-SIMPSON, J.
2. Ti.

Comment: A music score described in accordance with chapter 1 and chapter 5. The word 'Crucifixion' is capitalized, although not the first word of the title, because it is a religious event (Appendix A.19E); the same applies to 'Sacred Passion', while 'Holy Redeemer' represents Christ (Appendix A.19A). The GMD follows the title proper within square brackets. Although the title-page gives 'the Rev J. Sparrow-Simpson, M A', his title and degree are omitted, without marks of omission, in accordance with rule 1.1F7. The item is undated and only the century is certain, so it is recorded within square brackets. The physical description area begins with the specific material designation (score).

Main entry is under the composer (rule 21.19A), with added entries under the writer of the words (21.19A, 21.30A) and title (21.30J). Sparrow-Simpson is entered under the first part of his hyphenated name (22.5C3), and a reference will be necessary from the second half (26.2A3):

> SIMPSON, J. Sparrow-
> *see*
> SPARROW-SIMPSON, J.

Example 7

> HANDEL, George Frederick
> [Messiah. Selections]
> Highlights from Messiah [sound recording] / Handel. — London : Music for Pleasure, 1959. — 1 sound cassette (ca. 120 min.) : analog, stereo., Dolby processed. — Soloists and the Huddersfield Choral Society (chorus master: Herbert Bardgett); Royal Liverpool Philharmonic Orchestra, conducted by Sir Malcolm Sargent, organ: Eric Chadwick. — Contents: side 1. Comfort ye — Ev'ry valley — And the glory of the Lord — For unto us a child is born — Behold the Lamb of God, side 2. He was despised — Hallelujah — I know that my Redeemer liveth — Worthy is the Lamb — Amen. — Music for pleasure: TC CFP 40020.
>
> 1. Ti
> 2. ROYAL LIVERPOOL PHILHARMONIC ORCHESTRA
> 3. HUDDERSFIELD CHORAL SOCIETY
> 4. SARGENT, *Sir* Malcolm

Comment: A sound cassette described in accordance with chapter 1 and chapter 6. The title proper is followed by the GMD and the statement of responsibility is transposed to its correct position in the entry (rule 1.1F3); it precedes the title on the cassette. The trade name (Music for Pleasure) is given as the publisher rather than EMI Records (6.4D2). The physical description area begins with the specific material designation and is follows by an optional approximate duration, the type of recording, details of sound channels and (optionally) recording and reproduction characteristics (6.5). The speed, number of tracks and dimensions (including width) are not given as they are standard. Details of the performers are given in the note area rather than in the title and statement of responsibility area (6.1F1, 6.7B6) and the contents are recorded (6.7B18).

In accordance with the rule 21.23A, which says enter a sound recording of a musical work under the heading for that work, the main entry is under Handel. This is followed by the uniform title formulated in accordance with 25.27A and 25.6B3. Rule 21.23A states that added entries should be made under the principal performers if there are not more than three; Sargent, the Huddersfield Choral Society and the Royal Liverpool Philharmonic Orchestra are considered likely access points, as well as the title.

The use of the term 'analog' is introduced in the 1988 revision of AACR 2 in order to distinguish this type of recording from the newer compact disc, which is described as 'digital'. Compare the following physical descriptions:

1 sound disc : analog, 33⅓ rpm, stereo. ; 12 in.
1 sound disc : digital, stereo. ; 4¾ in.

Example 8

BRYANT, Martin
    Colossus chess [computer file] / by Martin Bryant. —
[Version] 4.00. — Computer program. — Doncaster : CDS
Software, c1986. — 1 computer cassette ; 3⅞ x 2½ in. + 1
instructions (28 p.) in container 22 x 18 x 2 cm. — Game. —
System requirements: Amstrad 8256/8512.

    1. Ti

Comment: A computer program described in accordance with chapter 1 and chapter 9. The GMD follows the title proper. Optionally, because a GMD has been used, the word 'computer' could be omitted from the file designation area (i.e. Computer program) and from the physical description (i.e. 1 computer cassette).

Main entry is under the person responsible for the intellectual content of the item (21.1A and 21.4A).

International Standard Bibliographic Description
For comparative purposes, the above entry is shown below as it would appear if it had been compiled according to ISBD(CF), the International Standard Bibliographic Description (Computer Files):

BRYANT, Martin
  Colossus chess [Computer file] / by Martin Bryant. —
[Version] 4.00. — Computer program. — Doncaster : CDS
Software, cop. 1986. — 1 computer tape cassette +
instructions (28 p.) in container, 22 x 18 x 2 cm. — Game. —
System requirements: Amstrad 8256/8512.

    1. Ti

The similarity of the entries is immediately obvious, although there are some
minor differences, i.e. the C of Computer file is capitalized, the copyright
date uses the abbreviation cop. rather than c., the specific material designation
has the word 'tape' added and no dimensions are given because they are
standard.

Example 9

  ALICE in wonderland [object]. — London : Spear, c1973. — 1
   game (board, 7 counters, cup, dice) ; in box 19 x 36 x 3 cm.
  + a short synopsis of the "Alice" stories by Gyles Brandreth
  (8 p. ; 22 cm.). — Based on the "Alice" stories by Lewis
  Carroll. — Instructions (on box lid) and synopsis of the "Alice"
  stories in English, French and Dutch. — For 2-6 players 6
  years onwards.

    1. CARROLL, Lewis

Comment: A game described in accordance with chapters 1 and 10 (three-
dimensional artefacts and realia). The GMD is given after the title proper.

The suggested added entry under CARROLL might seem surprising, but
the existence of the game could be helpful to the student of Lewis Carroll.
If the entry is provided, a reference will be required from Carroll's real name:

    DODGSON, Charles Lutwidge
     see
    CARROLL, Lewis

Gyles Brandreth's contribution would not appear to justify an added entry.

Example 10

THEATRE research international. — Vol. 1, no. 1 (Oct.
1975)- . — [London] : Oxford University Press for the
International Federation for Theatre Research, 1975- . —
v. : ill., plans, ports. ; 24 cm. — Three issues yearly. —
"Contributions appear only in English but articles are provided
with résumés in French" — T.p. verso. — Supersedes: Theatre
research = Recherches théâtrales. — ISSN 0307-8833

1. INTERNATIONAL FEDERATION FOR THEATRE RESEARCH

Comment: A printed serial described in accordance with chapter 1, chapter 12 and chapter 2. The second area, after the title and statement of responsibility area, is the numeric and/or alphabetic, chronological, or other designation area. The place of publication is given within square brackets because it does not appear on the item. The physical description area begins with the specific material designation (v. in this case) and is followed by details of illustrations and the height. There are notes giving the frequency (rule 12.7B1), language (12.7B2) and relationship with a previous serial (12.7B7). The previous serial had a parallel title in French. The GMD has been omitted.

Main entry is under title (21.1C) with an added entry under the responsible corporate body. A separate main entry will be made under the superseded title, with a note 'superseded by: Theatre research internation', and a *see* reference from the parallel title:

RECHERCHES théâtrales
   see
THEATRE research

Chapter Six
The subject approach: pre-coordinate indexing

For the person requiring information on a specific topic, the facility of a subject approach is essential. Using such an approach, the enquirer is able to find items which are available on a given subject. It is also helpful if items on subjects *related* to the specific subject of the enquiry can be traced. For example, the enquirer seeking titles dealing with the subject 'transport' should be made aware that there may be other relevant titles entered under 'railways', etc.

Little difficulty will be experienced in formulating subject entries for simple, single concepts such as 'chairs', or 'cleaning', or 'upholstery'. However, such simple concepts are necessarily and continually combined or coordinated to form more complex subjects, e.g. 'cleaning upholstery of chairs'. Now the formulation of subject entries becomes more problematic.

When concepts are combined or coordinated to form complex subjects, such coordination may be carried out by the *indexer* or by the *searcher*. The former is referred to as *pre-coordinate* indexing and the latter as *post-coordinate indexing*.

In pre-coordinate indexes, the complete context of a subject is, at some point, presented to the enquirer, e.g.:

Chairs : Upholstery : Cleaning

In post-coordinate indexing, only the constituent concepts are presented, e.g.:

Chairs

Upholstery

Cleaning

The searcher must carry out the process of combination or coordination. Post-coordination is considered more fully in chapter 7.

Pre-coordinate indexing

The normal book index is a pre-coordinate index. Here is an index entry from an encyclopaedia:

United States of America,
   motor car production

All of the constituent elements of the subject are given at the one point. Similarly, the subject entry in a manual library catalogue has traditionally been presented in this way.

The earliest form of subject catalogue is the *classified* form and this is the first of the pre-coordinate subject approaches which will be examined.

Classified catalogues

Systematically arranged catalogues have a long history; some date back to the thirteenth and fourteenth centuries and the classified approach probably remains the principal approach in the bibliographies and catalogues of Europe; this is certainly so in the United Kingdom. In a survey carried out by the authors in the late 1970s, 270 (81%) out of a total of 334 responding libraries used a classified catalogue and a further 7 libraries (2%) used a combination of a classified approach with some other inner form. The 270 libraries comprised 122 academic, 123 public and 25 special.[1] In the intervening years some of these libraries will have implemented online catalogues but this number is as yet too small to influence the overall trend.

A classified catalogue is usually arranged in the order of the scheme used for shelf arrangement in the library. Of course, it is possible to use broad classification on the shelves, which may allow for easy shelf maintenance, and a more detailed classification in the catalogue for speedy retrieval of specific items.

A classified sequence obviously requires alphabetical *indexes* to facilitate its use and the classified catalogue generally consists, therefore, of three sequences: a main sequence in classified order; an alphabetical author/title index; and an alphabetical subject index. The two alphabetical indexes may be combined if desired.

---

[1] Based on information received as part of a survey of indexers' reactions to PRECIS (see p.268).

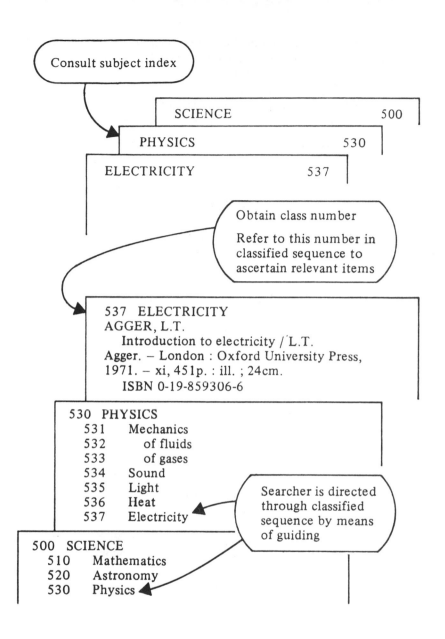

Consult subject index

| SCIENCE | 500 |

| PHYSICS | 530 |

| ELECTRICITY | 537 |

Obtain class number

Refer to this number in classified sequence to ascertain relevant items

537 ELECTRICITY
AGGER, L.T.
    Introduction to electricity / L.T.
Agger. – London : Oxford University Press,
1971. – xi, 451p. : ill. ; 24cm.
    ISBN 0-19-859306-6

530 PHYSICS
    531   Mechanics
    532   of fluids
    533   of gases
    534   Sound
    535   Light
    536   Heat
    537   Electricity

Searcher is directed through classified sequence by means of guiding

500 SCIENCE
    510   Mathematics
    520   Astronomy
    530   Physics

The subject approach in the classified catalogue

55

The classified sequence contains the *main* entries, i.e. those which provide the fullest information. It may also include *added* entries for subsidiary subjects and *analytical* entries for specific parts of an item.

The author/index entries may be simplified, although, when unit cataloguing is practised, such entries will be just as detailed as the main entries. This index sometimes contains more than its name suggests – such as entries under editors, illustrators, members of a cast, producers, directors, series and, indeed, any heading which could be used as a possible access point.

The subject index entries do not contain details of actual items but simply consist of the names of subjects and their class numbers. It is usual for the subject indexer to maintain an 'authority file' of class numbers showing the index terms which have been used under each number. This provides a quick check upon previous decisions and also ensures that appropriate subject index entries can be removed when the last book or other item on a subject has been withdrawn.

Indexing the classified catalogue

The subject index enables the searcher to discover the class number of any particular subject required. It can have an important secondary function, in that, as Melvil Dewey realized, it can bring together related topics which are *separated* by the classification. Such an index *complements* rather than repeats the classified sequence and is known as a *relative* index.

Chain procedure

Chain procedure, which was developed by S. R. Ranganathan, is a methodology which systematizes the preparation of index entries for the classified catalogue and which also achieves the secondary objective noted above, the collocation of 'distributed relatives'. A simple example of chain indexing (using Ranganathan's *Colon classification*) is:

Subject: The harvesting of the apple
Classificationl number: J371:7

Chain, i.e. the classification hierarchy for the subject working from general to special:

J	Agriculture
J3	Food
J37	Fruit
J371	Apple
J371:7	Harvesting

Index entries are produced by beginning with the last, or more specific 'link' in the chain and proceeding step by step through the chain, qualifying, where necessary, by a more general term or terms to indicate the subject context:

Harvesting: Apples: Agriculture	J371:1
Apples: Agriculture	J371
Fruit: Agriculture	J37
Food: Agriculture	J3
Agriculture	J

It is the process of qualification which leads to the production of a relative index. The subject 'Food', for instance, will not only be found in class J 'Agriculture' but also in other classes such as 'Cookery' and 'Medicine'. When items which deal with these aspects of the subject are added to a collection and indexed, the alphabetical index will assume the following appearance:

Food: Agriculture	J3
Food: Animal husbandry	KZ3
Food: Cookery	M31
Food: Medicine	L573

Thus the various aspects of the subject which are separated by the classification are brought together in the index.

The fact that chain procedure is dependent upon a classification scheme can present problems. The indexer must adjust terminology and spelling where necessary, watch for hierarchical 'faults' in the chain and remember to index synonyms. The chain may also need to be extended to ensure that the *specific* subject of an item is indexed. These processes can be illustrated by considering a further example.

The subject 'How to sail the Mirror dinghy' would be classified by the Dewey Decimal Classification (20th ed.) at 797.124 and the chain, taken directly from the scheme, would be:

790	Recreational and performing arts
797	Aquatic and air sports
797.1	Boating
797.12	With specific types of vessel
797.124	Sailboating

In a British library, this chain would be adjusted, altered and extended to give the following:

790	Recreation
796	Sports
797	Aquatic sports
	Water sports
797.1	Boating
797.124	Sailing
	Dinghies
	Mirror dinghies

which would result in the index entries:

Mirror dinghies: Sailing	797.124
Dinghies: Sailing	797.124
Sailing	797.124
Boating	797.1
Water sports	797
Aquatic sports	797
Sports	796
Recreation	790

It can be seen that chain is not a purely mechanical process, as is sometimes suggested, but a semi-mechanical process which requires the use of a certain amount of common sense in order to produce 'sought' entries. It is, however, a proven method and 106 (32%) of 334 libraries in the United Kingdom surveyed by the authors in 1977 were found to be using it.[1] It was also used with great success by the *British national bibliography* from its inception in 1950 up to 1970.

When it was decided to produce the *BNB* by computerized methods, investigation indicated that chain indexing could not easily be 'automated' owing to the fact that the method is directly related to a classification scheme with all of the hierarchical and other problems that this relationship presents. The special research team set up to examine techniques for adding subject data to the MARC record soon came to the conclusion that what was required was a new type of indexing system, to be completely independent of any particular classification scheme. This led to the development of PRECIS. (It should be reported, however, that in later years chain procedure was successfully 'automated' by a number of libraries, among which may be mentioned the London Borough of Barnet, Bedfordshire County, Coventry, Dorset County and Kingston Polytechnic. *See also* p.160.)

PRECIS

At first, PRECIS was referred to as a 'rotated' index but later the term 'shunted' was used to describe the way in which the computer manipulates the concepts in a subject statement to produce the various required entries. Unlike chain indexing, the 'context' is preserved at all entry points and the acronym actually stands for PREserved Context Index System. This conveys the intention of offering to the user a kind of 'precis' of the subject content of an item under every term which the indexer regards as significant enough to be used as an entry word. Authority files of the terms used are built up and maintained, thus ensuring that the same subject is consistently indexed under the same form of words whenever it appears.

---

[1] Based on information received as part of a survey of indexers' reactions to PRECIS (see p.268).

Unlike traditional alphabetical indexes and subject headings lists, but like the system developed by Coates for *British technology index* (now *Current technology index*), PRECIS consists essentially of a set of working procedures rather than a prescribed list of terms or phrases.

The system is based on the concept of an open-ended vocabulary, which allows terms to be admitted into the index at any time, once they have been encountered in the literature. When a term is admitted, the relationships with other terms are handled in two different ways, distinguished as the 'syntactical' and 'semantic' sides of the system.

All the elements of the syntax are embodied in a scheme of 'role operators', one of which is prefixed to each term in a string of terms summarizing the subject of a document. The position of each term in the string is normally determined by the ordinal value of its preceding operator.

Sample role operators are:

(0)   Location
(1)   Key system
(2)   Action; Effect of action
(3)   Performer of transitive action (agent, instrument)
(6)   Form of document; Target user
(p)   Part/Property

When allocating role operators, the recommended procedure is first to seek a term denoting action, then to look for the object of the action which will become the key system. For example, the subject 'Education of librarians in the United States' can be analysed into the concepts: 'Education', 'Librarians' and 'United States'. The 'action' is obviously 'Education'; 'Librarians' then becomes the key system and the 'United States' is clearly the location. The 'string' thus derived is therefore:

(0)   United States
(1)   librarians
(2)   education

The order of terms achieved by the operators is based upon a system of context dependency, each term setting the next term into its obvious context.

Computer instruction codes are added to the string and the computer will shunt each term through three basic positions in the index entries, thus:

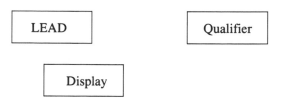

giving, for the example quoted above, the entries:

United States
Librarians. Education

Librarians. United States
Education

Education. Librarians. United States

Lower-case operators may be interposed at any point in the string. For example, for the subject 'design of aircraft engines', the string would appear as:

(1) aircraft
(p) engines
(2) design

giving the entries:

Aircraft
Engines. Design

Engines. Aircraft
Design

Design. Engines. Aircraft

The above syntactical side of the system is complemented by the semantic side which allows for the automatic production of references to link synonyms, related terms, etc., and a vast number of these are required. Examples of references which would be needed for the subject 'design of aircraft engines' are:

Motors *See* **Engines**

Aeronautics
See also **Aircraft**

PRECIS is a sophisticated automated indexing system offering a high degree of versatility. An attempt has been made to keep the above explanation reasonably simple. There are, for instance, additional role operators and a further group of operators known as connectives, which allow for a degree of articulation to be introduced into index entries, for example:

Drivers. Cars
Responsibility for safety of passengers

Libraries
Cooperation with museums

Detailed guidance on the construction of PRECIS strings is available in the form of a manual of use written by the system's originator, Derek Austin. A second edition of this manual was published in 1984[1] and this was followed in 1985 by a companion volume *PRECIS : a primer* by Mary Dykstra.[2]

PRECIS has been used in the *BNB* since 1971 and has also been used in the *Australian national bibliography, British education index, British catalogue of audiovisual materials*, catalogues of audio-visual materials published by the British Universities Film Council, and other bibliographical tools. A number of libraries have used PRECIS to construct their own indexes.

The document-specificity allowed by PRECIS has been compared favourably with the broad subject headings of LCSH (the list of *Subject headings used in the dictionary catalogs of the Library of Congress* which is described later in this text) but this document-specificity can have disadvantages when used with a classified catalogue because the notation (particularly in a scheme such as the Dewey Decimal Classification) may not have the same specificity as the index entry. It may, therefore, be necessary to consult several titles under one notation before finding the specific subject being sought. For this reason a one-stage index such as that introduced by Audrey Taylor into the Aurora High School Library, York County, Ontario (see p.62) has attractions.

Apart from the Canadian application of PRECIS noted above, there is additional evidence of North American interest. Mary Dykstra has found it to be vastly superior to LCSH[3] and an American public librarian (Rochelle R Reed) argued that specific information is wanted by the 'general' user in public libraries as much as by the subject specialist in academic libraries and that PRECIS is more adequate for this than LCSH.[4] Edward J. Blume of the Library of Congress and George F. Heise of the H. W. Wilson Company accepted the value of PRECIS as an indexing tool but were concerned about the administrative and economic implications of a change.[5] However, C. Donald Cook maintains that 'PRECIS has been adopted and is proving satisfactory in one of the major bibliographic agencies of the world. It cannot be ignored in North America'.[6] An introduction to the system, aimed specifically at North American audiences has also been published.[7]

---

[1] *PRECIS : a manual of concept analysis and subject indexing* / Derek Austin and Mary Dykstra. — 2nd ed. — London : British Library, 1984.

[2] *PRECIS : a primer* / Mary Dykstra. — London : British Library, 1985.

[3] *The PRECIS index system : principles, applications and prospects* ... / edited by Hans H. Wellisch. — New York : H. W. Wilson Company, 175-85.

[4] ibid., 195.

[5] ibid., 195.

[6] ibid., 193.

[7] *Introduction to PRECIS for North American Usage* / Phyllis A. Richmond. — Littleton, Colorado : Libraries Unlimited, 1981.

When the Library of Congress made a study of PRECIS in the late 1970s, the Library concluded that it liked it as a mode of accessing material. Unfortunately, adopting it as well as continuing the assignment of Library of Congress subject headings — a sine qua non, according to the views of the American library community — would have meant an increase in operating costs of approximately $1,000,000 per annum.

MOUNT ETNA
  Volcanic eruption, 1971 -- Illustrations
      REF 500.5 NAT Nature/science annual, 1972 edition. 1971

MOUNT WILSON OBSERVATORY See PALOMAR & MOUNT WILSON OBSERVATORY

MOUNTAIN BIOMES See ALPINE BIOMES

MOUNTAIN CLIMBING EXPEDITIONS See MOUNTAINEERING EXPEDITIONS

MOUNTAIN LIONS. Endangered species of mammals. Canada
  Conservation
      599.74428 WRI Eastern panther. Wright, Bruce S. Clarke, Irwin. 1972

MOUNTAIN SHEEP See BIGHORN SHEEP

MOUNTAINEERING EXPEDITIONS
  to 1960
      500.9 MIL Mountains. Milne, Lorus Johnson. 1969

MOUNTAINS
  See also
      ALPINE BIOMES
      ALPS
      MOUNT ETNA

MOUNTAINS
  Formation. Geological aspects
      500.9 MIL   Mountains. Milne, Lorus Johnson. 1969
      550 CAI   Anatomy of the earth. Cailleux, André. [1968]
      550 GAS   Understanding the earth. Gass, Ian Graham. [1971]
      551.4 WYC Rock, time, and landforms. -- Wyckoff, Jerome. [1st ed.]. -- [1966]

MOUSE See MICE

MOVEMENT
  See also
    KINESIOLOGY
    LOCOMOTION
    MOTION

MOVEMENT. Organisms
  Effects of light. Photobiology
      574.19153 WOL Photobiology. Wolken, Jerome J. [c1968]

MOVIES
  Film techniques. Psychological aspects
      001.5076 TER The mind benders. Teringo, J. Robert. 1969

Extract from one-stage PRECIS index — Aurora High School Library, Ontario, Canada

Despite these favourable comments, PRECIS has been criticized for being over-complex and one of the major reasons for this complexity is that PRECIS was designed to utilize the immense powers of the computer yet had as its main aim the production of a printed output. The British Library has been appreciative that the 'age of the printed index is drawing to a close and, at the same time, there is an increasing need for financial stringency'.[1] Thus there have been two prime factors to be considered where the future of PRECIS is concerned: cost-effectiveness and usefulness in an online interactive mode. Trotter has stated that three important features of PRECIS which need to be retained and exploited in an interactive automated environment are, first, the use of the open-ended, yet controlled and structured vocabulary that allows terms to be entered as encountered; second, the arrangement of terms into subject strings organized by principles of context dependency, so that the relationship between them is immediately comprehensible to the user; third, the fact that the system allows records to be re-used for subsequent titles on the same subject, thus increasing collocation of material as well as promoting cost-effectiveness.[2] Other elements traditionally associated with PRECIS can be dropped as they are not relevant to the new approach. When subject data is being searched online the distinction between terms as lead and non-lead becomes meaningless. Thus there is no need for the two-line index entry, nor for the shunting of terms. At a stroke this removes the need for complex manipulation of data to produce sophisticated output; PRECIS is reduced to its basic components. The result should be 'a subject authority system that contains the best of the basic qualities of the PRECIS system without its complexities, and also builds on PRECIS to produce a system that can be created, searched and displayed in an automated interactive environment'.[3] Working from these principles, a new subject system has been developed to replace PRECIS as from January 1991. This new system is called COMPASS.

COMPASS (COMputer Aided Subject System)[4]
The aim of COMPASS is to promote maximum recall of material. The user can then further refine the selection by using other data present in the bibliographic record, e.g. Dewey classification number. As COMPASS dispenses with most of the complex coding associated with PRECIS, it simplifies the indexer's task and thus greatly improves the turnaround time for records.

---

[1] *Developments in classification and indexing − Dewey and PRECIS* / Ross Trotter. − Paper delivered at seminar *New rules for old games* organized by The Library Association Continuing Education Department, 24 Oct 1989.
[2] ibid.
[3] ibid.
[4] The information on COMPASS presented here is taken from publicity and other material kindly supplied by The British Library National Bibliographic Service. For an explanation of fields, tags and the MARC record *see* Chapter 11.

COMPASS takes from PRECIS the following basic components:

1   an authority file of controlled terms and subject statements for use in bibliographic records
2   a network of related terms, from broader to narrower and between used and non-used terms.

From these two basic components has been built a system which will have a controlled indexing vocabulary with which complex subjects can be constructed in a consistent way and in which the vocabulary of terms can be linked in a thesaural network. After the core file of subject authority records has been established, work will begin on developing the network of related terms but it is unlikely that this will be completed before 1993.

The core file of authority records is being created using WLN software from the old PRECIS subject authority file. This has the advantage of providing some continuity between the old and the new subject data. The core file will not be fully in place until mid-1991 at the earliest.

The subject authority file is made up of two main types of records − terms and strings.

Term authority records are cither unitary expressions (single words) or compound expressions (more than one word) of simple concepts. They are divided into topical terms and geographical terms, identified by different field tags:

160.0   for topics
161.0   for geographical concepts

They have different subfield codes, so that unitary expressions are coded $a and compound expressions are coded $b, e.g.:

160.0$aPhysics   (unitary topical term)
160.0$bConcrete bridges   (compound topical term)

161.0$aFrance   (unitary geographical term)
161.0$bNew South Wales   (compound geographical term)

Term authority records control the vocabulary and provide the thesaural framework and so will be linked to other terms as appropriate. They can also be linked to bibliographic records if the terms constitute an adequate expression of the subject of the work.

String authority records consist of combinations of two or more terms expressing complex subject concepts. There is only one type − topical string records, which are identified by the field tag 160.1. Each contains unitary or compound expressions as defined above in any combination. To use such an expression it must already exist in the authority file as a term. Topical string authority records also have a third subfield − $c − to be used for connecting words, which are only present to show the relationship between the terms in the string and are not required in their own right, e.g.:

160.1$bMotor vehicles$aDesign$cApplications of$cComputers

As the topical terms and geographical terms are in separate fields, they can be more effectively controlled.

There are no geographic string records in the system; such data is added directly to the bibliographic record.

The subject records, as described above, form one part of a larger file of authority records including personal and corporate names. To avoid duplication, these names no longer form part of the subject record.

Greater control over choice of indexing terms will be exercised in the system. Differentiation of terms will be kept to a minimum, rather than letting it go unchecked as it did in PRECIS. Only one difference of modification will be allowed, thus 'Concrete bridges' is valid but not 'Reinforced concrete bridges'; 'Skimmed milk' and 'Powdered milk' are valid but not 'Skimmed powdered milk'. This is to ensure that expressions in strings exist in the authority file as terms.

When a British Library BNBMARC record is created, data from the subject authority file (along with headings from the name authority file) is added to the bibliographic data to form the whole record. The fields 660 (for topical descriptors) and 661 (for geographical descriptors) are used.

Names as subjects, topical terms and strings and geographical terms are held separately in the record. For example, Alistair Horne's biography of Macmillan contains:

    660.0$aPolitics
    661.0$bGreat Britain
    600.1$aMacmillan$hHarold$c1984-1986

and Michael Foot's biography of Aneurin Bevan would contain:

    660.0$aPolitics
    661.0$bGreat Britain
    600.1$aBevan$hAneurin

This allows the subject authority records 'Politics' and 'Great Britain' to be re-used, unlike PRECIS which requires a separate string for each biography.

The new system uses an 'holistic' approach and reflects the fact that in an automated catalogue environment access is made to the whole of the bibliographic record and its data elements. Subject information can be retrieved from many parts of the record, not only from standard subject headings and indexing terms.

With the introduction of COMPASS, subject data in the classified section of the *British national bibliography* appears in a numbered tracing as the last element of each entry (see p.243).

The greatest change is in the alphabetical subject index to the *BNB* where references are no longer included. To compensate for this, the British Library plans to produce a new thesaurus which will list all the authority terms together with their relationships. This should be published during 1991.

Behaviour therapy
Mentally handicapped persons. Behaviour therapy
616.891420874

Beliefs
Beliefs 140

Bells
Churches. Bells, *History* 786.8848094261

Benefits (Payments)
Benefits (Payments) 361.960941

Bereavement
Bereavement 306.88

Bicycles
Bicycles. Riding 796.6

Biochemistry
Biochemistry 574.192
Biochemistry. Terminology 574.192014

Bioengineering
Bioengineering 660.65

Biographies
Teaching. Biographies 371.10092

Biology
Biology 574
Biology *Related to* Christianity 261.55
Biology *Use of* Statistical mathematics 574.015195

Biotechnology
Biotechnology 547.005
Biotechnology 660.605
Biotechnology 660.60952
Biotechnology 660.6
Humans. Blood *Use of* Biotechnology 615.39

Birds
Birds 598
Birds 598.2941
Birds 598.297

Black persons
Black persons 363.20973
Black persons 973.0496073022
Black persons. Racial discrimination 323.11968

Black women
Black women 808.89896082
Teachers. Black women, *History* 371.10092

Blind persons
Blind persons. Personal adjustment 362.41092

Blood
Humans. Blood. Metabolic disorders *Role of* Calcium
616.399
Humans. Blood *Use of* Biotechnology 615.39

Bomber aircraft
Bomber aircraft, *History* 623.7463
World War 1. Bomber aircraft 940.44941

Bones
Humans. Bones. Surgery 617.3

Bonsai
Bonsai 635.9772

Books
Books. Trades 381.450020952

Boxing
Boxing 796.83092
Boxing, *History* 796.830922

Brain
Humans. Brain. Hypertension 616.8
Mammals. Brain. Receptors 599.0188

Breasts
Women. Breasts. Radiography 616.994490757

Breeding
Livestock. Breeding 636.0821

Bridge (Card games)
Bridge (Card games)

Cameras
Cameras 771.31
Cameras 771.32

Cameroon
Cameroon, *History* 966.11

Canals
Canals 386.46092
Canals 386.4809428
Canals. Cruising 797.1

Cancellations (Postage stamps)
Cancellations (Postage stamps) 796.567

Cancer
Humans. Cancer. Psychotherapy 616.99406
Men. Testes. Cancer 616.99463

Canoeing
Canoeing. Techniques 797.122

Capital
Capital 332.041

Capitalism
Capitalism 330.1220922
Capitalism 330.122
Humans. Social behaviour *Effects of* Capitalism 302

Carbohydrates
Organisms. Carbohydrates 574.19248

Carbon
Carbon 546.6811

Carbon dioxide
Climate *Effects of* Carbon dioxide 551.6

Care
Care 362.0425
Humans. Dementia. Care 362.2
Old persons. Care *Role of* Health services 362.63
Patients. Care 613
Patients. Care. Documentation 615.82

Carols
Carols 782.28

Carpentry
Carpentry 694

Cars
Cars 629.2222
Cars 629.28722
Cars, *History* 629.2222
Cars. Maintenance 629.28722
Cars. Rallying 796.72092

Cases (Law)
Cases (Law) 344.17084
Civil law. Cases (Law) 344.20725

Castles
Castles 914.1003
Castles, *History* 914.104859

Cataloguing
Rare books. Cataloguing 025.34160941

Catalysis
Catalysis 541.395

Catering
Catering. Management 647.95068

Catering establishments
Catering establishments 647.954105

Catholicism
Catholicism. Doctrines 230.2
Catholicism *Related to* Society, *History* 282.44

Catholics
Catholics, *History, 1691-1799* 305.620415

Cats
Cats 636.8
Cats. Veterinary medicine. Herbal remedies
636.70895321

BNB entries using COMPASS
Extract from issue no. 2123 30 Jan. 1991

```
001            b8623728#
008            890720$as1986$ben$e0$f1$g0$h0$i0$leng$nb$pW#
015.00:0/0 $ab8623728#
021.10:0/0 $a0408008245$bv$ccorrect#
024.00:0/0 $a25017789$c+UKX#
082.00:0/0 $a620.00420285$c20#
111.00:0/0 $aCAD 86$eConference$jLondon, England#
245.00:0/0 $aKnowledge engineering and computer modelling in CAD#
260.00:0/0 $bButterworth$c1986#
300.00:0/0 $aix,476p#
350.00:0/0 $a:40.00 : CIP rev.#
660.10:0/0 $aEngineering$aDesign$cUse of$aComputers#
911.00:0/0 $aInternational Conference on the Computer as a Design
               Tool$i7th$k1986$jLondon, England$xSee$aCAD 86
               (Conference : London, England)#


001            b8701366#
008            891018$as1989$ben$e0$f0$g0$h1$i1$leng$nb$oh$pW#
010.00:0/0 $a86-23914#
015.00:0/0 $ab8701366#
021.10:0/0 $a0198127529$bx$cv.1$d:55.00#
021.10:0/1 $a019812337X$bx$cv.2$d:55.00#
021.10:0/2 $a0198123388$bx$cv.3$d:55.00#
024.00:0/0 $a26001305$c+UKX#
082.00:0/0 $a320.941$c20#
100.10:0/0 $aHalifax$hGeorge Savile$fMarquis of$c1633-1695#
245.14:0/0 $aThe works of George Savile Marquis of
               Halifax$eedited by Mark N. Brown#
260.00:0/0 $aOxford$bClarendon$c1989#
300.00:0/0 $f3$nv.$ifacsims$c23cm#
350.00:0/0 $aNo price : CIP rev.#
490.00:0/0 $aOxford English texts#
504.00:0/0 $aIncludes index#
660.00:0/0 $aPolitics#
661.00:0/0 $bGreat Britain#
700.11:0/0 $aBrown$hMark N.#
900.10:0/0 $aSavile$hGeorge$fMarquis of Halifax$xSee$aHalifax,
               George Savile,$xMarquis of,$x1633-1695#
```

BNB UKMARC records with new subject data in fields 660 and 661. Subject fields
no longer used (as from 1991) are:

083 (verbal feature heading)

690, 691, 692 (PRECIS string, SIN (Subject Indicator Number) and RIN
    (Reference Indicator Number))

Fields 050 (Library of Congress classification number) and 650, 651 (Library of
Congress subject headings) will also no longer be used

For an explanation of fields, tags and the MARC record *see* Chapter 11

Keyword indexing

Apart from the classified catalogue, the other predominant inner form at the beginning of the nineteenth century was the author catalogue. 'Subject' entries began to appear in such catalogues as the tendency to use 'catchwords', extracted from the titles, became more pronounced, e.g.:

Cookery, Everyday
Costume, A history of
Gardening, The concise encyclopedia of
Nursing, Pictorial home

A prominent advocate of the use of 'subject' words, i.e. catchwords, taken from titles, was Andrea Crestadoro. In 1856 Crestadoro produced a code of rules which he later (1864) applied to a catalogue of the Manchester Public Library.

One of the problems encountered with catchword-from-title indexing is that, very often, the title is *not* expressive of the subject content of a work. For example, *How to hold up a bank*, *Keep off the grass*, *The monstrous regiment* and *Out of the dinosaurs* are concerned, respectively, with the subjects civil engineering, drugs (marijuana), literary criticism and the evolution of the National Lending Library! Because of this, a more systematic method of selecting subject headings was favoured by many librarians. Perhaps the first was Charles C. Jewett, who wrote his important pamphlet *On the construction of catalogs of libraries* in 1852. Jewett's ideas were strongly reinforced by the publication of Cutter's major code of 1876.

However, the use of catchwords did not completely disappear. One major bibliography, Whitaker's *Books in print* (previously the *Reference catalogue of current literature*) has utilized them for many years, giving entries such as:

Cancer research, Mathematical models on (Wheldon) . . . /

With the advent of the computer, catchword indexing took on a new lease of life. It requires the minimum of intellectual effort and is, therefore, eminently suitable for mechanization. H. P. Luhn is generally recognized as having reintroduced the method under its new name of *keyword* indexing, in the United States, in the 1950s.

Many such keyword systems rely upon the automatic selection, by a computer, of the more important terms from the title of a document as index entries. The titles are printed out in an alphabetical sequence of these selected terms, e.g.:

                    The BINOMIAL theorem
                 Primary EDUCATION
                            GYMNASTICS for schools
            The teaching of MATHEMATICS
                            PRIMARY education
            Gymnastics for SCHOOLS
                            The TEACHING of mathematics
            The binomial THEOREM

Words not required as index entry points are placed on a 'stop' list and the computer is programmed to ignore them. Words such as 'the', 'for', 'of' and 'in', i.e., articles and prepositions, are obvious candidates for such treatment, but any word considered unnecessary as an indexing term may be included.

The above example illustrates KWIC (Key-Word *In* Context) indexing (see also p.159). Another similar method is KWAC (Key-Word *And* Context) which is illustrated below:

BINOMIAL	The binomial theorem
EDUCATION	Primary education
GYMNASTICS	Gymnastics for schools
MATHEMATICS	The teaching of mathematics
PRIMARY	Primary education
SCHOOLS	Gymnastics for schools
TEACHING	The teaching of mathematics
THEOREM	The binomial theorem

Some indexes are referred to as KWOC (Key-Word *Out-of* Context). These are very similar to KWAC indexes and differ only in the fact that the lead term is not repeated but is replaced by an asterisk, e.g.:

BINOMIAL	The * theorem
THEOREM	The binomial *

Some computerized keyword indexes have also included authors' names as entries. Examples are WADEX (Word and Author inDEX) and the AKWIC (Author and Key-Word In Context) index (see p.160).

Various attempts have been made to increase the efficiency of keyword indexing. One such technique was developed in the late 1960s at Ohio State University. This is referred to as 'Double-KWIC coordinate indexing'. The normal KWIC index provides access via only a single concept but Double-KWIC facilitates speedy coordination with other concepts. This is achieved by taking a word or phrase that would normally appear in the KWIC index column and using this as a main term, with the remaining context being rotated to create an ordered list of subordinate entries, e.g.:

NOMENCLATURE
    FLUORINATED MOLECULES   THE * OF HIGHLY
    HIGHLY FLUORINATED MOLECULES   THE * OF
    MOLECULES   THE * OF HIGHLY FLUORINATED

As with KWOC, the original location of the main term in the complete context is identified by an asterisk.

As the index expands, it will begin to take on the following appearance:

NOMENCLATURE
    BIOCHEMICAL *   THE ORGANIZATION AND FUNCTIONING OF
    CARBOHYDRATE *
    CHEMISTRY   THE * OF ORGANIC
    FLUORINATED MOLECULES   THE * OF HIGHLY
    FUNCTIONING OF BIOCHEMICAL *   THE ORGANIZATION AND
    HIGHLY FLUORINATED MOLECULES   THE * OF
    MOLECULES   THE * OF HIGHLY FLUORINATED
    ORGANIC CHEMISTRY   THE * OF
    ORGANIZATION AND FUNCTIONING OF BIOCHEMICAL *   THE

Although easy-to-produce, automated keyword indexes still have to face the problem referred to earlier, that of titles which are not indicative of subject content. It is possible, however, to 'enrich' indexes by the inclusion of additional indexing terms and it is also possible to suppress terms which are meaningless as subject index entries. The title *Keep off the grass* could be enriched by the addition of the indexing terms 'drugs' and 'marijuana' and have the other words in the title suppressed to give the entries:

Drugs   Keep off the grass
Marijuana   Keep off the grass

Once this is done, however, an *intellectual* element enters into the indexing process; it can no longer be automatic and we are approaching a 'choice of alphabetical subject heading' situation. It should also be noted that with the transition to online interactive interrogation of databases, the hard-copy keyword index is becoming much less common.

Alphabetical subject catalogues
The major difference between keyword indexing and the true alphabetical subject catalogue is that the latter attempts to bring together all books on the one subject at the *one* place. For instance, *The book of the bird* and *An introduction to ornithology* would not be indexed as:

Bird, The book of the
Ornithology, An introduction to

but one term would be chosen as the term under which both books are to be entered, e.g.:

70

BIRDS
   The book of the bird
   An introduction to ornithology

and a *reference* would be made to direct the searcher from the unused term to the one where information may be found, e.g.:

ORNITHOLOGY
   see
BIRDS

Terms which best express the subject matter of documents should be chosen and it is important that these terms be *specific*. A book on alsatians should be entered under 'Alsatians' and not under 'Dogs'; although, again, a reference can direct the searcher from the broader term, e.g.:

DOGS
   see also specific breeds, e.g.
ALSATIANS

Terms which may be used are entered in authority lists. Such lists not only contain terms which may be used as headings but also indicate references which should be made from unused terms (*see* references) and from related terms (*see also* references). For example, an entry for the term 'Halloween' might appear in an authority list thus:

Halloween
   Make *see* references from: All Hallow's Eve
                                Hallow-Eve
   Make *see also* references from: Folk lore
                                Manners and customs

   This entry indicates that of the three possible headings for this subject, 'Halloween', 'All Hallows' Eve' and 'Hallow-Eve', the one that *must* be used is 'Halloween'. References should then be made to this heading: *see* references from the two rejected names; and *see also* references from the broader related terms: 'Folk-lore' and 'Manners and customs'. The indexing language is therefore *controlled* and it can thus be said to be *artificial*.

   The first such authority list was *Subject headings used in the dictionary catalogs of the Library of Congress* published in 1914. Today, there are many such lists in a variety of subject areas and they are now generally referred to as *thesauri*. However, the LC list is *not* a thesaurus (see below).

Library of Congress subject headings
This authority list has gone through many editions. It is the most comprehensive list of subject headings in existence and automated methods are used to

71

produce it. The 13th edition, 1990,[1] contains subject headings created by cataloguers and used in cataloguing at the Library of Congress from 1898 through to December 1989. It is now sold as an annual subscription. Information about new and changed headings is contained in MARC tapes, in *L. C. Subject headings weekly lists*, in the quarterly *LCSH* in microfiche, and in the *Cataloging service bulletin*. The entire subject authority file is now also available on CD-ROM.[2]

Approved subject headings are listed in bold type, e.g. **Chemistry, Rivers,** etc. A heading may be followed by the code (*May Subd Geog*), which shows that the heading may be subdivided by place, and by Library of Congress class numbers (thus the list can act to a limited extent as a general index to the classification scheme). A scope note indicating the meaning or application of a heading may be given and then references associated with the heading are listed in groups. A new departure from the 11th edition is the use of accepted abbreviations such as BT and NT, now generally found in thesauri (see p.99), to express relationships (it should be noted, however, that the LCSH list is *not* a thesaurus − see p.98).

Here, for instance, is the entry for 'Halloween' as it appears in the LC list:

Halloween (*May Subd Geog*)
    [*GT4965*]
    UF All Hallows' Eve
       Hallow-Eve
    BT Manners and customs
    NT Halloween decorations
       Jack-o-lanterns

Note the similarity between this entry and that shown on p.71. For example, under UF, i.e. Use For, are those terms which have been considered for use but rejected. These rejected headings will be found in the alphabetical list but in light-face type and the indexer is directed to the preferred heading, e.g.:

All Hallows' Eve
    USE Halloween

Links to other subject headings are found under BT (Broader Terms) and NT (Narrower Terms) reflecting hierarchical relationships in which super-ordination and subordination are clearly stated.

---

[1] *Library of Congress subject headings* / prepared by Subject Cataloging Division Processing Services. — 13th ed. — Washington : Library of Congress. Cataloging Distribution Service, 1990. — Available also as cumulative microform ed. updated every three months.
[2] *CDMARC subjects*. — Washington : Library of Congress. Cataloging Distribution Service. — 1 computer laser optical disk. — Cumulates every three months.

Associate relationships are expressed by RT (Related Terms), e.g.:

Ornithology
RT Birds

Birds
RT Ornithology

General SA (See Also) references may also be made to an entire group of headings as an economy measure, e.g.:

Dog breeds
SA *names of specific breeds, e.g.* Bloodhounds,
Collies

The application of Library of Congress subject headings requires extensive use of subject subdivisions as a means of combining a number of different concepts into a single heading. Complex topics may therefore be represented by subject headings followed by subdivisions. Some subdivisions are given in the list but many more may be assigned according to certain rules. For example,

Hallmarks
—Forgeries

will be found in the list but

Motor vehicles
—History

will not. However, the latter heading can be constructed by the indexer from supplied instructions.

Here are a few more examples of actual entries from the LC list; note the scope note under the **Great Awakening** entry:

Gravity waves
[*QA927 (Mathematical)*]
UF Waves, Gravity
BT Gravity
Hydrodynamics
Waves

Grease
USE Lubrication and lubricants
Oils and fats

Great Awakening
> [*BR520*]
>
> Here are entered works dealing with the revival of religion
> that occurred in the American colonies in the 18th century
> UF Awakening, Great
> BT Religious awakening—Christianity
>   United States—Church history—Colonial period, ca. 1600-1775
> RT Evangelical Revival

In using the list, if it is decided that 'Gravity waves' is an appropriate
heading, then, as it is given in bold type, it may be used as the subject heading
under which details of the relevant item will appear. References will then
be made as instructed, i.e.:

Subject heading: GRAVITY WAVES

References: WAVES, GRAVITY
> *see*
> GRAVITY WAVES
>
> GRAVITY
> *see also*
> GRAVITY WAVES
>
> HYDRODYNAMICS
> *see also*
> GRAVITY WAVES
>
> WAVES
> *see also*
> GRAVITY WAVES

Note that the new symbols such as USE and NT need not necessarily be
used in library catalogues. Those who wish to continue to make cross-
references in the manner to which they have become accustomed should do so.

Although there are currently over 180,000 entries in LC subject headings,
including many personal names and corporate headings, clearly it is impossible
to list all such names and these may be assigned as subject headings by the
indexer. Authority records for such headings may be found in the *Name
authorities* cumulative microfiche edition.[1]

---

[1] *Name authorities.* — Microform ed. — Washington : Library of Congress. Cataloging
Distribution Service. — The annual subscription consists of four cumulative quarterly
issues plus a fifth issue which cumulates all 1987-90 data. The 1977-86 cumulation should
also be purchased in order to acquire the complete file.

An important auxiliary aid to the list is the *Subject cataloging manual : subject headings*, a third edition of which was published in 1989, updated in 1990.[1]

Library of Congress subject headings have received severe criticism over recent years: 'The weaknesses of Library of Congress subject cataloging are well known ... and the only hope for adequate subject access is through fundamental changes in the national standard'.[2] The introduction of the new format with accepted thesaural abbreviations (such as BT, RT, etc.) did nothing to stem this criticism: 'The fact of the matter is that the LCSH list is not a thesaurus, not any more now than it ever was. To attempt to make it into one simply by changing the codes on the existing syndetic structure is both misleading and impossible to achieve. Even more serious, *the attempt is professionally irresponsible, for by adopting at this time the well recognised codes for thesauri and applying them to LCSH, the LC Subject Cataloging Division has in single stroke violated nearly all of the international guidelines and standards for thesaurus construction that have been published in the last 15 years and are readily available'.[3]*

Headings such as: 'Television and children' and 'Children and death' are cited as being clearly subject headings and not legitimate candidates for a thesaurus, which would list the constituent concepts. Further, the relationship:

Television and children
BT Mass media and children

is seen to be fundamentally invalid because 'neither "Television and children" nor "Mass media and children" is a term'. 'Since by definition thesauri consist of terms and their relationships, the only possible valid use of the thesaural code "BT" would be to denote the relationship between the two terms "Television" and "Mass media", e.g.:

Television
BT Mass media

The inconsistency of the syntax used in the LC list is also criticized, as the following headings illustrate:

---

[1] *Subject cataloging manual : subject headings.* — 3rd ed. — Washington : Library of Congress. Cataloging Distribution Service, 1989. 1990 subscription includes one 1989 and two 1990 updates.

[2] Database limitations & online catalogs / Michael J. Simonds, *Library journal* 109 (3) 15 Feb 1984.

[3] LC subject headings disguised as a thesaurus / Mary Dykstra, *Library journal* 113 (4) 1 Mar 1988.

Automobile driving on mountain roads
Cogs (sailing ships)
Combat in the Bible
Cooperative marketing of farm produce
Miraculous drought of fishes (Miracle) in art
Stability of airplanes, Lateral
Sewage disposal in rivers, lakes, etc.
Micro-organisms, Effect of drugs on
Peer review of research grant proposals

The author from whose work the above examples are taken[1] goes on to write: 'North America has never bothered to grasp the significance of the research on analytico-synthetic classification that has been undertaken in the rest of the world'.[2]

Sears' List of subject headings

This list (13th edition, edited by Carmen Rovira and Caroline Reyes, New York : Wilson, 1986) is a simplified version of the Library of Congress list, intended for small and medium-sized libraries. The first edition was published in 1923. General omissions, such as names of persons, are similar to those of the Library of Congress list, but many other headings are excluded if it is felt that they would be used only in large libraries. For example, the heading 'Great Awakening' is absent from Sears. As well as exclusions, there are also modifications to meet the needs of smaller collections.

However, the Sears format is very similar to that of the Library of Congress list, and a cataloguer who is used to working with one can easily adjust to the other. Here is a simple example of an entry from Sears:

Skis and skiing
  See also **Water skiing**
  x Skiing, Snow
  xx **Winter sports**

The resemblance to the Library of Congress layout is quite marked, and headings and references are selected in the same way. Previous editions of Sears, however, have suggested that the '*see also*' element be interpreted as '*consider using*'. If it is desired to use the more specific heading 'Water skiing', then the cataloguer must turn to this heading. If it is not desired to use the more specific heading, then the cataloguer forgets all about it; no references are made to it. This would seem to be a more sensible way of using such a list for it avoids references which lead *away* from chosen headings. In fact Sears instructs that *see also* references are made from the

---

[1] ibid. (i.e. ref. 3 previous page)
[2] ibid.

general to the specific and *not* from the specific to the general. In addition, such references cannot be made without knowing whether the library has material under the other subjects, as *see also* references are concerned entirely with guiding the reader from headings where information has been found to other headings under which materials on related or more specific aspects of the subject are listed.

In Sears, common subdivisions (e.g. Bibliography, History, Research) are listed alphabetically at the front of the work, together with a list of 'key' headings to be used as examples for subdividing headings of a similar type. Examples of these key headings are **Chicago**, for subdivision under names of cities and town, and **English language**, for subdivision under various languages. Sears, like LCSH, has been criticized on the grounds of inconsistency but some amendment has been made in more recent editions. Thus, different heading formats such as:

Hospital libraries
and
Libraries, Special

have disappeared. The latter heading now appears as:

Special libraries

However, there are still some oddities, for example:

Classification, Dewey Decimal

which is a clear corruption of a name, and why is there no 'Classification, Library of Congress'?

Dictionary catalogues
When an alphabetical subject catalogue is combined with entries under authors, titles and other headings, then the result is a *dictionary* type of catalogue in which, as the name implies, all entries are presented in one alphabetical sequence. The main entry in such catalogues is the author entry and other 'added' entries, including the subject entry, may be simplified if required.

Very few libraries in the United Kingdom use an alphabetical subject approach, yet this form of catalogue is pre-eminent in the United States. The American 'subject approach' is still largely based upon the two lists of subject headings (*Library of Congress* and *Sears*) just described. These tools reflect the principles laid down so many years ago by Cutter.

The subject approach in the dictionary catalogue is illustrated overleaf. The subject heading and the references have been formulated using Sears.

Chain procedure in the dictionary catalogue
It is possible to use other methods such as chain procedure instead of a published list of subject headings for the construction of subject entries.

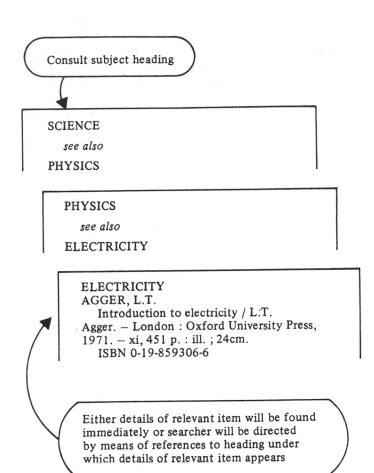

The subject approach in the dictionary catalogue

Silberstein, Laurence J. (Laurence Jay), 1936-
    Martin Buber's social and religious thought; alienation and the quest for meaning. 358p $40 1989 New York Univ. Press
    ISBN 0-8147-7886-0   LC 88-25575
Silcox, Harry C., 1933-
    Philadelphia politics from the bottom up; the life of Irishman William McMullen, 1824-1901. 175p $29.50 1989 Balch Inst. Press; Associated Univ. Presses (London)
    ISBN 0-944190-01-4 (Balch Inst. Press)
    LC 88-70766
The silence of Bartleby. McCall, D. pa 1989 Cornell Univ. Press
Silent films

Catalogs
    Magliozzi, R. S. Treasures from the film archives. 1988 Scarecrow Press

United States
    Wyatt, E. M. More than a cowboy. 1988 Wyatt Classics
Siliceous deposits of the Tethys and Pacific regions; James R. Hein, Jeleja Obradović, editors. Q 244p il 1989 Springer-Verlag (NY)
    ISBN 0-387-96704-4   LC 88-31137
    Sel. presentations given at the 3rd International Conference on Siliceous Deposits, held in Yugoslavia, Sept., 1986
Silicon
    Properties of silicon. 1988 INSPEC; Institution of Electrical Engs.
Silicon crystals
    Shimura, F. Semiconductor silicon crystal technology. 1989 Academic Press (San Diego)
Silicon nitride
    Silicon nitride in electronics. 1988 Elsevier
Silicon nitride in electronics; [by] V.I. Belyi [et al.] (Materials science monographs, 34) Q 263p il 1988 Elsevier
    ISBN 0-444-42689-2   LC 86-16805
Silk painting
    Kennedy, J. Painting on silk. £10.95 1988 Dryad Press (London)
Silk Road

Guide-books
    Shafi, I. M. Silk road to Sinkiang. 1988 WajidAlis
Silk road to Sinkiang. Shafi, I. M. 1988 WajidAlis
The silk vendetta. [large print ed] Holt, V. 1988 Hall, G.K. & Co.
Sillars, Stuart
    The welfare state. Q il pa £2.75 1988 Macmillan Educ.
    ISBN 0-333-43838-8
Silva, M. Fernanda da (Maria Fernanda), 1938-
    (ed) See NATO Advanced Study Institute on Materials Modification by High-fluence Ion Beams (1987: Viana do Castelo, Portugal). Materials modification by high-fluence ion beams
Silva, Maria Fernanda da *See* Silva, M. Fernanda da (Maria Fernanda), 1938-

Extract from Cumulative book index *(Oct 1989) illustrating how entries under author,* title, subject, etc. *are all combined in the one dictionary arrangement.*

79

The method is similar to that described on p.56, but a subject heading and appropriate references are produced rather than a series of index entries, e.g.:

Subject heading MIRROR DINGHIES
(*specific* subject):

References: DINGHIES
            see also specific names, eg
            MIRROR DINGHIES

            SAILING
            see also
            DINGHIES and specific names, eg
            MIRROR DINGHIES

            BOATING
            see also
            SAILING

            WATER SPORTS
            see also
            BOATING

            AQUATIC SPORTS
            see
            WATER SPORTS

            SPORTS
            see also
            WATER SPORTS

            RECREATION
            see also
            SPORTS

Such headings and references are very similar to those produced by a printed list (in the 'Electricity' example on p.78, the heading and references would, in fact, be exactly the same) but, because chain is linked directly to classification, it is perhaps possible to achieve greater consistency. Printed lists are notorious for not adhering to classificatory principles.

This is not to suggest that there are no problems with regard to the application of chain to the dictionary catalogue. For example, it may well be necessary to invert the last two links in the chain to provide more helpful headings, e.g.:

BIRDS — Nutrition rather than NUTRITION — Birds
and
BIRDS — Great Britain rather than GREAT BRITAIN — Birds

Care must also be taken to 'pick up' relevant references between subjects in different classes.

The allegedly simple alphabetical sequence of author, title and subject headings can become extremely complex as the catalogue grows and difficulties can be encountered in both filing and retrieval. Because of this, some academic and other large libraries have separated subject from other entries to form a 'divided' catalogue.

Advantages and disadvantages of dictionary and classified catalogues

The major advantages of the dictionary catalogue are its single sequence (unless it is 'divided') and its alphabetical order, which is easy to understand. However, alphabetical order can separate closely related topics, e.g. Arithmetic, Geometry, Mathematics, Trigonometry, etc. All of these subjects would be brought together by a classified arrangement.

An alphabetical subject catalogue can, however, complement the classified shelf arrangement by bringing together aspects of a subject which the classification scheme has had to scatter ('distributed relatives'); for example, works on coal mining and economics of coal mining will be collocated under the headings COAL — Mining, and COAL — Mining — Economics. This can also be done in the subject index to a classified catalogue.

Unfortunately the notation of a classification scheme may well be bewildering to the user and, of course, a classified arrangement can only be as good as the scheme on which it is based.

The dictionary catalogue is often referred to as a 'direct' catalogue and the classified catalogue as an 'indirect' catalogue. The subject approach in the latter must always involve at least two steps. It should be remembered, however, that the subject approach in the dictionary catalogue is only direct if the user selects the subject heading chosen by the cataloguer at the *first* attempt: in a survey in 20 public libraries in the 1950s, S. J. Butcher found that this did not happen in 30% of the cases investigated.[1]

The alphabetico-classed catalogue

The alphabetico-classed catalogue attempts to combine the advantages of a classified catalogue with the simplicity of an alphabetical subject catalogue, by providing alphabetically arranged broad subject headings with alphabetically arranged subdivisions. There are few examples of such catalogues today, perhaps because compromises are never entirely successful.

---

[1] Cataloguing in municipal libraries / S. J. Butcher, pp. 93-103. *In Cataloguing principles and practice : an inquiry* / edited ... by Mary Piggott. — London : Library Association, 1954.

Main entry

> 537 ELECTRICITY
> AGGER, L.T.
>   Introduction to electricity /
> L.T. Agger. — London : Oxford
> University Press, 1971. — xi,
> 451 p. : ill. ; 24 cm.
>   ISBN 0-19-859306-6

Main entry

> AGGER, L.T.
>   Introduction to electricity /
> L.T. Agger. — London : Oxford
> University Press, 1971. — xi,
> 451 p. : ill. ; 24 cm.
>   ISBN 0-19-859306-6
>
>   537

Author/title entries

> INTRODUCTION to electricity /
>   L.T. Agger. — 1971.
>   537

> AGGER, L.T.
>   Introduction to electricity. —
> 1971.
>   537

Added entry (title)

> INTRODUCTION to electricity /
>   L.T. Agger. — 1971.
>   537

Subject index entries

> SCIENCE   500

> PHYSICS   530

> ELECTRICITY   537

Added entry (subject)

> ELECTRICITY
> AGGER, L.T.
>   Introduction to electricity. —
> 1971.
>   537

References

> SCIENCE
>   *see also*
> PHYSICS

> PHYSICS
>   *see also*
> ELECTRICITY

Entries are in three separate sequences, or two if the subject index is combined with the author/title index

All entries are filed in one alphabetical sequence unless the catalogue is 'divided', ie the subject entries separated

Comparison of 'classified' and 'dictionary' forms of catalogue

Parts of the original British Museum subject index used the alphabetico-classed principle, as can be seen from the following extracts:

PHYSICS — APPLIED AND INDUSTRIAL PHYSICS
        — COSMICAL PHYSICS
        — MATHEMATICAL PHYSICS

Here the main heading PHYSICS is subdivided alphabetically. However, other subdivisions of Physics (e.g. ELECTRICITY, MAGNETISM and RELATIVITY) are given headings in their own right, so that the alphabetico-classed principle is not used throughout the index.

A more obvious example of the alphabetico-classed principle is seen in the following examples of headings which were taken from the Bodleian Library's PPE (Philosophy, Politics and Economics) Library:

ECONOMICS — Advertising
ECONOMICS — Agricultural economics
ECONOMICS — Capital and profit
ECONOMICS — Commerce (general)
ECONOMICS — Industries
ECONOMICS — Industries — Chemicals
ECONOMICS — Industries — Clothesmaking
ECONOMICS — Industries — Coal

Alternative forms of cataloguing

The dictionary versus classified form of catalogue debate is now rapidly decreasing in relevance because of the multi-access capability which the computer offers. The current Liverpool Polytechnic Library microfiche catalogue is one example of a catalogue which has abandoned a single traditional inner form. It combines a classified catalogue with a non-conventional subject index and an alphabetical catalogue which includes Key Word And Context index entries.

Here is an example of an entry which appears in the classified sequence:

```
301.41 KIN
    WOMEN AND WORK : SEX DIFFERENCES AND SOCIETY / by
    King, J.S. — H.M.S.O., 1974   £0.31   0-11-360665-6
    Manpower Pap., 10
SHELVED AT 301.41 KIN EXCEPT WHERE INDICATED:
Walton Ho.: 2 copies
Walton Ho. Reserve: 1 copy
Mt. Pleasant (Business): 1 copy
F.L. Calder Pamphlets: 1 copy
```

This would be indexed in the alphabetical subject index under:

```
WORK
    WORK : SEX DIFFERENCES : SOCIOLOGY
    301.41
```

```
SOCIOLOGY
    WORK : SEX DIFFERENCES : SOCIOLOGY
    301.41
```

```
SEX DIFFERENCES
    WORK : SEX DIFFERENCES : SOCIOLOGY
    301.41
```

In the alphabetical catalogue, headings are alternated over the basic description shown in the classified entry above to provide entries under all relevant access points including keywords, e.g.:

```
WORK
    WOMEN AND WORK : SEX DIFFERENCES AND SOCIETY / by
    King, J.S. — H.M.S.O., 1974   £0.31   0-11-360665-6
    Manpower Pap., 10
SHELVED AT 301.41 KIN EXCEPT WHERE INDICATED:
Walton Ho.: 2 copies
Walton Ho. Reserve: 1 copy
Mt. Pleasant (Business): 1 copy
F.L. Calder Pamphlets: 1 copy
```

Similar entries would be made under KING, J.S., MANPOWER PAP.10, SEX DIFFERENCES and WOMEN

This is an interesting example of the flexibility which the computer has brought to the inner form of catalogues. Liverpool Polytechnic is, however, currently changing to the Dynix system. The microfiche catalogue with its keyword facility will be retained after the change but only until online public access is implemented.

More about pre-coordinate indexing methods

Pre-coordinate methods, as used in library catalogues and printed indexes/bibliographies, often attempt to indicate the complete context of a subject. The concepts which together make up the context of the subject can be presented in a variety of ways. For example, the subject 'Cleaning the upholstery of a chair' could be indexed as:

Cleaning: Upholstery: Chairs
Cleaning: Chairs: Upholstery
Upholstery: Chairs: Cleaning
Upholstery: Cleaning: Chairs
Chairs: Upholstery: Cleaning
Chairs: Cleaning: Upholstery

The number of possible permutations can be calculated by the formula $n \times nx\,(n-1) \times (n-2) \times (n-3)$ etc., where n equals the number of concepts present. In the above instance, the calculation would be $3 \times (3-1) \times (3-2)$, i.e. $3 \times 2 \times 1 = 6$. It can be seen that the number of entries required rapidly increases as the subject becomes more complex. For a subject containing only seven concepts, full permutation to cover all possible approaches would lead to an incredible 5,040 entries. This is completely unacceptable. With pre-coordinate indexes, therefore, the problem has always been how to *reduce* the number of entries whilst retaining an acceptable degree of efficiency in the system.

Two methods by which a reduction in the number of entry points in a pre-coordinate index can be achieved have already been examined. These are chain procedure and the 'shunting' procedure used in PRECIS. Other methods include:

Cycled or cyclic indexing which involves the movement of the first lead term to the last position, and this process is continued until each element or concept has occuped the lead position once.

Rotated indexing is a method in which each element in turn becomes the main heading under which an entry is to be filed, but there is no change in the citation order. The entry element is indicated by underlining.

SLIC indexing, or Selective Listing in Combination, first introduced by J. R. Sharp at ICI Fibres Ltd, involves the combination of elements in *one direction only* and the exclusion of combinations which are contained in larger groups.

The principles underlying these methods may be demonstrated by taking as an example a subject containing three elements which may be represented by A, B and C.

The entries obtained would be as follows:

Chain:	A B C	PRECIS:	A B C	Cycling:	A B C
	B C		B C		B C A
	C		A		C A B
			C		
			B A		

Rotation:	A B C	SLIC:	A B C
	A B C		A C
	A B C		B C
			C

85

Now, taking the actual example, 'Cleaning the upholstery of a chair', the various entries would be:

Chain: Cleaning:Upholstery:Chairs
            Upholstery:Chairs
            Chairs

PRECIS: **Cleaning**. Upholstery. Chairs
            Upholstery. Chairs
              Cleaning
            Chairs
              Upholstery. Cleaning

Cycling: Cleaning:Upholstery:Chairs
            Upholstery:Chairs:Cleaning
            Chairs:Cleaning:Upholstery

Rotation: <u>Cleaning</u> : Upholstery : Chairs
            Cleaning : <u>Upholstery</u> : Chairs
            Cleaning : Upholstery : <u>Chairs</u>

SLIC: Cleaning: Upholstery: Chairs
            Cleaning: Chairs
            Upholstery: Chairs
            Chairs

It can be seen that all of these methods do reduce the number of entries required and as the complexity of a subject increases, this reduction becomes more dramatic.

It should be stressed that the above examples are intended only as an *illustration* of the application of the various methods. In practice there would be other factors involved; for instance, the 'chain' would be provided by the classification scheme in use. In addition, in a system such as PRECIS, references would also be required.

A few further points are worthy of note:
1   In chain, PRECIS and SLIC, the citation order of the elements plays an important role
2   There is a close relationship between the rotated index and KWIC indexing
3   Indexes such as PRECIS and SLIC are intended mainly for use in computerized systems.

The methods so far described are not the only pre-coordinate indexing methods that could be employed. There are a number of other systems, many of which have been specifically designed for the generation of entries by computer. Some examples are briefly described below.

86

Articulated subject indexing

An element of articulation can, of course, be a feature of indexing methods such as the previously described PRECIS, but the term ASI has become specifically associated with the system developed by Michael Lynch and his colleagues at the University of Sheffield Postgraduate School of Librarianship and Information Science (renamed the Department of Information Studies in 1981). This involves the manipulation, by a computer, of a natural language sentence describing the subject of a document to bring certain elements to the file position in turn. Unlike most other indexing methods, prepositions and conjunctions, etc., are not discarded but used − sometimes as signals instructing the computer to print out in a certain manner. Brackets are also used for this purpose, so that the input:

[Cleaning] [Upholstery] of [chairs]

would be manipulated by the computer to obtain the index entries:

chairs
   upholstery of, cleaning

upholstery
   of chairs, cleaning

cleaning
   upholstery of chairs

This simple example illustrates that the system is designed to enable the searcher to reconstruct the sentence with the minimum of effort and this is still possible with far more complex sentences.

A computerized system which has much in common with Lynch's articulated subject indexing is NEPHIS (NEsted PHase Indexing System). It appears to be less sophisticated but is probably easier to implement than the Lynch system. NEPHIS was developed in Canada by Craven.[1] In common with the system described above, it also uses brackets and other symbols in the input and, in normal circumstances, both the Lynch system and NEPHIS would produce identical or closely similar entries for the same item.

A manual and a workbook for NEPHIS (for use with a microcomputer) have been produced by the College of Librarianship Wales.[2,3]

---

[1] NEPHIS : a Nested Phase Indexing System / T.C. Craven, *Journal of the American Society for Information Science* 28 1977 107-14.
[2] *Manual for teaching NEPHIS and KWAC* / C.J. Armstrong and E.M. Keen. — Aberystwyth : College of Librarianship Wales, 1981.
[3] *Workbook for NEPHIS and KWAC* / C.J. Armstrong and E.M. Keen. — Aberystwyth : College of Librarianship Wales, 1981.

POPSI (POstulate-based Permuted Subject Indexing)

S. R. Ranganathan has made a significant contribution to the theory and practice of indexing. POPSI is yet another example of his influence for, in their description of the system, Neelameghan and Gopinath suggest that term selection and organization be guided by 'the postulates and principles of the General Theory of Library Classification' as formulated by him.[1] Because of the involvement of Ranganathan and the fact that the system is closely linked with classification, there is a vague relationship between POPSI and chain procedure, but this relationship is vague. In POPSI, the lead term, or terms, appears on a first line and there is a complex set of rules for determining the composition of the terms on this line. On a second line appears a constant modifier which, in effect, provides the complete context of the subject, e.g.:

Chairs
Chairs, Upholstery ; Cleaning

Upholstery, Chairs
Chairs, Upholstery ; Cleaning

Cleaning
Chairs, Upholstery ; Cleaning

It is emphasized that this is a simple, simulated example of how the above subject might appear in POPSI form.

Current technology index

Another prominent figure in subject work has been E. J. Coates. Coates analysed various possible approaches in his book *Subject catalogues*[2] and developed his own theory for the formulation of headings for compound subjects based upon a 'significant order' of thing-material-action. As editor of *British technology index*, Coates was able to translate his theories into practice.

The entry under which details of an item may be found looks almost like an 'inverted' chain index entry. The subject used as an example above would probably appear as indicated below, the layout shown being that adopted when *British technology index* changed its name to *Current technology index* in 1981. *CTI* is computer produced.

---

[1] Postulate-based Permuted Subject Indexing (POPSI) / A. Neelameghan and M.A. Gopinath, *Library science with a slant to documentation* 12 1975 79-87.

[2] *Subject catalogues : headings and structure* / E.J. Coates. — London : Library Association, 1960. Reissued with a new preface, 1988.

CHAIRS : Upholstery
Cleaning

References to cover other approaches would be made from right to left:

CLEANING
See
Chairs : Upholstery : Cleaning

UPHOLSTERY
See also
Chairs : Upholstery

Headings under which information can appear are in bold type. Unused headings are in light face type.

It has been possible to give only the briefest descriptions of the various indexing methods in this work. For those readers requiring further detail, reference should be made to Foskett[1] and Wheatley.[2] The former is an admirable treatise of current thought and practice with regard to the subject approach to information. The latter, which is a report to the British Library Research and Development Department, is generally referred to by its acronym MOPSI and is an extensive survey of subject indexes. It is now somewhat dated but, for those who wish to see what a particular type of index looks like, whether it is keyword, articulated, cycled, SLIC, chain, etc., a considerable number of examples are reproduced. It should also be noted that these are *printed* indexes, even though they may be computer produced. As indicated in the case of PRECIS (p.63) the format of a printed index may not be relevant or suitable to online retrieval.

Citation indexing

One subject indexing method is unique and does not fit comfortably into any particular category. This is *citation indexing*, which is based upon the principle that if a certain author writes in a subject field in which a person is interested, then articles which *cite* this author are also likely to be of interest. This principle has long been established in legal circles, since lawyers often base their arguments upon previous decisions, and the earliest known application of the principle was a legal index. *Shepard's citations* of 1873.

The concept becomes clearer if one recognizes the processes that one goes through when reading a textbook. The reader examines the information on a particular theme in the textbook and then notes the references given relating to earlier works on the same subject. These references provide *previously published* sources for further reading. Citation indexing works like this *but in reverse* in that it leads to *newer* rather than *older* material.

---

[1] *The subject approach to information* / A.C. Foskett. — 4th ed. — London : Bingley, 1982.
[2] *A manual on printed subject indexes : report to the British Library Research and Development Department* / Alan Wheatley. — Aberystwyth : College of Librarianship, Wales, 1978.

Eugene Garfield of the Institute for Scientific Information (ISI), Philadelphia, pioneered the principle in information science generally, and ISI publishes the two best known citation indexes: *Science citation index* and *Social sciences citation index*. In these and similar indexes, citations are sorted automatically by computer and alphabetical listings under authors *cited* and sources, that is *citing* authors, are compiled. A permuted subject index may also be available.

Here is a simple entry from *Social sciences citation index*:

BRYSON R
74 J EDUC RES 68 11
FELDMAN KA   RES HIGH ED   30 583 89

This entry indicates that an article by R. Bryson, which appeared in the 1974 *Journal of education research* Vol. 68, p. 11, has been cited by K. A. Feldman in *Research in higher education* Vol. 30, p. 583 1989. By referring to the *Source index* under Feldman, further details relating to this author's article, e.g. the title, will be found.

When citation indexing is considered, note must be taken of *bibliographic coupling*. Two articles are *coupled* if they both cite the *same* additional article as a reference. Obviously, the strength of the coupling increases according to the number of common references; and when this is considerable it is likely that the two articles deal with very much the same subject.

Chapter 7

The subject approach:
post-coordinate indexing and thesauri

Post-coordinate indexing was developed in the early 1950s by Mortimer Taube as a means of dealing with the many research reports acquired by the US Armed Services Technical Information Agency (ASTIA).

A prerequisite of post-coordinate indexing is that each item to be indexed is given as 'accession' number by which it can be identified. The subject content of the item is then analysed into its constituent concepts and each concept is indexed to that number. Simple, single concepts were referred to by Taube as 'uniterms'. If, for instance, the item which deals with the subject 'cleaning upholstery of chairs' is the fifty-fourth item to be added to the stock of a library or information service, then simple, manual, post-coordinate indexing cards for that item might appear as follows:

					CLEANING				
0	1	2	3	4	5	6	7	8	9
		32		54					

					UPHOLSTERY				
0	1	2	3	4	5	6	7	8	9
	1			54		26			

					CHAIRS				
0	1	2	3	4	5	6	7	8	9
20	1			54					19

All of these index cards contain the number 54 entered, or 'posted', in the column appropriate to the last digit in the number. This is known as terminal digit posting and is a device intended to facilitate searches by comparison.

This simple indexing process completed, the cards are filed in an alphabetical sequence.

If an enquirer subsequently asks for information on 'cleaning upholstery of chairs', each of the concepts which together make up this complex subject is identified and the cards representing these concepts extracted from the alphabetical file. The cards are then compared for common numbers.

A scan of the three cards shown above will reveal that item no. 54 probably deals with the required subject. This item can then be traced by this number, or, if some arrangement of items other than a simple numerical one is employed, by means of an intermediate accessions register.

Each post-coordinate indexing card carries the number of all items to which the particular index term applies. In the above example, for instance, item no. 32 must deal with some aspect of the subject 'cleaning'; item no. 26 deals with some aspect of 'upholstery'; and items no. 19 and no. 20 with some aspect of 'chairs'. Item no. 1 deals with 'upholstery of chairs'.

In a 'manual' system, the numbers are 'written' in; but numbers can also be 'entered' by punching holes in certain positions. Cards can then be compared by holding them up to the light (hence 'peek-a-boo' cards) or by placing them on a 'light box'. The light will 'shine through' if there is a common number, i.e. a hole in the same position, on all of the cards being compared. Cards of this type are referred to as optical coincidence cards, or feature cards.

CLEANING										
0		0	1	2	3	4	5	6	7	8	9
1		0	1	2	3	4	5	6	7	8	9
2		0	1	2	3	4	5	6	7	8	9
3		0	1	●	3	4	5	6	7	8	9
4		0	1	2	3	4	5	6	7	8	9
5		0	1	2	3	●	5	6	7	8	9
6		0	1	2	3	4	5	6	7	8	9
7		0	1	2	3	4	5	6	7	8	9
8		0	1	2	3	4	5	6	7	8	9
9		0	1	2	3	4	5	6	7	8	9

Representing numbers by holes punched in appropriate positions. Read down and then across, thus '32' and '54' are punched on the above card. Note that terminal digit posting is still employed.

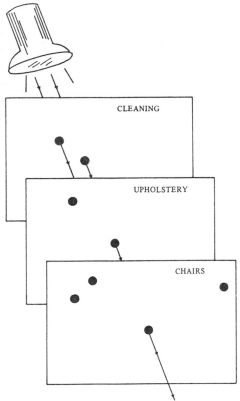

Searching with 'peek-a-boo' or optical coincidence cards

Advantages and disadvantages of post-coordinate indexing
The two major problems of pre-coordinate indexing, namely the considerable number of possible methods of entry and the question of the citation order in which the constituent elements of a compound subject are to be presented, are both overcome in a post-coordinate system. The number of index cards required is similar to the number of concepts that make up the subject being indexed, When searching, these cards may be extracted in any order and citation order is therefore irrelevant.

Some people consider that post-coordinate indexing speeds up the processes of indexing, filing and searching. However, there are some disadvantages. Browsing in a numerical sequence presents difficulty. As previously pointed out, a more useful order can be adopted and an intermediate accessions register employed but this involves the maintenance of an extra record.

In a system which uses optical coincidence cards, the number of items which can be indexed is limited by the number of 'holes' which can be punched on one card. This may mean multiple indexes for larger collections.

Commercially produced optical coincidence post-coordinate indexing card. Items numbered 27, 224 and 347 deal with the subject 'Dyslexia'. Actual size of card 13½ × 8 in.

Terminology can be a real problem. An item may, for instance, be indexed under 'tankers' and if an enquirer searches for information on 'ships', the item, although relevant, will not be retrieved. Another searcher might be looking for information on the 'tanker' as a form of road transport. In this case the item would be retrieved but it would be irrelevant. Such a retrieval of irrelevant information is referred to as a 'false drop' and there is said to be 'noise' in the system. False drops can easily occur. A further example might be the retrieval of a document on the 'teaching of history' in response to a request for information on the 'history of teaching'. The problem of 'noise' may be tackled by the use of 'roles' which follow the indexing term and indicate its context, e.g. history (subject of study) *and* history (of a subject), or tankers (ships) *and* tankers (road vehicles). A further device designed to eliminate noise is the 'link', which connects related terms within the context of a document. An item on 'Interfacing online catalogues with CD-ROM databases' should not be retrieved in response to a search for information on 'CD-ROM catalogues'. Such retrieval can be avoided by numbering 'online' and 'catalogues' 54 and 'CD-ROM' and 'databases' 54A, thus linking the related terms. Some authorities consider that the value of roles and links is limited and that the advantages to be gained are not worth the effort involved.

A post-coordinate index is not a tool that one can let an 'irresponsible' searcher use, as cards can easily be left 'lying around' and not refiled; thus the system is soon a chaotic mess. It is possible to print out post-coordinate indexes in book form, provided at least two copies of the index are available. They can then be laid side by side and entries compared for common numbers. Such an index is known as a *dual dictionary*, but it obviously has limitations — especially when more than two indexing terms apply to an item.

The 'Termatrex' method of post-coordinate indexing utilizes a clever system of 'visible' numbers so that cards can easily be 'scanned' to select appropriate index entries. Cards can, therefore, be filed in random order and there is no need to maintain a strict alphabetical sequence.

Boolean searching

As described above, when searching in a post-coordinate index, elements present in a complex subject must be searched for individually. Concept cards are extracted and compared in order to identify common numbers which *may* relate to documents relevant to an enquiry. Thus, when searching for the subject 'the teaching of mathematics', the cards for 'teaching' and 'mathematics' are extracted and compared. This could be represented pictorially by using two circles, circle 'A' for all documents on 'mathematics' and circle 'B' for all documents on 'teaching'. The search requirement is indicated by the shaded area:

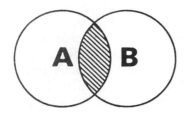

This type of search is referred to as an 'and' search, i.e. 'teaching *and* mathematics', and the above pictorial representation relates to the 'Venn' diagram based on the Boolean algebra of sets, hence 'Boolean' searching.

Searches can be broadened by reducing the number of concepts or elements. In the example 'the teaching of mathematics', disregarding 'mathematics' would broaden the search to all documents on 'teaching'. If a search were begun using three or more concepts, each of these could be discarded in turn to give various combinations of those remaining. For example, where the subject 'cleaning of upholstery of chairs' is concerned, the discarding of 'cleaning' would give 'upholstery of chairs', the discarding of 'upholstery' would give 'cleaning chairs', and the discarding of 'chairs' wold give 'cleaning upholstery'.

Post-coordination and automation

Manual and feature card post-coordinate systems such as those described are now very few in number because such systems have, in many cases, been superseded by automation. However, it was thought advantageous to retain the above explanation because the *principles* are so important. They are important because one of the great advantages of post-coordination is the ease with which it can be applied in automated systems. Post-coordinate indexing relates very closely to the 'inverted file' (see p.148) and many computerized information retrieval systems make use of the method. Boolean searching is often introduced as an important search facility in such systems.

The most common Boolean logic is the one already noted, the logical product or 'and' search:

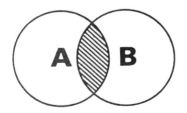

Logical *product* − the 'and' search
Symbolized as A.B, A × B or (A) (B)
All documents dealing with 'mathematics' and 'teaching'

It may well be that what is required is all documents dealing with 'teaching' and/or 'mathematics'; that is, on 'mathematics' only, on 'teaching' only, or with both 'teaching and mathematics'. This situation could again be represented pictorially.

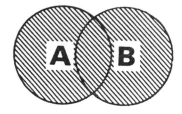

Logical *sum* the 'or' search
Symbolized as A + B
All documents on 'mathematics' *or* 'teaching'

A search could also be made for all documents dealing with 'mathematics' excluding those covering the 'teaching of mathematics':

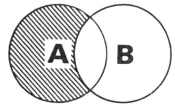

Logical *difference* — the 'not' search
Symbolized as A—B
All documents on 'mathematics' but *not* 'the teaching of mathematics'

Lastly a search could be made for all documents dealing with 'teaching' or 'mathematics' but not the 'teaching of mathematics':

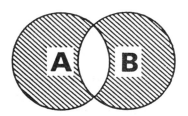

Exclusive 'or' search
Symbolized as (A + B)—(A × B)
All documents on 'mathematics' *or* 'teaching' but *not* the 'teaching of mathematics'

The value of the latter two searches is limited, as they can result in failure to retrieve relevant items. For example, if a search is being conducted on the pattern: 'Computers' and 'Information retrieval systems' not 'Chemistry', then an item dealing with the 'computerized information retrieval systems in physics and chemistry', which is relevant, would be rejected.

Conversely the logical product is obviously of prime importance.

Boolean logic can be used to illustrate coordination in information retrieval. Using 'search logic' in this way, search 'patterns' are developed. A typical pattern might be:

$$\begin{pmatrix} A \\ or \\ B \end{pmatrix} \quad and \quad \begin{pmatrix} A_1 \\ or \\ B_1 \end{pmatrix} \quad not \quad \begin{pmatrix} A_2 \\ or \\ B_2 \end{pmatrix}$$

For instance, if information were required on the classification and cataloguing of maps and charts, excluding atlases or globes, then the search pattern could be displayed graphically as:

$$\begin{pmatrix} Cataloguing \\ or \\ Classification \end{pmatrix} \quad and \quad \begin{pmatrix} Maps \\ or \\ Charts \end{pmatrix} \quad not \quad \begin{pmatrix} Atlases \\ or \\ Globes \end{pmatrix}$$

In automated systems, where the human intellectual element is not present and the computer merely does as it is instructed, such search formulations can be of value.

However, despite the wide use of Boolean in online systems, not everyone is convinced that this is the best search methodology. Hildreth, for instance, states that 'Much research and experience with Boolean retrieval systems (including OPACs) indicates clearly and repeatedly that Boolean search formulation syntax and retrieval techniques are not very effective in search performance and not very usable or efficient search methods for end-users'.[1] 'Determined explorers and the just plain curious need a flexible, rich, contextual subject search and browsing mode which offers plenty of navigation and trail-blazing options' (see also p.267).[2]

Thesauri

Whether a manual or an automated system is in use, similar problems will be encountered in relation to terminology.

If terms are selected from the title or text of an item and used, without alteration or manipulation, as index entries, then this is referred to as *natural language* indexing. If, however, the selected terms are 'translated' into 'authorized' terms as presented in a prescribed list, then the indexing language becomes *controlled* or *artificial*. As previously indicated, these lists are now generally referred to as 'thesauri'.

A thesaurus differs from a conventional authority list such as the Library of Congress list or Sears in that a listed term need not necessarily be used alone but may be coordinated with other terms. The relationships between terms may also be more clearly defined.

---

[1] *The online catalogue : developments and directions.* — edited by Charles R. Hildreth. — London : Library Association, 1989. 19.
[2] ibid. 22.

The following is a typical thesaurus entry; it indicates a non-preferred term and related terms. The meanings of the abbreviations, which are now standard in many thesauri, are: UF Use for; BT Broader terms; RT Related terms; NT Narrower terms:

Expenses
- UF   Allowances
- BT   Financial benefits
- NT   Family allowances (provided by firm)
          Travel allowances
- RT   Compensation
          Grants
          Gratuities
          Loans

Entries will also be found in the alphabetical list for non-preferred terms, i.e. those which may *not* be used. Where the above example is concerned, the entry for the non-preferred term 'Allowances' would appear as:

Allowances USE Expenses

The reader should note that there is a close affinity between the relationships revealed by the above entry and the process of classification. Indeed it can be advantageous initially to compile a faceted classification in a particular subject area and then to derive an alphabetical thesaurus from the classification schedules. This can lead to greater consistency and efficiency and ensure that the thesaurus is based upon firm principles. Some thesauri are in fact published as a 'thesauro-facet' type presentation, i.e. an alphabetical authority list together with the faceted classification from which the list has been derived. In such a case, the thesaurus also acts as an index to the classification scheme. Here, for example, is an entry from the *London education classification*:[1]

Analysis   Butr
- SN   Examination of research data; distinguish
          from philosophical analysis
- BT   Research technique
- NT   Computing
          Statistical analysis
- RT   Interview
          Questionnaire
          Survey

---

[1] *London education classification : a thesaurus/classification of British educational terms* / Douglas and Joy Foskett. — 2nd ed. — London : University of London, Institute of Education Library, 1974.

Butr is the classification number or code for 'Analysis'. By referring to this number in the classification schedules the user can examine the structure of the classification for this particular subject.

The above entry also introduces a further abbreviation: SN for Scope Note, which provides an indication of the scope of the term and the way in which it may be used.

When a classification scheme is combined with an alphabetical listing of terms, it is not absolutely necessary for relationships to be shown in the latter. They could be included in the classified sequence as the following extract from the *London classification of business studies*[1] illustrates:

JDF   Price mechanism
          SN *Many works on "price theory" really deal with*
                microeconomics and should be classed at JD
          UF Commodity prices
                Consumer prices indexes
                Prices
                Prices indexes
                Price theory
          RT Price stability JNKF
                Pricing BM
          For prices of specific commodities synthesise with Class K

JDFB   Resale prices

JDFC   Resale price maintenance
          RT Consumerism and consumer protection BT

Broader terms and narrower terms are not listed in this thesaurus since they are shown by the classification hierarchy: Resale prices is a 'BT' for 'Resale price maintenance' and an 'NT' for 'Price mechanism'.

Not all thesauri use the standard abbreviations and symbols shown in the preceding examples. Some may use the more traditional *see* and *see also* references, e.g.:[2]

Unemployment *see also* Redundancy
Unions *see* Trade unions

---

[1] *London classification of business studies* / K.D.C. Vernon and Valerie Lang. — 2nd ed. / revised by K.G.B. Bakewell and D.A. Cotton. — London : Aslib, 1979.
[2] *Management information retrieval : a new indexing language* / John Blagden. — Rev. ed. — London : Management Publications, 1971.

The preceding examples illustrate the fact that thesauri are available for a wide range of subjects and use varied methods of presentation. In addition, abbreviations such as BT and NT are abbreviations of English-language terms and therefore language-dependent. The British Standard Institution's *Guidelines for the establishment and development of monolingual thesauri* (BS 5723:1979) recognized this fact and suggested that a more neutral or language-independent system of symbols might be preferred for foreign-language or multi-lingual thesauri. A tentative system of possible symbols was proposed:

→   precedes the preferred term
=   precedes the non-preferred term
<   precedes the broader term
>   precedes the narrower term
—   precedes the related term

These symbols were subsequently used in the *BSI Root thesaurus*.[1] BSI had for some considerable time recognized the need for a comprehensive, adaptable thesaurus and invested the equivalent of 20 man-years, together with the corresponding financial outlay, into the development of this thesaurus. It is an authoritative guide to technical terminology and it is claimed that the combination of a logical structure and computer generation means that 'specialized' thesauri can be produced quickly and easily to suit particular requirements.

In line with 'thesauro-facet' practice, the thesaurus features a subject display as well as an alphabetical list. Sample entries:

Lignite   JFD.D
=   Brown coal
<   Coal

Mineral waxes   JOW
=   Waxes (mineral)
<   Mineral oils
>   Petroleum jelly

Nuclear containment structures   JSK
=   Containment structures (nuclear)
—   Nuclear technology

Nuclear energy
→   Nuclear power   JG

---

[1] *BSI root thesaurus.* — Hemel Hempstead : BSI, 1981. — 2v. A second edition was published in 1985.

Thesauri can provide help with terminology difficulties and lead to greater consistency in indexing. Nevertheless, it has yet to be proved that a controlled-language index is more efficient than one which uses natural language. However, it should also be noted that even in natural-language systems, appropriate thesauri may be used as 'memory joggers' in searches.

A standard which addresses itself specifically to alphabetical indexing, with particular reference to controlled indexing languages as found, for example, in thesauri is: *Recommendations for examining documents, determining their subjects and selecting index terms*, published by the British Standards Institution.[1]

---

[1] *Recommendations for examining documents, determining their subjects and selecting indexing terms.* — London : British Standards Institution, 1984. — (BS 6529).

Chapter 8
Analysis

AACR 2

Analysis is defined in AACR 2 as 'the process of preparing a bibliographic record that describes a part or parts of an item'. Chapter 13 of the Rules deals with analysis and four ways of achieving analysis are described.

First, if the item is part of a monographic series or a multipart monograph and has a title not dependent on that of the comprehensive item, the analytical entry may be prepared in terms of a complete bibliographical description of the part, with details of the comprehensive item given in the series area (rule 13.3A):

KUŽVART, Miloš
    Prospecting and exploration of mineral deposits / Miloš Kužvart and Miloslav Böhmer. — Amsterdam ; Oxford : Elsevier Scientific, 1978. — 431 p. ; 25 cm. — (Developments in economic geology ; 8). — Published in co-edition with Academia, publishing house of the Czechoslovak Academy of Sciences, Prague. — ISBN 0-444-99876-4.

Second, the individual parts of an entry may be displayed in the note area, normally in the form of a contents note (rule 13.4A):

BÖTTCHER, C.J.F.
    Theory of electric polarization / C.J.F. Böttcher. — 2nd completely rev. ed. by O.C. van Belle... [et al.] — Amsterdam ; Oxford : Elsevier Scientific, 1973-1978. — 2 v. ; 24 cm. — Contents: Vol. 1. Dielectrics in static fields — Vol. 2. Dielectrics in time-dependent fields / by C.J.F. Böttcher and P. Bordewijk. — ISBN 0-444-41019-8.

An analytical name-title added entry may then be made for each individual part (rules 13.2A and 21.30M1):

BORDEWIJK, P.
    Dielectrics in time-dependent fields
BÖTTCHER, C.J.F.
    Theory of electric polarization...

If more bibliographic description is required for a part that can be obtained

103

by displaying it in the note area, the 'in' analytic may be used (rule 13.5A). This consists of a description of the part analysed, followed by the word '*In* (italicized, underlined, or otherwise emphasized) and the citation for the whole item, consisting of the name and/or uniform title heading (if appropriate), title proper, statement(s) of responsibility when necessary for identification, edition statement, numeric or other designation (of a serial) or publication details (of a monograph):

REVIEW of biology and fisheries for smaller cetaceans :
report and papers from a meeting of the Subcommittee on
Smaller Cetaceans, International Whaling Commission, in Montreal,
April 1-11, 1974 / Edward Mitchell special editor. — p. 875-1240.

In FISHERIES RESEARCH BOARD OF CANADA. Journal... — Vol. 32 (1975)

PEMBERTON, Max
The ripening rubies / Max Pemberton. — p. 21-40 ; 22 cm.

In The RIVALS of Sherlock Holmes : early detective stories /
edited and introduced by Hugh Greene. — London : Bodley Head, 1970.

The citation following the word '*In*' is known as the 'In' analytic note.

The fact that all of the above examples apart from Pemberton were taken from the catalogue of the British Library (Science Reference Library, now the Science Reference and Information Service) indicates clearly that it is possible for different forms of analysis to be used in one library system.

The fourth method of analysis is the use of multi-level description (rule 13.6). Here the descriptive information is divided into two or more levels, which are made distinct by layout and/or other means. At the first level, only information relating to the item as a whole is recorded. At the second level, information relating to a group of parts or to the individual part being described is recorded. If information at the second level relates to a group of parts the information relating to the individual part is recorded at the third level. The following example is taken from the *BNB*:

Comprehensive biochemistry / edited by Marcel Florkin and Elmer
H. Stotz. — Amsterdam ; Oxford : Elsevier Scientific, 1962-

Vol. 19A : Amino acid metabolism and sulphur metabolism /
[edited by] Albert Newberger, Laurens L.M. van Deenen. —
1981. — xviii, 481p. : ill. ; 23 cm.
Includes index.
ISBN 0-444-80257-6

The application of the ISBDs to the description of component parts

A fifth draft of the recommendations for an International Standard Bibliographical Description for Component Parts — ISBD(CP) — was published in 1981. The original brief of the relevant IFLA Working Group was to prepare an ISBD for Analytics — ISBD(An), but the Group felt that 'Components' was a more appropriate term. The considerable substantive criticism of the 1981 draft indicated that there was far more than simple editorial work to be done in completing the task that had been originally set for the Working Group. An impasse was reached and the Group was disbanded in 1983. Subsequently, an *ad hoc* group was formed to readdress the problem, although with a somewhat different brief, and this eventually led to the publication of *Guidelines for the application of the ISBDs to the description of component parts* in 1988.[1]

The *Guidelines* are designed to assist those who prepare descriptions of component parts of publications (chapters of books, articles in serials, tracks from sound recordings, etc.) for use in catalogues, bibliographies, indexes or abstracting services. They are intended to apply only to the description of component parts that are issued with, in, or as part of a 'host' item (the publication (book, serial, sound recording, etc.) in which a component part is contained), and are dependent on the host item for purposes of bibliographic identification or access. They take as their starting point the International Standard Bibliographic Descriptions and must be used in conjunction with the ISBD appropriate to the material or type of publication represented by the component part itself as well as the host item in which the part is contained.

The description of the component part comprises four distinct segments:

1 the description of the component part
2 a linking element relating the description of the component part to the identification of the host item
3 the identification of the host item
4 details on the location of the part within the host item.

The *Guidelines* produce a result similar to that obtained using AACR 2's 'in' analytics but there are differences: the location of the part within the host item, e.g. the relevant pagination of a printed text, is given *after* the identification of the host item instead of (as in AACR 2) with the description of the component part. This is in line with many people's preferences, but the logic of AACR 2's rule is that the description is given in two clear stages — first the component part and then the host item.

The following is the 'Pemberton' example on p.104 given in accordance with the ISBD *Guidelines*:

The ripening rubies / Max Pemberton.

In: The rivals of Sherlock Holmes : early detective stories / edited and introduced by Hugh Greene. — London : The Bodley Head, 1970. — p. 21-40.

Below are given the ISBD(CP) and AACR 2 entries for a periodical article:

Alphabetization in indexes : experimental studies / James Hartley, Lindsey Davies and Peter Burnhill.

In: The indexer — Hatfield, Herts : Society of Indexers. — ISSN 0019-4131. — Vol. 12, no. 3 (April 1981), p. 149-153.

---

[1] *Guidelines for the application of the ISBDs to the description of component parts* / International Federation of Library Associations and Institutions. — London : IFLA UBCIM, 1988.

Alphabetization in indexes : experimental studies / James Hartley, Lindsey Davies and Peter Burnhill. — p. 149-153 ; 24 cm.

In The INDEXER. — Vol. 12, no. 3 (April 1981)

Subject analysis

AACR 2 and ISBD(CP) are, of course, concerned only with author-title analysis. Equally important — much more important in some kinds of libraries — is subject analysis. If an alphabetical subject catalogue is used, it is necessary only to provide an additional subject heading for the part analysed and then to follow the normal rules for author-title analysis:

POLLUTION
POLLUTION control : the hard decisions / Robert V. Hansberger. —
  on reel 5 of 9 film reels (30 min.) : sd., col. ; 16 mm.

In DRUCKER, Peter F. Managing discontinuity. — Rockville, MD. :
BNA Communications ; Peterborough : Guild Sound & Vision, 1971.

In the case of a classified catalogue it is necessary to classify the part analysed and to conclude the entry with a 'shelved at' note, showing where the item itself is shelved:

AZM/JNED 773
POLLUTION control : the hard decisions / Robert V. Hansberger. — on reel
  5 of 9 film reels (30 min.) : sd., col. ; 16 mm.

In DRUCKER, Peter F. Managing discontinuity. — Rockville, Md. : BNA
Communications ; Peterborough : Guild Sound & Vision, 1971.

shelved at AA 773

Subject index entries must then be made for the part:

Films *see under subject*
Pollution: Social responsibility of industry   AZM/JNED
Industry: Social responsibility   AZM
Social responsibility of industry   AZM

(The classification scheme used in the above example is the second edition of *The London classification of business studies*.)

Policy

Rule 13.1 of AACR 2 states that cataloguing agencies have their own policies regarding analysis. In an individual library, the extent to which analysis is made will depend upon such factors as the purpose of the library (including the extent to which comprehensive literature searches are carried out), the purpose and use made of the catalogue, the number of staff available, and the availability and effectiveness (including currency) of published indexing and abstracting services and online services.

Author analysis may be used for plays, poems and other literary works in collections; significant conference papers (including papers by members of staff of an academic institution or the parent body of a special library); and for local authors in a public library.

Title analysis is often confined to anonymous works but may also be used for plays in collections.

Subject analysis can be very useful in special departments of public or academic libraries (especially in local collections), as well as in special libraries. It is particularly valuable for combating the problem of 'scatter' (i.e. the appearance of a component part on one subject in a host document dealing with a totally different subject, as in the 'pollution control' example above or, perhaps, an article on personnel management in a journal on engineering); for recording significant contributions to a subject such as papers at conferences or in symposia; and when there is no other material in the library on a particular subject.

Analysis can result in much more effective exploitation of a library's stock, allowing significant articles, chapters, sections, pages or even paragraphs to be highlighted. Care should be taken to ensure that the library catalogue is not bulked unnecessarily by insignificant entries, however, and that the library is not duplicating the work of an external service. Many subjects and many forms of material, such as a large amount of audio-visual material, are not covered by such services, and libraries might consider using staff released by having cataloguing done centrally on such tasks as analysis.

Analysis and computerized cataloguing

Analysis presents special problems where computerized cataloguing is concerned. Either a separate record must be created for each analytical entry, or the cataloguing record for the item as a whole must cater for the inclusion of the extra detail relating to the component part or parts. In the former case, the analytical record must be linked to the record for the item as a whole or contain a suitable *In* statement in a note. In the latter case, the system must allow for the relevant analytic fields to be accessed in an appropriate manner.

The UKMARC format, for example, utilizes the second methodology. It provides field 505 for contents notes and caters for the related analytical sub-records by the repetition of fields and the addition of level numbers (consisting of single digits) which inform the computer that the field refers to an analytical entry within the record for the item as a whole (the main entry). 'Thus for the book *Three plays of 1972* some fields are required to describe the book as a whole but other fields are needed to describe each individual play.' [1] Analytical records are made only for three or less works contained in a publication.

In W. A. Munford's *Penny rate : aspects of British public library history, 1850–1959* there appears a separate section by Joan Edmondson entitled *Mechanics' institutes and public libraries.* Here are selected fields from a machine-readable record as they might appear if the work were catalogued according to UKMARC. For an explanation of fields, tags and the MARC record see Chapter 11.

---

[1] *UKMARC manual.* — 2nd ed. — London : British Library. Bibliographic Services Division, 1980. 5/2.

100.10$aMunford$hW.A.#
245.10$aPenny rate$baspects of British public library history, 1850-
1950$eW.A. Munford#
505.00$aIncludes: Mechanics institutes and public libraries$eJoan
Edmondson#
100.10:1$aEdmondson$hJoan#
245.10:1$aMechanics institutes and public libraries#

The contents note from the main entry is shown in field 505 and the level digit ':1' in the 100 and 245 fields for the Edmondson contribution indicates an analytical level. (The level digit for the record for the whole item, i.e. the main entry, is zero). If further component parts required analytical entries then the level digits 2 and 3 would be used to indicate that fields related to these analytical records.

In Mitev, *et al.*, it is maintained that 'Fortunately records with analytical entries are fairly rare'.[1] However, as noted above, the actual number would depend on the policy of the individual library. The library referred to by Mitev is the Polytechnic of Central London where less than 2% of all records were found to require analyticals.

The UKMARC policy is that analytical entries are made only for three or less works contained in a publication. Thus entries would be made for each of the individual plays in *Three Restoration comedies* but not for the individual plays in *Six Elizabethan tragedies*. This policy obviously has had to be introduced for reasons of economy, which is perfectly justifiable and understandable, but such decisions could clearly lead to user confusion.

Conversely, of course, there is no reason why the bibliographic record should not be enhanced to cater for more adequate analysis. The provision of additional access points by the inclusion of information from contents pages or back-of-the-book indexes might radically improve not only subject access but also the analytical function. There is also the possibility of access to articles in serials, the CLR survey (see p.267) found that many OPAC users would like such information to be accessible. The availability and effectiveness (including currency) of hard-copy and online indexing and abstracting services and the possible duplication of information already available would have to be considered here.

Just how much analysis can be undertaken, no matter how desirable, will depend therefore on the various factors mentioned above, in both this and the previous section on 'Policy'. 'Ideally, the record format should enable it to be displayed appropriately according to which level it was accessed by, but this would entail heavy overloads'.[2]

---

[1] *Designing an online public access catalogue : Okapi, a catalogue on a local area network /* Nathalie Nadia Mitev, Gillian M. Venner and Stephen Walker. — London : British Library Board, 1985. 43.
[2] ibid.

Chapter 9
Filing

Filing is often regarded as something of a chore, but it is a very important chore because a misfiled entry is a lost entry. It is also a chore which demands a considerable amount of skill, particularly if a dictionary catalogue containing (in one sequence) entries under author, title and subject is used.

Some codes of cataloguing rules have included filing rules, including Cutter's *Rules for a dictionary catalog* and the Vatican code.

AACR 2

The uniform-titles rules in AACR go some way towards solving some filing problems, such as the arrangement under voluminous authors and under classics and sacred books. The AACR heading, for example, ensures that the parts of the Bible are filed together and then subfiled by language:

Bible. *English*
Bible. *French*
Bible. *N.T. English*
Bible. *N.T. French*
Bible. *N.T. Epistles. English*
Bible. *N.T. Epistles. French*

and the application of the optional uniform-titles rules for collections ensures that Shakespeare's complete works, complete plays or complete poems are collected regardless of title or language:

SHAKESPEARE, William
  [Plays]
  The complete plays of Shakespeare...

  [Plays]
  Shakespeare's dramatic works...

[Plays. German]
Die Schauspiele von Shakespeare...

[Poems]
The poetry of Shakespeare...

[Poems]
Shakespeare's complete poems...

[Poems]
The verse of Shakespeare...

[Works]
The complete Shakespeare...

[Works]
Shakespeare...

[Works]
The works of Shakespeare...

[Works. French]
Les oeuvres de Shakespeare...

Omission of designation of function (e.g. editor, compiler, translator) from the heading, as allowed in AACR, eliminates one filing problem — whether to file works written by an author in a different sequence from those he has translated, edited or compiled. The use of alternative headings, instead of traditional unit entry, removes amother filing problem — how to subfile entries for which a person or corporate body has been given an added entry. For example:

LONDON, Keith
The computer survival handbook : how to talk back to your computer / by Susan Wooldridge and Keith London...

clearly subfiles under the title; but if traditional unit entry is used:

LONDON, Keith
WOOLDRIDGE, Susan
The computer survival handbook...

there is the problem of whether to subfile under the title or under the main entry heading (Wooldridge).

Berghoeffer
An interesting filing system was introduced by Professor Christian W. Berghoeffer for the Frankfurter Sammelkatalog towards the end of the nineteenth century, involving the division of the catalogue into three sections — a personal section, a geographical section, and a title section. In the personal section initials and forenames of authors are ignored, and all titles are arranged in one alphabetical seqence under each surname. The Berghoeffer system,

110

```
BAYNES, KEN
  THE ART OF THE ENGINEER, KEN BAYNES AND FRANCIS PUGH.
  LUTTERWORTH, 1981.  240P. ILL(SOME COL.).
  2E, 4D
  0 7188 2506 3
BAYNES, KEN
  GORDON RUSSELL.  DESIGN COUNCIL, 1980.  ILL.
  2X
BAYNES, J
  THE JACOBITE RISING OF 1715.  CASSELL, 1970.  ILLUS. BIBLIOG.
  1R, 2B, 4B, 4D2, 4M, 4Z
  0 304 93565 4
BAYNES, HELTON GODWIN
  MYTHOLOGY OF THE SOUL.  A RESESARCH INTO THE UNCONSCIOUS FROM
  SCHIZOPHRENIC DREAMS AND DRAWINGS.  (NEW ED.).  RIDER, 1969.
  1R
  0 09 098740 3
BAYNES, K
  THE RAILWAY CARTOON BOOK.  DAVID & C., 1976.  ILL.
  4M2, 7S, 7T, 7W
  0 7153 7354 4
```

Sample entries from Cheshire Libraries microfiche catalogue illustrating the partial Berghoeffer filing. Forenames are ignored and titles file alphabetically within surnames

which is claimed to save filing and searching time, is particularly useful for union catalogues. Cheshire County Library now ignores initials and forenames of personal authors in the arrangement of entries for its microfiche catalogues.

The computer and filing

One advantage of computerized cataloguing is that it removes the drudgery of filing, since this can be done automatically by the computer. Each 'character', (numeral, letter, punctuation mark or symbol) is allocated a number within the machine and this facilitates sorting and merging. For example, in ASCII (the American Standard Code for Information Interchange) an upper-case A is 65, an upper case B is 66, an upper case C is 67, and so on. The computer, when comparing A and B, will 'know' that A comes before B because it has a lower numeric value. However, this does not solve all of the problems that will be encountered and library applications may require special programming arrangements in order to overcome:

1   certain difficulties posed by a pre-determined character order
2   the fact that the computer cannot think like a human being.

Where (1) is concerned, for instance, if upper-case letters have less value than lower-case letters (in ASCII the lower-case letters a−z are represented by the codes 97–122) then *The story of David Copperfield* and *The story of O* will file *before The story of aviation*, even though the latter comes *first* in alphabetical order.

With regard to (2), the computer could be instructed to 'ignore initial articles' and it would file *A tale of two cities* under 'tale' — but would it then file *A for Andromeda* as 'for Andromeda'? We shall also have to instruct the computer to ignore 'un', 'une', 'ein', 'eine', 'der', 'die', 'das', etc., since it does not know what an initial article is. And how would it distinguish between *Die fledermaus* and *Die retouching*? One solution to this problem is to ignore initial articles when cataloguing, regardless of what the cataloguing rules say.

There are also the problems of 'as if' filing (e.g. file abbreviations or numbers as if spelt out in the language of the title) and the tradition of filing personal names before the same word representing places, subjects, titles, etc.

Use can be made of filing control characters to provide a 'print as' or 'file as' routine. The XII Legion, for instance, could be entered as:

| The XII | 12th | Legion |

with control characters interposed to achieve the following:

The XII	12th	Legion
Print but do not file by	File by but do not print	Print and file by

Filing rules
The first code of rules dealing specifically with computer filing was published in 1966.[1] BLCMP published its own code of rules in 1971[2] and three major codes of filing rules, all compiled with the computer in mind, were published in 1980: *ALA filing rules*; *Library of Congress filing rules*; and *BLAISE filing rules*:

ALA filing rules[3]
ALA filing rules is the successor to *ALA rules for filing catalog cards* (2nd ed. 1968), but it is stated in the introduction that 'since the present rules are based to a much greater extent than their predecessors on the "file-as-is"

---

[1] *Computer filing of index, bibliographic and catalog records* / Theodore C. Hines and Jessica L. Harris. — Newark, NJ : BroDart Foundation, 1966.
[2] *Code of filing rules* / Birmingham Libraries Co-operative Mechanisation Project. — Birmingham : BLCMP, 1971.
[3] *ALA filing rules* / Filing Committee, Resources and Technical Services Division, American Library Association. — Chicago : ALA, 1980.

principle, and since the new rules are applicable to bibliographic displays in other than card formats, the work should be considered as new, and not as another edition'.

The rules are presented in two parts — General Rules and Special Rules. The Special Rules apply to 'situations encountered in the arrangement and display of bibliographic records with relative infrequence; for the most part they are extensions of, rather than exceptions to, the General Rules' (p.2).

There are considerably fewer rules than in the previous ALA filing rules and the exceptions and alternative rules, which were strong features of the earlier works, have been largely eliminated.

The rules are intended to be applicable to the arrangement of bibliographic records, whether by manual or automated means. 'Although the Committee was initially constituted as the Computer Filing Committee of RTSD, and although it has frequently had occasion to consider machine-related developments . . . , its major considerations have rested in the area of human utilization of bibliographic files' (p.4). Nevertheless, the emphasis on the 'file-as-is' principle (i.e. the principle that character strings should be considered for filing in exactly the form in which they appear — emphasizing what they *look* like rather than what they *sound* like or what they *mean*) makes the rules far more suitable for computer filing than were their predecessors.

Library of Congress filing rules[1]

The *Library of Congress filing rules* are more elaborate than the *ALA filing rules*. There are twice the number of rules and there is a tendency to adhere to some traditional 'classified' arrangements, no doubt because of the problems which radical changes would pose for the huge Library of Congress catalogues.

The rules replace *Filing rules for the dictionary catalogs in the Library of Congress* (1956) and the provisional *Filing arrangements in the Library of Congress catalogs* by John C. Rather (1971). They 'have been designed to enable the Library of Congress, with the least possible effort, to arrange large bibliographic files to satisfy a variety of needs' (p.1). They are presented in five sections:

1 a preliminary note defining the filing terms used in the rules
2 general rules
3 special rules
4 a discussion of aids to catalogue use
5 an appendix providing additional information on optional rules to be used in arranging older styles of catalogue entries.

---

[1] *Library of Congress filing rules* / prepared by John C. Rather and Susan C. Biebel, Processing Services. — Washington : Library of Congress, 1980.

Emphasis is on the 'file-as-is' principle and it is stated on p.7 that 'although the primary concern was to obtain arrangements that are relatively easy for humans to achieve and use, the final test of the practicality of a rule was whether a computer could be programmed to apply it efficiently'.

BLAISE filing rules[1]

The BLAISE rules had their origins in the report of a Working Party on Computer Filing set up by the Library Association Cataloguing and Indexing Group.[2] The British Library Filing Rules Committee started work in 1973 and circulated various drafts of the rules for comment before publication.

The rules were drafted according to the principles developed by the International Organization for Standardization (ISO). They are presented in four section: (1) Order of characters; (2) Exceptional treatment of certain combinations of characters; (3) Filing and non-filing elements in headings and uniform titles; (4) Order of entries. There are two appendices dealing with (A) Additional Roman characters and (B) Arrangement of entries for works of 'complex' authors.

The BLAISE rules differ from the ALA and Library of Congress rules in one unfortunate respect. They do not contain an index.

Filing problems

Whether manual filing or computer filing is used, decisions have to be made with regard to a number of problems, and the three main codes of rules do not always agree on these decisions. Some of the major problems will now be considered, though obviously in a more simplified manner than is done in the three codes.

'Word by word' v 'letter by letter'

All 'characters' (i.e. spaces, punctuation marks, numbers and letters) are allocated values within a computer. A space usually has less value than any other character, which means that 'word by word' (or 'nothing before something') is an easier system to program. All three sets of rules adopt this method rather than the 'letter by letter' (or 'all through' or 'solid' system), which ignores spaces and files alphabetically according to the letters of the heading regardless of whether or not they form complete words.

---

[1] *BLAISE filing rules* / British Library Filing Rules Committee. — London : British Library, 1980.

[2] Filing by computer / report of the Working Party on Filing Rules, *Catalogue and index* (27) Autumn 1972.

Word by word	*Letter by letter*
Air and space resources	Air and space resources
Air conditioning	Air conditioning
Air cushion vehicles	Aircraft
Air Force	Air cushion vehicles
Air pollution	Airfields
Air transport	Air Force
Aircraft	Air pollution
Airfields	Airports
Airports	Air transport

Many people prefer 'letter by letter', if only because it can rectify inconsistencies or confusion which can arise because certain words may be written either as one word or two. For example, PRESS MARK is used in L. M. Harrod's *Librarian's glossary* but PRESSMARK in T. Landau's *Encyclopaedia of librarianship*; the 'letter by letter' system would bring the two forms together but the 'word by word' system would separate them.

Order of characters
The BLAISE rules stipulate the following basic order of filing characters:

spaces, dashes, hyphens and diagonal slashes (given equal filing value)
ampersand
arabic numerals
roman alphabet letters
other alphabet letters

ALA and LC are similar but add full stops (periods) to the first group of punctuation symbols; also ALA either ignores the ampersand in filing or (optionally) files it as if spelled out in the appropriate language.

BLAISE and LC	*ALA (1)*	*ALA (2)*
over & out	over 5 bridges	over 5 bridges
over 5 bridges	over and above	over and above
over and above	over-anxiety	over & out
over-anxiety	over-credulous	over-anxiety
over-credulous	over & out	over-credulous
over/under	over/under	over/under
overcoat	overcoat	overcoat

Initial articles
Initial articles at the beginning of headings, titles, etc. are normally ignored unless they form an integral part of a proper name heading:

J. Bibby and Sons (name heading)
Eine kleine Nachtmusik
The merchant of Venice
A midsummer night's dream
A tale of two cities
The taming of the shrew
W. H. Smith (*firm*) (name heading)

As stated on p.112, the computer will need to be programmed very carefully if it is to ignore initial articles in all languages; it might be better to omit them from catalogue entries.

Initials and acronyms

BLAISE files initials and acronyms as words, not as individual letters, whether or not they contain full stops. If, however, the initials are separated by spaces, they file as letters. ALA and LC file them as letters if they are separated by marks of punctuation or spaces:

BLAISE	*ALA + LC*
L E A *see* LEA	L.C.
LADSIRLAC	L E A
The last rose of summer	L.I.R.G.
L.C.	LADSIRLAC
LEA	The last rose of summer
L.I.R.G.	LEA
Love among the ruins	Love among the ruins
LUTIS	LUTIS

M', M^c, Mc and Mac

BLAISE files the prefixes M', M^c, Mc and Mac occurring in names of Scottish or Irish origin as Mac. When, however, they occur in names of other languages, they are filed as given. ALA and LC *always* file them as given, which seems more appropriate to computer filing. The computer will have considerable difficulty in recognizing whether or not the name is of Scottish or Irish origin!

BLAISE	*ALA + LC*
M'Alpine, Neil	Macdonald, Ronald
McCluskey, Hugh	Machinery
Macdonald, Ronald	Madden, James
McDowell, Malcolm	M'Alpine, Neil
Machinery	M'Bengui, Mamadou
Madden, James	Mcanyana
M'Bengui, Mamadou	McCluskey, Hugh
Mcanyana	McDowell, Malcolm

Other abbreviations
All three codes arrange abbreviations exactly as written, so the computer does not have to work out what they mean:

Down among the dead men
Dr. Finlay's casebook
The Saint returns
St. John
St. Petersburg
A streetcar named desire

Same word as author, title, subject, etc.
ALA arranges identical headings alphabetically by the words following, while BLAISE and LC prefer 'classified' groupings. BLAISE arranges:

Personal forenames
Personal surnames
Corporate names
Subjects (other than personal or corporate names or titles of works)
Titles

and LC's arrangement is:

Personal forenames
Personal surnames
Place names
Thing (corporate body)
Thing (topical subject heading)
Titles

BLAISE
Mark
Mark, 1250-1301
Mark III
Mark, *Saint*
Mark *(family)*
Mark,   , *Dr.*
Mark, A.S.
Mark, Andrew
Mark, Andrew, 1901-
Mark, Andrew, *Solicitor*
Mark (Andrew) and Sons *see*
Mark (Somerset)
Mark (Somerset). *Education Department*

Mark (German coin)
The mark of Cain   (title)
Mark Twain's boyhood   (title)

LC
Mark
Mark III
Mark, 1250-1301
Mark, *Saint*
Mark,   , *Dr.*
Mark, A.S.
Mark, Andrew
Mark, Andrew, 1901-
Mark, Andrew, *Solicitor*
Mark family
Mark (Somerset)
Mark (Somerset). *Education Department*
Mark (Andrew) and Sons *see*
Mark (German coin)
The mark of Cain
Mark Twain's boyhood

ALA
Mark
Mark,   , *Dr.*
Mark III
Mark, 1250-1301
Mark, A.S.
Mark, Andrew
Mark, Andrew, 1901-
Mark, (Andrew) and Sons *see*
Mark, Andrew, *Solicitor*
Mark family
Mark (German coin)
The mark of Cain
Mark, *Saint*
Mark (Somerset)
Mark (Somerset). *Education Department*
Mark Twain's boyhood

Some would argue that the simplicity of ALA's arrangement makes it more attractive for an *alphabetical* catalogue and more geared to the needs of the computer, while others consider the separation of personal names to be a disadvantage. LC, with its artificial separation of place names and corporate names, is particularly complex.

Arrangement of subject headings

Unlike ALA, which ignores punctuation in favour of straightforward alphabetical arrangement, LC arranges subject headings as follows:

Heading
Heading followed by a dash and subject subdivision(s)
Heading followed by a comma and additional words
Heading followed by parenthetical qualifier

BLAISE has no rules for this problem, the implication being that straightforward alphabetical arrangement is used.

LC	ALA
MANAGEMENT	MANAGEMENT
MANAGEMENT – Encyclopaedias	MANAGEMENT BY OBJECTIVES
MANAGEMENT – Theories	MANAGEMENT – Encyclopaedias
MANAGEMENT, Industrial	
MANAGEMENT (FOOTBALL TEAMS)	MANAGEMENT (FOOTBALL TEAMS)
MANAGEMENT BY OBJECTIVES	MANAGEMENT, Industrial
	MANAGEMENT – Theories

See also references

All three codes file *see also* references *before* entries for the same heading. This is logical, as it prevents the possibility of a catalogue user spending some time searching through the entries under a particular subject heading only to find that he should really be consulting some other heading.

Unit entries

BLAISE points out that, when arranging unit entries under an added entry heading, the main entry heading should be ignored:

BRECH, E.F.L.
URWICK, L.F.
   The making of scientific management / by L.F. Urwick and E.F.L. Brech ...

BRECH, E.F.L.
   Management : its nature and significance ...

In the above example, all the entries under Brech are arranged alphabetically by title and the intervening main entry heading (Urwick) is ignored.

BS1749

The British Standards Institution, when preparing a new version of *British Standards recommendations for alphabetical arrangement and the filing order of numbers and symbols*,[1] took into account the BLAISE rules and, with permission, used some of the examples from this work. The ALA and LC rules were also consulted. However, BLAISE, ALA and LC all adopt a 'word by word' rather than a 'letter by letter' order; the British Standard maintains that 'the nature purpose or tradition of a list may determine the choice of filing method' and therefore does not recommend one or the other.

Conclusion

The above points demonstrate that, as Ayres[2] has pointed out, filing is not always 'as easy as ABC'. It is unfortunate that, although librarians in the English-speaking world have now reached agreement on how to *compile* catalogues and bibliographies, they are so far from agreement on how to *arrange* them. Further, commercially available software packages may have in-built sort routines which follow different directions.

---

[1] *British Standard recommendations for alphabetical arrangement and the filing order of numbers and symbols.* — Hemel Hempstead : British Standards Institution, 1985. (BS1749: 1985).

[2] It's not as easy as ABC / Fred Ayres, *Catalogue and index* (54) 1979 1-3, 8.

Chapter 10
Physical forms of catalogue

A catalogue may be presented in any one of a number of different physical forms:

Printed: A conventional book-type format.

Guardbook: A 'scrapbook'-type format. Entries are 'pasted in'. Space is left for new additions and extra strips of linen may be bound in to enable further pages to be inserted.

Card: Entries are on cards which file into 'trays' or 'drawers' housed in cabinets. Standard cards are 12.5 cm × 7.5 cm. Rods may be inserted through holes in the bottom of the cards to help retain them in trays.

Sheaf: A loose-leaf binder format providing some of the convenience of the book. Usually each entry is on a separate 'slip' of paper but there may be a number of entries on each slip or page.

Visible index: 'Office'-type equipment which may consist of strips mounted in a frame or cards held flat, hinged, and with the edge of each card protruding to make the heading 'visible'.

Microform: A form in which entries are greatly reduced and 'printed' upon film. A suitable 'reader' which magnifies the film and projects it on to a screen is required. Microfilm may be on a single reel, but more usually it is housed in a cassette containing two reels so that the film can be wound backwards and forwards within its container. Microfilm may come in:

comic mode, i.e.   or *cine mode*, i.e.

P1	P2	P3	P4	P5	P6

P1
P2
P3
P4
P5
P6

Microfilm readers will, therefore, usually allow rotation of the image through 90 degrees. Microfiche is a transparent 'card'-type format. A reduction of 42× would give 200 frames per card. Microfiche has the advantage of direct access to a particular frame whereas microfilm requires a 'serial' search through the film to reach a required entry point. Microfiche can also be presented in comic or cine mode and is very often in double-column format:

comic mode   *cine mode*

P 1		P 2		P 3	
Col	Col	Col	Col	Col	Col
1	2	1	2	1	2

P 1	
Col	Col
1	2
P 2	
Col	Col
1	2
P 3	
Col	Col
1	2

Machine-readable: A format which permits input and storage (on disc, tape, etc.) for manipulation in a computer. Access may be online or offline. Online systems are linked directly with the computer, which can thus be used immediately for processing and searching. Results are displayed on a screen or visual display and may also be output to disc or printed in hard copy. The computer may be a 'stand-alone' microcomputer or a larger mini- or mainframe computer accessed by remote terminals. Such terminals may be 'intelligent' or 'dumb'; the former have processing power of their own, the latter do not. The use of a microcomputer as a terminal provides a typical example of 'intelligence'. Offline relates to operation without continuous communication with the computer. Data must be processed in 'batches' which limits utility and flexibility. A useful analogy is to think of online as a telephone system and offline as a postal service.

A recent offshoot of the machine-readable format has been CD-ROM (Compact Disc – Read Only Memory). CD-ROMs are optical discs which are written and read by a laser beam (the narrowest form of read/write head currently available). Data is impressed on the surface as a series of pits of variable length and the discs can store vast amounts of data in digital form. For example, the British Library's *General catalogue of printed books to 1975* has recently (late 1989) been launched: 178,000 pages from 360 folio volumes on three small discs. To read a disc, a suitable microcomputer fitted with a CD-ROM drive is required.

In the nineteenth century, the most common physical form was the printed book, but its main disadvantage, the fact that it is out of date as soon as it is printed, led to the wide use of the more flexible card and sheaf forms.

These remained the major forms until the mid-twentieth century when the influence of business equipment began to be felt. This influence manifested itself not only in the appearance of visible index formats, but also in the use of machines to help automate the production of book-type catalogues, thus facilitating the constant updating that is required. Entries could, for instance, be recorded on punched cards which were sorted mechanically and the information thereon printed out by the use of electronic accounting machines, ready for reproduction by photography or offset printing. The sequential camera could also be utilized. Entries could be typed on cards upon which further information was punched, thus enabling the cards to be sorted and collated by machine. A camera would photograph the typed portion of the cards in sequence and the product was a photographic negative which could be cut and formatted into pages and printed out by a lithographic process.

Such photographic and offset lithographic methods enabled the catalogues of large research libraries to be effectively transformed into book-form catalogues for sale. Examples were the British Museum *General catalogue of printed books* and the *National union catalog*. The acquisition of such tools dramatically increases the bibliographic resources of any library.

However, it is the computer which has brought about the greatest revolution. Catalogue entries can not only be stored and sorted automatically, but the resultant computer output can be utilized in several ways. For instance, the computer 'print out' itself can be used as a 'master' and then reproduced by xerography or some other method. Photocomposition may also be used, the page master in this case being a photographic negative. Alternatively, output on magnetic tape may be processed into a microform (COM − Computer Output Microform). All of these computer-produced formats, however, manifest the same major disadvantage as the more traditional printed book form: they are out of date as soon as they are produced and regular updates are required.

The one form which facilitates continuous updating, with amended entries being available to the user as soon as they are input, is the online catalogue. Online public-access catalogues are becoming more and more common and many may be accessed from outside the particular library via remote terminals. The JANET (Joint Academic NETwork), for example, provides access to a number of the online public-access catalogues of academic libraries in the United Kingdom (see also p.222).

The CD-ROM catalogue is used in a very similar way to online access and may provide excellent search facilities but it is an *offline* format and, like microform, is out of date as soon as it is produced. Currency may therefore be a problem. One great advantage of the CD-ROM is its transportability, a complete catalogue can easily be sent by post. This gives the opportunity to place library catalogues in hitherto unlikely places.

In the United States, it was the large research and academic libraries which tended to lead the way in computerization. Computers were first applied to library techniques in the early 1950s, Taube's post-coordinate indexing system (see p.91) proving eminently suitable for mechanization, but the first application of computers to cataloguing processes was not to come until some ten years after this. The first proposal for a single machine-readable record from which multiple products, such as printed catalogue cards and subject bibliographies, could be obtained is probably to be found in a 1960 report to the Douglas Aircraft Company.[1] The automated production of catalogue cards began here in 1961.

The first computerized catalogues in the United Kingdom were produced by public libraries, the London boroughs becoming the pioneers when they were faced with the problems of amalgamation in the mid-1960s.

Today, with the extremely rapid developments that have taken place in the last decade, a vast number of libraries all over the world are applying the computer to cataloguing or other library processes. Centralized computerized services are available and the network (see p.190) has become the norm.

Despite the widespread use of the computer and the fact that a number of libraries provide online access, a great many catalogues in traditional format such as card or sheaf will continue to exist for some years. Indeed, paradoxically, the computer is often used to produce catalogue cards. Thus a very sophisticated process is followed by tedious manual filing in the monstrous space-eaters which the card catalogues of large libraries have become.

At the present time, therefore, it remains relevant to compare and contrast the various physical forms. The *best* physical form would need to possess as many as possible of the following attributes:

1 It must be easy to use
2 It must be easy to keep up to date
3 It must be easy to 'scan', i.e. to glance over a number of entries at once
4 It must be easy to produce multiple copies
5 It must take up as little space as possible
6 It must be easy to 'guide'.

The table on p.127 indicates how the different forms match these requirements.

---

[1] *Study of and proposal for a mechanised information retrieval system for the Missiles and Space Systems Engineering Library* / L.R. Bunnow. — California : Douglas Aircraft Company, 1960.

Using a microfiche catalogue

CALDER, N.
WHAT THEY READ AND WHY: THE USE OF TECHNICAL LITERATURE IN THE ELECTRICAL AND ELECTRONICS INDUSTRIES / by Calder,N. - 1959
x-85-002329-6
SHELVED AT 620.7 CAL EXCEPT WHERE INDICATED:
Walton No.: 1 copy

CALDER, P.R.
Common Sense about a Starving World / by Calder,P.R. - 1962
-85-017937-7
Canada Bronze Series - No. 10
SHELVED AT 338.19 CAL EXCEPT WHERE INDICATED:
Walton No.: 1 copy

CALDER, R.
MEN AGAINST THE DESERT / by Calder,R. - 2 ed. - Allen and Unwin, 1958   x-85-006074-8
SHELVED AT 910.4 CAL EXCEPT WHERE INDICATED:
I.M. Marsh: 6 copies

CALDER, R.
MEN AGAINST THE FROZEN NORTH / by Calder,R. - Allen and Unwin, 1957.   x-85-006077-4
SHELVED AT 910.4 CAL EXCEPT WHERE INDICATED:
I.M. Marsh: 1 copy

CALDER, S.
TRAVELLERS SURVIVAL KIT U.S.A. AND CANADA / by Susan Griffith & Simon Calder. - Vacation Work, c1985   £5.95   0-907638-38-4
SHELVED AT 917 GRI EXCEPT WHERE INDICATED:
Walton No.: 1 copy

CALDER MARSHALL, A.
THE INNOCENT EYE: THE LIFE OF ROBERT J. FLAHERTY / by Calder Marshall,A. - Allen, 1963   x-85-070092-9
SHELVED AT 791.43023 FLA EXCEPT WHERE INDICATED:
I.M. Marsh: 1 copy

CALDER-MARSHALL, A.
LONE WOLF: THE STORY OF JACK LONDON: THE BALLADS OF GEORGE R. SIMS. / by Calder-Marshall,A. - Hutchinson, 1961   x-85-070557-4
SHELVED AT 823.8 CAL EXCEPT WHERE INDICATED:
I.M. Marsh: 1 copy

CALDER MARSHALL, A.
WISH YOU WERE HERE: ART OF DONALD MACGILL / by Calder Marshall,A. - Hutchinson, 1966   x-85-043326-3
SHELVED AT 741.60 CAL EXCEPT WHERE INDICATED:
Byrn St.: 1 copy

CALDER VALLEY
HALIFAX AND CALDER VALLEY / by Yorkshire and Humberside Economic ... - H.M.S.O., 1966   x-85-051267-8
SHELVED AT 338.0942 CAL EXCEPT WHERE INDICATED:
Walton No.: Booktec: 1 copy

CALDERA, T.
INDAIN: LA DEMOCRACIA CRISTIANA EN AMERICA LATINA / by Caldera,T. - Ediciones Ariel, 1979. Spanish   x-85-010794-5
SHELVED AT 320.98 CAL EXCEPT WHERE INDICATED:
Walton No.: 1 copy

CALDERBANK, G.
THE TECHNOLOGY OF SUSPENDED CABLE NET STRUCTURES / by Frances Chaplin, Geoffrey Calderbank and ... construction Press ..., 1984   0-900459-051-5
SHELVED AT 624.1771 CAL EXCEPT WHERE INDICATED:
Mr. Pleasant (Architecture): 1 copy

CALDERDALE
CARING FOR THE VISITOR: THE CALDERDALE INTERPRETIVE STRATEGY STUDY / Civic Trust ... 1986   £6.00   0-900459-051-5
SHELVED AT 711.558094 CAL EXCEPT WHERE INDICATED:
Mr. Pleasant (Architecture): 1 copy

CALDERDALE LOCAL EDUCATION AUTHORITY
TEACHING ENGLISH AS A SECOND LANGUAGE: REPORT OF A FORMAL INVESTIGATION BY THE COMMISSION FOR RACIAL EQUALITY INTO THE TEACHING OF ENGLISH AS A SECOND LANGUAGE IN CALDERDALE LOCAL EDUCATION AUTHORITY ..., 1986. No price D-
SHELVED AT 428.24 COM EXCEPT WHERE INDICATED:
I.M. Marsh: 2 copies

CALDERHEAD, J.
EXPLORING TEACHERS' THINKING / edited by James Calderhead. - Cassell, 1987   £10.00   0-304-31303-1
SHELVED AT 371.102 CAL EXCEPT WHERE INDICATED:
I.M. Marsh: 4 copies

CALDERHEAD, J.
HOSPITAL(S) FOR PEOPLE: A LOOK AT SOME NEW BUILDINGS IN ENGLAND / James Calderhead, prod. by King Edwards Hospital Fund for London, for Dept. of Health and Social ... 1975   ill. £3.50   0-900890-47-8
SHELVED AT 725.51 REA EXCEPT WHERE INDICATED:
Mr. Pleasant (Architecture): 1 copy
Byrn St.: 1 copy

CALDERHEAD, J.
TEACHERS' CLASSROOM DECISION-MAKING / James Calderhead. - Holt, Rinehart and Winston, 1984   £3.95   0-03-910515-2
SHELVED AT 371.102 CAL EXCEPT WHERE INDICATED:
I.M. Marsh: 2 copies

Extract from Liverpool Polytechnic Library microfiche catalogue (see also p.83-4)

	Easy to use	Easy to keep up to date	Easy to scan	Easy to produce multiple copies	Bulky	Easy to guide	Other factors
Printed	Yes	No	Yes	Yes	No	Yes	
Guardbook	Yes	Yes, with some effort	Yes	Feasible but improbable	Yes	Yes	Time-consuming to compile. Withdrawals are a problem
Card	Debatable	Yes	No	No	Yes	Fairly easy	One user can monopolize a complete section
Sheaf	Yes	Yes	No, unless multiple entries to page which makes updating difficult	Not usual but it is possible	Yes	No	'Binding mechanisms can be awkward. Sheaf slips are flimsy
Visible index	Yes	Yes	Yes	No	Depends on type	Yes	
Microform	Debatable	Yes	Yes	Yes	No, microform's big advantage	Yes	Requires a machine to 'read'
Machine readable online access	Depends upon the system; generally speaking the answer is yes but some training may be necessary	Yes, the easiest of all forms	No unless multiple entries can be displayed on screen and page up/down scrolling facilities provided. Other search facilities may compensate where scanning is not possible	Multi-user access can be catered for and terminals can be placed in remote locations	A terminal may be quite small even as small as a portable typewriter but minicomputers or larger may need a special room to house them	The interactive nature of the system facilitates the provision of on screen help and guidance	By far the most flexible and powerful form
Machine-readable CD-ROM	As for online access catalogues above	Yes – but can be costly	As for online access catalogues above	Yes, but a workstation will be required for each disc or the system must be networked	No, a complete catalogue on a disc can easily be sent via the postal service but to access the disc a microcomputer with CD-ROM drive is required	As for online access catalogues above	Transportability. Useful for union catalogues

Comparison of physical forms of catalogue

127

The above table enables some general comparisons to be made but it does not address all of the points which may have to be considered. One further question, for example, is that of cost. This is a difficult question: direct comparisons cannot be made because of influencing factors such as size and type of library, computer availability, access to centralized services, cataloguing objectives, and so on. Nevertheless, some general observations may be made.

No one form of catalogue, either in terms of staff or materials, can be said to be cheap to produce. However, the cost of conventional forms is increasing all the time; the price of print and paper, for instance, has soared in recent years. As the cost of traditional forms rises, so the cost of computers and computer time diminishes with advancing technology and increased usage. The microform catalogue can be reproduced easily and cheaply from computer output (a matter of pence rather than pounds in the United Kingdom). There are, of course, the costs of producing the initial machine-readable version of the catalogue, which may be considerable. The cost of producing the master of a CD-ROM catalogue is also very high. 'In effect, the running costs of a CD-ROM based catalogue for any library will be comparable with the hardware maintenance costs for a standalone online system in the same library'[1] and therefore 'the CD-ROM catalogues does not appear to provide a practical alternative to a minicomputer OPAC'.[2] 'The number of discs produced is effectively irrelevant to the general level of cost since the run-on costs of CD production are miniscule'[3] and, for this reason, the CD-ROM catalogue can have advantages as a union catalogue. The CD-ROM may also be a viable form where the catalogue of a very large library can be offered for sale in considerable numbers.

Cost must also be linked with benefits (cost-benefit analysis − see p.236). One of the great virtues of both the microform and the CD-ROM catalogue is transportability; a complete library catalogue can be carried round in one's pocket (although appropriate equipment will be required to access it).

However, where benefits are concerned, there is no doubt that the online public-access catalogue offers enormous advantages − 'The online catalog is a far more powerful instrument than any of its predecessors'.[4]

---

[1] As simple to use as a card catalogue : can you put your library catalogue on CD-ROM? / Tony McSean and Neil Smith, *Vine* (74) Aug 1989 25-30.
[2] ibid.
[3] ibid.
[4] The online catalog revolution / Frederick G. Kilgour, *Library journal* 109 (3) 15 Feb 1984 319-21.

Microcomputer and compact disc drive
(Illustration reproduced from The British Library Bibliographic Services
newsletter *(46) June 1988)*

Searching an online public-access catalogue via a keyboard-free terminal. When a search begins, the screen displays user instructions and the words 'author', 'title' and 'subject'. Beneath the surface of the screen are heat-sensitive pads. Users touch the word on the screen to indicate what they require. The screen displays a broad alphabetic selection prompted by the first touch. The user narrows this down by repeating the touch procedure until the desired item appears. With another touch, full details of this item are displayed. The first library to provide this type of access to the public catalogues is reported to be the Chicago suburb of Evanston.[1]

---

[1] 'The moving finger' accesses / Cherry Susan Spaeth, *American libraries* 12 (1) Jan 1981 14-17.

Not only does the public-access catalogue overcome the problems of the printed book and COM forms, e.g. lack of currency, filing difficulties, multiple sequences etc., but it offers other advantages. The following is a list of the possibilities as seen by the developers of the University of California's MELVYL system:[1]

1 It could be easily updated − in real time or overnight − and hence would be much more up to date

2 It could be more accurate because corrections and changes could be made easily and immediately

3 It would allow faster catalogue searching for the user because the computer could do the searching and display the results within a few seconds

4 It could provide for searching under multiple terms, or keywords, not just the initial words of the headings chosen in the cataloguing process

5 It could allow combinations of terms or keywords to limit or define a search more precisely

6 The interactive nature of an online system could make it easier to provide guidance to the user in finding and locating material

7 The filing rule problems would be greatly lessened, both for librarians and users, because the computer would both store and retrieve all the information

8 A variety of display formats could be used (and chosen) by the user

9 The terminals used for the online catalogue could be used to provide access to other databases, or terminals already in use for other purposes could be used to access the union catalogue.

'In contrast with the existing card catalogs on most of the campuses, an online catalog could also be much more complete; it could display several entries at once, on the same screen, to facilitate browsing; it could be more portable (that is, terminals could be installed at various locations on campus, even in dormitories and offices); and the terminals would not only occupy less space but would allow greater flexibility in providing space for them.'

No wonder that the final University plan, then, 'strongly endorsed the online catalog' as the form of the new proposed system.

There is one problem associated with the online catalogue, of course, and that is that, being machine-based, it could break down. A library may consider it necessary to have a spare processor available or to maintain some form of back-up catalogue in hard copy or COM. The provision of a hard-copy back-up would obviously be expensive and time consuming and hardly cost-beneficial. However, it may well be, as Perry suggests, that 'producing some kind of COM catalogue on an infrequent basis is a very good idea.'[2]

---

[1] In-depth : University of California MELVYL *Information technology and libraries* 1 (4) Dec 1982 351-71 *and* 2 (1) March 1983 58-115.

[2] The implementation of an online public catalogue / Niall Perry *In Introducing the online catalogue : papers based on seminars held in 1983* / edited by Alan Seal. — Bath University Library Centre for Catalogue Research, 1984. 43.

Chapter 11

Using a computer

Data, files and records

The prime function of a computer is to store information, the latter being referred to as 'data'. This data can then be manipulated and extracted according to specific instructions. Such instructions are known as computer 'programs'.

Data is organized into 'files' and a 'database' can consist of one or more files. A file will contain a number of similar 'records' and each record is made up of elements called 'fields'.

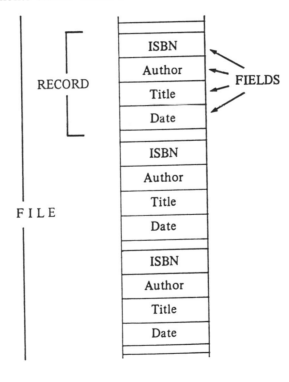

In library applications a 'file' might be, for example, a catalogue. The 'record' then becomes each individual entry in the catalogue and the 'fields' are the elements within the entry, e.g. ISBN, author, title, date, etc.

Fields may be in 'fixed' or 'variable' format. A fixed field is one of a specific length in terms of characters (a character being a single letter, digit, punctuation mark, symbol, or space). With fixed fields, the computer is able to calculate which field it is handling at a given time by a count of characters from the beginning of the record. With variable fields, each field may contain a varying number of characters. The length of records and constituent fields will now differ. The beginning and end of each record and each field must therefore be marked by 'tags', or 'indicators', which the computer can recognize. The characters used as tags must be unique and used for this purpose only. They must not occur elsewhere in the record. An alternative to the special symbol indicating the end of each variable field is a 'record and field length count' field, included at the beginning of the record.

Variable fields offer obvious advantages but they are more difficult to manipulate and to search.

It should be noted that even if variable-length format *is* used, certain fields, e.g. accession number, may still be of fixed length. The record will therefore consist of a mixture of fixed and variable-length fields.

Whether the format is fixed or variable, it must be stressed that all of the records in a file must have a similar format, with elements cited in a consistent order, although a particular element, e.g. a series, may not be present in every record.

Key field

One field may have a higher status than other fields and is therefore called the *key* field because, when searching for a particular record within a file, it would normally be this field which would act as a unique identifier. The key field will usually be the first. The ISBN or International Standard Book Number (see Glossary) could be utilized for this purpose. Alternatively, an in-house running number could be generated. In this latter instance, numbers can be made 'meaningful' to the cataloguing agency. For example, the first digit could indicate whether the item is fiction, non-fiction, audio-visual material, etc.; other digits could indicate the library or branch to which the item is allocated, and the remaining digits would comprise a unique identifier.

The key field could, of course, be something other than a number, e.g. the author. More than one field might also comprise the key, either concatenated or used separately.

Record organization

As the organization of a catalogue record relates directly to the catalogue entry, similar criteria to those indicated on p.24 apply and the manner in which a record is organized will depend upon the requirements of the particular cataloguing agency. A reasonably short, fixed-field format might well be suitable for some library systems, as such records are easier and quicker to compile and to search and they do provide a workable 'finding list' type catalogue. A fixed-field input form used by Clwyd Library Service is reproduced on p.135. Here the author field is limited to 60 characters and the title field to 85 characters. On the other hand, a national library would find such a fixed format unacceptable because elements of bibliographic data are of widely differing and unpredictable lengths.

Standardization

A library which acts unilaterally and uses an in-house record format will encounter a further problem. It will be unable to exchange bibliographic data with other institutions, as the record formats will be incompatible.

A clear distinction must therefore be made between a local, or in-house, format and a communication, or exchange, format. An in-house format is primarily concerned with efficient and cost-effective computer processing for the particular institution concerned. The exchange format's main objective is to provide a record structure which is hospitable to the needs and requirements of a wide variety of systems. In order to achieve this objective, the organization of the record must be standardized.

There are three things to be considered:[1]
1   the basic structure or framework of the record
2   the field names (sometimes called designators, labels, or attributes)
3   the record contents or data.

Some degree of standardization can be applied to all three of these. With regard to (1) and (2) the best known record format is the MARC (MAchine Readable Cataloguing) format. MARC conforms to *Anglo-American cataloguing rules*, 2nd edition, (AACR 2). In the English-speaking world and in some other countries, e.g. Norway, the latter is the major current standard for the description of a bibliographic item and for selecting and formulating the access points through which the item may be retrieved. AACR 2 is, therefore, apart from certain aspects of the subject approach, also important in relation to (3).

---

[1] *Compatibility issues affecting information systems and services* / prepared by F. Wilfrid Lancaster and Linda C. Smith for the General Information Programme and UNISIST. — Paris : Unesco, 1983.

Notes on the Clwyd Library Service input form reproduced below

The catalogue data is entered on the form offline and is subsequently input online by an operator to an in-house system. The resultant database is used for the production of microfiche catalogues which are updated monthly. In addition, the data is transferred to the ASSASSIN[1] package to form the basis of an online system.

The CATEGORY field is used to divide stock into fiction/non-fiction, adult/junior, English/Welsh, lending/reference.

The SUB-CATEGORY field is used to denote special collections, e.g. local studies, large print, video, etc.

The AUTHOR field includes only the first named author, editor, compiler, etc.

The TITLE field includes subtitle and series statement if the available number of characters is sufficient.

The EDITION is expressed as, for example, 02ED.

In the LOCATIONS field, each of the 50+ branches and mobiles has a two-letter mnemonic, e.g. BU = Buckley, CQ = Connahs Quay. This is followed by the number of copies, e.g. CQ2, RL3, WR1 . . .

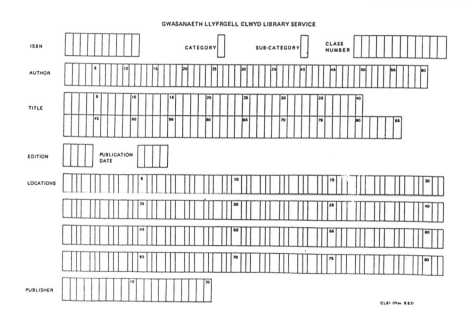

Field field input form used by Clwyd Library Service, UK
(actual size 11¾ × 8¼ inches)
Author field limited to 60 characters. Title field limited to 85 characters.
Publisher field limited to 20 characters

---

[1] ASSASSIN was originally developed for internal use at ICI Agricultural Division. It was publicly released in 1972 and at various times since then has been further enhanced. It has become widely recognized for information handling and has been purchased by a number of organizations.

135

MARC format

The MARC format is a variable-length field format and each element must therefore be tagged for identification. As noted above, MARC conforms to AACR 2 and the description of an item formulated according to these rules would contain various areas as described on p.33.

The MARC tag for the title and statement of responsibility area, for example, is 245. This is followed by an indicator which provides the machine with certain other information and then subfield codes to identify the various elements within the area.

Here is a title and statement of responsibility tagged according to MARC:

245   10 $aBorn free$ba lioness of two worlds$eby Joy Adamson#

The tag 245 is followed by the digits 1 which indicates that a title entry will be required (otherwise 0) and 0 which indicates that no characters are to be ignored when filing (otherwise 2, 3, or 4 if the title began with an indefinite or definite article). The $a is the subfield code for the title proper, the $b is the subfield code for other title information, a subtitle in this instance, and the $e is the subfield code for the statement of responsibility. The field is terminated with a hash mark (#).

The heading for the main access point (usually the responsible person or body) would be tagged with a number beginning with 1. 100 is the tag for a person as main entry heading and the indicator 10 reveals that this is a person with a single surname. $a is the subfield code for the entry element and $h for other parts of the name, i.e.:

100   10 $aAdamson$hJoy#

The tag for the publication area is 260. The digits 00 indicate that the publisher is not the main entry heading. The subfield codes are $a for place, $b for publisher, and $c for date, i.e.:

260   00 $aLondon$bCollins$c1960#

Three areas of the entry have now been tagged and identified:

100   10 $aAdamson$hJoy#
245   10$Born free$ba lioness of two worlds$e by Joy Adamson#
260   00 $aLondon$bCollins$c1960#

Other areas would be tagged and identified in a similar fashion to complete a full MARC record.

On pp.138 and 139 is a reproduction of an illustrative and shortened version of a MARC input form, with an abbreviated schedule of field tags, indicators and subfield codes, as used for teaching purposes at Liverpool Polytechnic. The form is shown completed with details relating to a sample item.

Evolution of MARC

MARC came into being in the United States in 1966 with a pilot project which involved the weekly distribution of machine-readable tapes to 16 selected libraries. These libraries processed the tapes through their own computing facilities, the most common requirement being, at that time, the production of catalogue cards.

A more advanced version of the scheme, using what became known as the MARC II format, became operational in 1967 with, initially, about 50 libraries receiving tapes on a subscription basis. In that same year, the British National Bibliography began work upon the development of a MARC system in the UK and tapes were being distributed to libraries by 1969.

MARC I had certain limitations; MARC II made the record format much more flexible. Variable length fields are used and each record is capable of holding a vast amount of information (up to 6,000 characters in the UK format, although the average is 1,000 characters)[1] and a considerable number of elements. Apart from all of the information which would be found in a full description by AACR 2, there are many additional fields, e.g. Dewey decimal and Library of Congress classification numbers, Library of Congress subject headings, PRECIS or COMPASS, subject index entries, etc. Any of these elements may be used as a means of approach. In addition, provision is made for information of 'local' significance to be included, for example a library 'holdings' note.

The MARC format caters (as does AACR 2) for a variety of library materials, monographs, serials, music, etc. The system is no longer confined to Britain and the United States. Many countries, including Australia, Canada, France, Germany, Netherlands, Japan, Scandinavia and South Africa have agreed to work to the same MARC format standard.

MARC now spreads its influence across the whole spectrum of library activity; including selection, ordering, cataloguing, information retrieval, production of bibliographies, etc. MARC can now be accessed online and the system is at the heart of many library networks.

Despite its widespread use, the MARC record, based, as it is, on AACR 2, remains an automated version of a manual catalogue entry. Because of this, the question of whether MARC is the most suitable format for machine-based systems must be asked, although no recognized new form of record has yet been established (see also pp.29−30).

An overview of MARC and other international exchange formats is provided by Gredley and Hopkinson.[2]

---

[1] *UKMARC manual.* — 2nd ed. — London : British Library. Bibliographic Services Division, 1980. 2/1.

[2] *Exchanging bibliographic data : MARC and other international formats* / Ellen Gredley and Alan Hopkinson — Ottawa ; London : Canadian Library Association ; Library Association, 1990.

Liverpool Polytechnic

School of Information Science and Technology

MARC FORMAT CATALOGUING SHEET

ISBN 021	021 00 $a 0340058099 #
Accession number 029	029 00 $a 17643 #
Personal author or responsible body 100	100 10 $a Sommerfelt $h Alf #
Uniform title 240	
Title 245	245 10 $a Norwegian $b a book of self-instruction in the Norwegian Riksmal $d Alf Sommerfelt #
Edition 250	250 00 $a New ed. $c completely rev. and enlarged by Ingvald Marm #
Publication details 260	260 00 $a London $b Hodder and Stoughton $c 1967 #
Physical description 300	300 00 $a xiv, 281 p. $c 18 cm #
Series 400	440 00 $a Teach yourself books #
Library's holdings 998	998 00 $a 01: H01 #

MARC input form used for teaching purposes at Liverpool Polytechnic, completed in accordance with the abbreviated statement of field tags, indicator and subfield definitions shown opposite. (It should be noted that these do not incorporate amendments to the UKMARC format announced in 1990 to take effect from January 1991. For example, 245 $d is no longer used. All statement of responsibility information is now held in repeated 245 $e subfields.)

Tag	Indicator	Subfield code	Definition
021	00	$a	ISBN
029	00	$a	Accession number
100	10		Person entered under single surname
		$a	Entry element
		$e	Additions to names, eg Sir, Dame
		$h	Forenames
	20		Compound surnames
		$a	Entry element
		$e	Additions to names
		$h	Parts of name other than the entry element
110			Corporate headings
	10		Government bodies
		$a	Entry element
		$c	Subordinate agencies – repeated when necessary
	20		Corporate bodies other than govts. and confs.
		$a	Entry element
		$c	Subordinate headings – repeated when necessary
111	00		Conference headings
		$a	Entry element
		$i	Number
		$j	Location
		$k	Date
240	10	$a	Uniform title
245	00		No title entry required
	10		Title entry required
		$a	Title proper
		$b	Other title information
		$d	Statement of responsibility – simple, single author
		$e	Statement of responsibility differing from, or adding to, info. in $d, eg 'edited by', etc
250	00	$a	Edition statement
		$c	Statement of responsibility relating to edition
260	00		Publisher not main entry heading
	10		Publisher main entry heading
		$a	Place
		$b	Publisher
		$c	Date
300	00	$a	Pagination
		$b	Illustration
		$c	Size
440	00	$a	Series title
		$v	Number
998	00	$a	Library's holdings note, eg 01:H01, ie 'One copy in Humanities Library'

On this input form, the information to the left of the vertical line refers the cataloguer to the schedules given above. Cataloguing data is to be written in the boxes to the right of the vertical line, together with the appropriate tags, indicators and subfield codes. Each field must be marked at the end by a 'field terminator', i.e. #.

It should be noted that in the MARC format tags ending in '9' and tags 950-998 are reserved for local needs.

In the United Kingdom, the MARC Users' Group (MUG) provides a forum for users of MARC records. The Group organizes a programme of conferences and meetings. Certain of the proceedings and various other monographs produced by members of the Group have been published.

Tag	Field
001	85018556#
020	ᵦᵦ$a0882339389$b(set : alk. paper)#
050	00$aPG3015.5.R6$bB76 1986#
082	00$a891.7/09/145$v19#
100	10$aBrown, William Edward,$d1904-#
245	12$aA history of Russian literature of the romantic period /$cWilliam Edward Brown#
260	0ᵦ$aAnn Arbor :$bArdis,$c1986#
300	ᵦᵦ$a4 v. :$bill. ;$c24 cm.#
500	ᵦᵦ$aIncludes bibliographies and indexes.#
650	ᵦ0$aRussian literature$y19th century$xHistory and criticism.#
650	ᵦ0$aRomanticism$ySoviet Union.#%

Selection of fields from a USMARC record[1] (above) and the cataloguing entry derived from that record (below)

```
Brown, William Edward, 1904-
    A history of Russian literature / William Edward
Brown. -- Ann Arbor : Ardis, 1986.
    4 v. : ill. ; 24 cm.
    Includes bibliographies and indexes.
    ISBN 0-88233-938-9 (set : alk. paper).
    1. Russian literature--19th century--History and
criticism.  2. Romanticism--Soviet Union.   I.  Title.
PG3015.5.R6.B76 1986
891.7'09'145--dc19                              85-18556
```

[1] Adapted from a USMARC record given in: *UNIMARC in theory and practice : papers from the UNIMARC Workshop, Sydney, Australia, August, 1988* / edited by Sally H. McCallum and Winston D. Roberts. London : IFLA UBCIM Programme, 1989, 88.

UNIMARC

The MARC format is undoubtedly the world's most important bibliographic record format and certain other standards, e.g. the international standard ISO 2709 (format for bibliographic information interchange), have derived from it.

The last 20 years have seen the evolution of a number of national MARC formats. Each of these follows ISO 2709 but, because of certain continuing differences in cataloguing practice, there are national variations in tag assignments and data definition.[1] Thus, initially, one national agency wishing to process the MARC data of another national agency had to write a special computer program to do so, and separate programs would be needed for every such format that the agency wished to make use of, meaning costly *multiple* conversion programs.

This led to the development of UNIMARC by IFLA. It was not possible to design one format that would meet equally the requirements of all MARC users but UNIMARC was intended to be a *communication* format, which would make it possible to write and maintain only *two* conversion programs − one from the national format to UNIMARC and one from UNIMARC to the national format. UNIMARC standardizes content designators for a core element, a 'descriptive block', which takes special account of ISBD. The IFLA International Office for UBC (now UBCIM) published *UNIMARC : universal MARC format* in 1977 and a second edition, which added specifications for cartographic materials, appeared in 1980. In the same year, the national libraries of Britain, Australia, Canada and the United States committed themselves in principle to exchanging records in the UNIMARC format.[2] A test involving nine national libraries was commissioned by the International MARC Network Study Steering Committee in 1981. The Deutsche Bibliothek analysed the results, which demonstrated that the use of the format would be facilitated by interpretation.[3] Thus in 1982 the British Library and the Library of Congress collaborated on the production of such an interpretative document: the *UNIMARC handbook* edited by Alan Hopkinson (IFLA, 1983).

A meeting of UNIMARC users was held in 1986, under the auspices of the International MARC Programme at the British Library. At this meeting a number of proposals for minor changes to UNIMARC were considered and specifications for several non-book forms of material were finalized. In 1987, the 1980 UNIMARC format and the *UNIMARC handbook* were merged into a single definitive publication: *UNIMARC manual*.

---

[1] *UNIMARC in theory and practice : papers from the UNIMARC Workshop, Sydney, Australia, August, 1988* / edited by Sally H. McCallum and Winston D. Roberts. London : IFLA UBCIM Programme, 1989. 1.

[2] ibid.

[3] ibid. 2

Exchange records in UNIMARC format are now offered by the national bibliographic agencies of a number of countries, including the Federal Republic of Germany, France, Hungary, Portugal, South Africa and Taiwain. The IFLA UBCIM (Universal Bibliographic Control International MARC) Programme continues to promote and maintain the UNIMARC format. A basic principle of UBC is that national agencies who so desire may take advantage of cataloguing work being carried out in the country in which a particular item originated[1] and, given the cooperation and effort, not to mention the financial outlay, of all national MARC users, UNIMARC could make a significant contribution.

Input of data

Cataloguing may be carried out 'offline' or 'online'. Where the offline mode is concerned, a form such as that shown on p.135 is normally completed by the cataloguer and this is then passed to an operator for inputting to the computer, hence the name 'input form'.

With an online system, records are input to the computer *direct*, usually via a keyboard. Online direct data entry is now becoming commonplace. The process may well begin by the cataloguer being presented with a list of options, or 'menu', from which the required operation will be selected, e.g.:

1 ADD RECORD
2 AMEND RECORD
3 DELETE RECORD

If 'Add record' is chosen, a series of prompts may appear, in some form, on the screen, so that a new record may be created, e.g.:

```
ENTER ISBN
?
```

```
ENTER ISBN
? 0 13 093963 3
ENTER AUTHOR
?
```

---

[1] UNIMARC / Henriette D. Avram and Sally H. McCallum, *IFLA journal* 8 (1) 1982 50−4.

```
ENTER ISBN
? 0 13 093963 3
ENTER AUTHOR
? CLIFTON, H.D.
?
```

```
ENTER ISBN
? 0 13 093963 3
ENTER AUTHOR
? CLIFTON, H.D.
ENTER TITLE
? BUSINESS DATA SYSTEMS
```

In the example given above, the particular field content must be entered before the next prompt appears. More usually, however, the prompts will appear all at once as a workform, e.g.:

```
ISBN:
Title:
Responsibility:
Edition:
Publisher:
Date:
Classification:
```

In this instance the length of the input line may denote field lengths, e.g.:

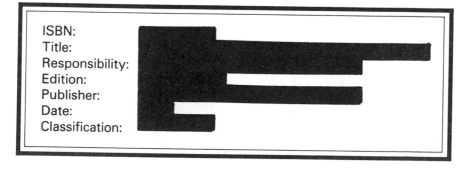

In some 'form-filling' online systems, the 'form', i.e. the screen format, can be tailored to meet specific user requirement.

The initial menu shown on p.142 indicates that it is necessary to have data maintenance facilities, e.g. amendment and deletion, as well as creation. Movement about a workform for the purpose of editing is made possible by, for example, cursor keys, usually marked on the keyboard by arrows. Full screen editing is increasingly being provided, with some systems incorporating word-processing type facilities.[1]

An alternative to editing on a workform is the use of commands, e.g.:

CHANGE AUTHOR ROBINSON

which means change the content of the author field to ROBINSON.

Some systems make use of a combination of the various methods, e.g. menu and command mode, or menu and form-filling mode.

```
TITLE     Office practice terms
RESPONS   Hewitt, Josephine
EDITION
PLACE     Edinburgh
PUBLISHER Chambers
DATE      1987
PHYS_DESC iv, 152 p. ; 18 cm.
SERIES    (Chambers commercial reference)
NOTES     A–Z guide to key words and phrases for business students and workers
          in commerce
ISBN      0 550 18061 3
CLASS_NO  HF5547.5
```

Cataloguing record input using the form-filling method. In this case the database management system dBase IV was used. This system permits the user to define the record format and, in this example, the format follows AACR 2

---

[1] *Library systems : a buyer's guide* / Juliet Leeves. — 2nd ed. — Aldershot : Gower, 1989. 9.

It will, of course, be necessary for the cataloguer to be able to search the database in order to ascertain whether a record for a particular item is already present. The cataloguer or operator must have ready access to an enquiry mode and therefore the initial menu will include an option such as SEARCH FOR RECORD. In a form-filling system, the search term might be entered in the appropriate field on the workform, e.g.:

```
ISBN: 0851573584
Title:
Responsibility:
Edition:
Publisher:
Date:
Classification:
```

whilst in a command-based system, searches will usually be entered by means of a command followed by the search term, e.g.:

SEARCH NUMBER 0851573584

Commands and field names may be abbreviated, e.g.:

s/n/0851573584

and use may be made of codes, e.g.:

SEARCH AUTHOR HUNT,ERI,J

or

s/a/HUNT,ERI,J

Searching is referred to here from the cataloguer's point of view and not necessarily the user's. Online searching by the user is discussed on p.161.

When a catalogue record for a particular item is retrieved by a search, it may not be one that the searching agency itself has generated. It could, in a centralized or cooperative system (see p.191), be an already existing record compiled by some other agency or library. The searching agency must then decide whether it wishes to use this record, in whole or in part, as a basis for its own cataloguing.

A retrieved record will be displayed on the screen, perhaps more than one screen, and any required amendments or additions (e.g. local data) can then be made to suit the individual library. Such amendments will be made as previously indicated, by cursor control, editing commands, and so on. Display formats can be complex, especially if MARC is used, and careful checking will be necessary.

If a relevant record is not retrieved, the searching agency will then create one and, if the agency belongs to a cooperative network, this record can then be made available to other participants.

Some cataloguing agencies like to print out records in hard copy after input for checking. Such a printout is referred to as a diagnostic.

```
    RECORD CARD

    CLASS      [                                                    ]
    AUTHOR-1   [                                                    ]
    AUTHOR-2   [                                                    ]
    TITLE-1    [
                                                                    ]
    TITLE-2    [                                                    ]
    SUBJECT    [                                                    ]
    PUBLISHER  [                                                    ]
    DATE       [                    ]            CATEGORY  [   ]
    ISBN       [              ]        NUMBER  [                    ]
    LOCATED    [                                                    ]
    BUDGET-No.    [      ]     PRICE  [        ]    COPIES    [     ]
    DATE-ORDERED  [        ] REQUEST-BY [                           ]
    TOTAL-HELD    [        ] BUDGET-COMMITTED [ ] BUDGET-SPENT [   ]
    DATE-RECEIVED [        ] COPIES-ORDERED [   ] TO-COME [        ]
    DISCOUNT        [    ]   ORIGINAL-PRICE [        ]
    TRAP        [                                     ]    PAGE >>

    Record Number  [                ]       Press <F1> to search
```

```
    RECORD CARD

    AUTHOR-3   [                                                    ]
    AUTHOR-4   [                                                    ]
    AUTHOR-5   [                                                    ]
    AUTHOR-6   [                                                    ]
    MEDIA      [                                                    ]
    EDITION    [                                                    ]
    CORPORATE-NAME [                                                ]
    VOLUME     [                 ]     COLLATION [                  ]
    SERIES     [                                                    ]
    NOTES-1    [                                                    ]
    NOTES-2    [                                                    ]
    PRECIS-1   [                                                    ]
    PRECIS-2   [                                                    ]
    CONFERENCE  [                                                   ]
    REFERENCE   [                                                   ]

    INVOICE     [          ]     ORDER-NUMBER [        ]  S-O [ ]
    SUPPLIER    [  ] DELIVERY [  ] COUNTY-REF  [                   ]

    Press <DO> when you have finished          <HELP> for Help
```

ONLINE INPUT SCREENS – ST HELENS COLLEGE, UK (OPAC)
(Fretwell-Downing's 'Lending Library' system)

146

Storage and manipulation of data

It is not essential for the cataloguer to be familiar with the way in which records are stored and manipulated after input; this is more the concern of the system designer and computer programmer. Nevertheless, some knowledge of basic general principles helps towards a better understanding of the overall computerized cataloguing system.

Records will not be arranged like materials on the shelves of a library, with new records being introduced into their correct places in the sequence as items are acquired. It is possible to do this but it is not the most practical solution. Indeed, records may *never* need sorting into classified order, or author order, etc., *unless* it is desired to output the catalogue in an eye-readable form. If the computer is online, a flexible search facility may be all that is required.

'But surely', the reader might say, 'it is necessary to have records in some sort of order, otherwise how would they be found?' Not so. In the simplest form of database − a single file containing just one type of record − it is possible, for instance, to search through the file, record by record, in order to find the particular record(s) that contain required information. With a small file this is perfectly feasible but larger systems need a faster and more flexible approach. There are various methodologies that may be used and the information given below is intended merely to illustrate one or two of these.

For example, as we have seen, it is possible to use a 'key' field by which the record can be found more quickly. The key field might be the author field and, if the records were ordered by this field then it would be quite easy to locate a record containing a specific author's name. However, the records need not be *physically* stored in author order as they would be on a shelf or in a manual author catalogue; a system of pointers can be used to represent the required arrangement.

The structure shown below is known as a one-way linked list and processing is always done by following the links. Because the links establish the order, the data need not be continually moved as items are added or deleted, all that is necessary is to amend the pointers.

Start

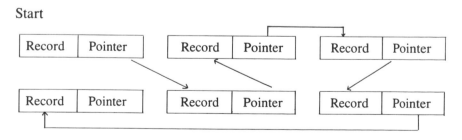

Having a single 'key' will not, of course, help if a search needs to be done on some other record element. If the key field is the author field, then what if one wishes to search for a title or subject? To cater for this facility, one of the more common answers is the 'multi-indexed' system, in which a number of indices are created to point to records in the main file. One multi-indexed method often used in library-type applications is the *inverted file*.

Whereas the normal record contains field identifiers, or attributes, together with the field contents, e.g.:

Author Shakespeare

an inverted list shows the *content* followed by a complete list of record identifiers, e.g.:

Shakespeare 1, 5, 7, etc.

A group of inverted lists comprises an inverted file and this may be completely or partially inverted, depending upon whether all fields are included as lists.

MASTER FILE				
Record	Author	Title	Publisher	Date
1	MORLAND	FISHING	HAMLYN	1982
2	HANSFORD	LET'S PLAY CHESS	OCTOPUS	1980
3	EDWARDS	FISHING FOR BEGINNERS	COLLINS	1978
4	PRITCHARD	RIGHT WAY TO PLAY CHESS	ELLIOT	1950
5	STEAN	SIMPLE CHESS	FABER	1978
6	PRITCHARD	LET'S GO FISHING	OCTOPUS	1980

AUTHOR INVERTED LIST	KEYWORD FROM TITLE INVERTED LIST
EDWARDS 3	CHESS 2 4 5
HANSFORD 2	FISHING 1 3 6
MORLAND 1	
PRITCHARD 4 6	
STEAN 5	

Partially inverted file

148

Complex search routines are facilitated by matching the list of identifiers for one search term against the list of identifiers for another. If searching for a book by Pritchard on chess, for example, records 4 and 6 would be matched against 2, 4 and 5 to reveal that record 4 is the only record containing both elements. Readers may recognize that this methodology has much in common with post-coordinate indexing as explained on p.96.

It is possible to link the contents of more than one field to provide some form of 'coded' search facility. Below, for example, is an inverted list under an author/title 'key' derived from the first four letters of the author and the first three of the title:

AUTHOR/TITLE KEY INVERTED LIST
EDWAFIS 3
HANSLET 2
MORLFIS 1
PRITLET 6
PRITRIG 4
STEASIM 5

If vocabulary control is required, then provision for 'authority' files will have to be made, so that when an index entry is added to the system this may be compared with those already in use. Any necessary adjustment can then be made to ensure consistency and to avoid indexing the same author or subject, etc., under different forms of entry term.

Angling
USE FISHING

FISHING
Use for Angling

An alternative to a separate authority file, and possibly a more efficient means of authority control, would be to use the actual index file as the authority file, e.g.:

SUBJECT ACCESS INVERTED FILE
ANGLING
GO TO FISHING
CHESS
2
4
5
FISHING
1
3
6

If desired, both terms could be fully maintained in the access file, e.g.:

SUBJECT ACCESS INVERTED FILE
ANGLING
1
3
6
CHESS
2
4
5
FISHING
1
3
6

The user will automatically retrieve the same records regardless of whether 'Angling' or 'Fishing' is used as the search term.

When a subject authority list indicates more complex relationships between terms, it is referred to as a thesaurus (see p.98).

It should be clear from the above that the computer is capable of performing various valuable 'clerical' functions on the data that is stored within it. Sorting, rearranging, updating and searching are just some of the more obvious tasks which the computer can undertake much more quickly and efficiently than can be achieved manually. The librarian contemplating automation of the cataloguing process must remove the blinkers imposed by the restrictions of the traditional 'author, title, subject' approach and think in terms of the tremendous flexibility that the computer can offer. What is more, this flexibility can be achieved without any of the tedium which has been the constant lot of those faced with the task of maintaining a card or sheaf catalogue.

Output of the data

Data can be output in various arrangements and, as noted in chapter 10, in various physical forms, e.g. print-out on paper for book type catalogues, or on cards for card catalogues, or onto magnetic tape in machine-readable form and subsequently onto microfiche. Records can be sorted into classified order for output with the classification number as first element, or into alphabetical order with the author as first element. There is no need to keep multiple records within the computer store. All of this can be achieved from one complete record for each item.

Alternatively, online access can be provided.

Online catalogues and cataloguing

Before proceeding to discuss the online catalogue, it must be emphasized that not all online catalogues are *public* catalogues. An often encountered combination, for instance, has been an online access facility for library staff and an offline, e.g. microfiche, catalogue for the user. However, the online public-access catalogue is an innovation that overshadows all other events in the history of cataloguing during the past decade. An online public-access catalogue (OPAC) 'is a library catalogue accessed via a computer terminal for the benefit of library users'.[1]

OPAC's were introduced in the United States in the late 1970s as an offshoot of the online real-time circulation systems which had been available from the early years of that decade. As part of the circulation system, some form of enquiry module was provided for library staff and, as this facility was developed and became more powerful, it was a logical step to extend the provision to the library user.

The honour of being the first library in the United Kingdom to introduce online public access must probably go to the University of Hull where a Geac circulation system was acquired in 1980 and an associated OPAC went live in 1981.

---

[1] *Online catalogues* / Stephen Walker. London : British Library Board, 1988. (Library and information briefings). 2.

Early online public-access systems were designed to run on a minicomputer (or larger) but, as early as 1980–1, libraries were also applying the smaller microcomputer to a variety of tasks. A full online public-access catalogue was, however, a difficult facility to implement on a microcomputer, mainly because of the small storage capacity, both immediate-access and secondary, which such machines had at that time. A number of floppy discs were required to hold a full catalogue, even in a small library with a stock of only a few thousand volumes. By 1982 the coming of the hard disc, with its vast storage capacity, made cataloguing on a microcomputer a more feasible possibility and suitable commercial packages began to appear. By 1983, for instance, the University of Buckingham had an online public-access facility (LIBRARIAN from Eurotec), which was based upon a Comart Communicator with a 20-megabyte hard disc. This would accommodate up to 40,000 catalogue entries and related indexes.

The bibliographic utilities (see p.200) tended to differ from commercial systems such as Geac in that they usually ran on mainframes rather than minicomputers; they were (and are) based upon MARC records; and they provided a different, and sometimes more sophisticated, type of search facility. In this guise, working on a remote-access basis, it was not easy to provide an online public-access catalogue. In more recent years therefore, there has been a tendency for the utilities to add local standalone dedicated systems to the services which they provide.

Thus the two developmental paths, commercial suppliers and cooperatives, started to converge. Commercial systems began to offer more flexible access facilities and more structured records (i.e. MARC cataloguing) than they had hitherto and the networks moved towards standalone systems.

The term 'online catalogue' can, in fact, be a misnomer for, as Seal points out, the advent of integrated systems has made it less relevant to distinguish between acquisition, catalogue and circulation records.[1] Perhaps, therefore, a more correct phrase might be 'online access to library files'.[2] 'The greatest virtue of automated database systems is that they permit a single file of information, once converted to machine-readable form, to serve several different functions.'[3] It should be possible for an OPAC (Online Public Access Catalogue) user, and prospective borrower, to ascertain the answer to questions such as: 'Is the item that I have selected available?'; 'If not, when is it likely to be available?' – thus linking the circulation control and cataloguing functions. Ultimately, when an item is not in stock, the user will be able

[1] *Introducing the online catalogue : papers based on seminars held in 1983*. Bath University Library. Centre for Catalogue Research, 1984. 1.

[2] ibid. 9.

[3] *The future of the catalog : the library's choice* / S. Michael Malinconico and Paul J. Fasana. Knowledge Industry, 1979.

to transmit his/her request onward to other libraries and information centres, or even to an appropriate bookseller. Electronic order transmission has already begun, albeit on a relatively small scale, and writers such as Bonk[1] maintain that increasing automation in the book trade and in libraries will lead to a new type of bookseller/library interface and relationship.

Catalogue output on CD-ROM

A CD-ROM catalogue has been defined as a 'MARC-based compilation of bibliographic records distributed on CD-ROM with accompanying software enabling it to perform some or all of the following functions:

1 local public-access catalogue
2 union catalog in support of interlibrary loan
3 reference database of bibliographic information
4 resource data file for extraction of records to be used in retrospective conversion, card production, ongoing additions to a local online database'.[2]

The CD-ROM catalogue is claimed to be 'a good medium for library catalogs because, for the moment, it offers the best combination of large data-storage capacity, reasonable production cost and computer-based searchability'.[3]

However, McSean and Smith point out that 'CD-ROM is an offline medium. CD-ROM based catalogues will suffer all the disadvantages familiar to us from fiche, printout and other more traditional forms of offline catalogues. The two most frequent enquiries which we and our users make are:

(a) circulation status information
(b) information about the latest acquisitions

Therefore, this characteristic has to be seen as a considerable disadvantage'.[4] In addition, unless a large number of discs (at least in the hundreds) are to be produced, unit cost of production will be alarmingly high. The verdict of McSean and Smith therefore is that because of the offline and economic factors, for the individual library, CD-ROM does not appear to provide a practical alternative to a minicomputer OPAC. Circumstances where they are worthy of consideration include: union catalogues (most North American sales have been for use as union catalogues); promotion and outreach (CD-ROM can take the catalogue into previously inconceivable places); and use in very large libraries, where there may be factors (e.g. the possibility of catalogue sales) which will transform economic arguments.

---

[1] Integrating library and book trade information / Sharon C. Bonk, *Information technology and libraries* 2 (1) Mar 1983 18-25.
[2] CD-ROM catalogs : the state of the art / Karl Beiser, *Wilson library bulletin* 63 (3) Nov 1988 25-34.
[3] ibid.
[4] As simple to use as a card catalogue : can you put your library catalogue on CD-ROM? / Tony McSean and Neil Smith, *Vine* (74) Aug 1989 25-30.

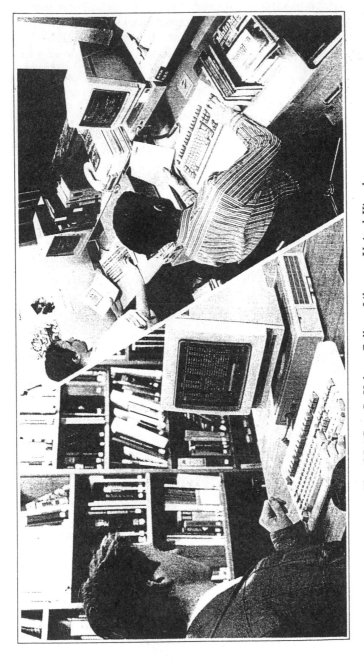

The OPAC at St Helens College Library, United Kingdom.
Staff inputting records to catalogue (right) and user searching the catalogue (left)

Thus it can be seen that opinions vary from 'CD-ROM is a viable alternative to expensive online systems' to 'CD-ROM is something similar to microform, i.e. offline and out of date'.

The latter opinion, however, ignores the important fact that microform search facilities are similar to manual catalogues whereas CD-ROM offers the same flexibility as online searching. Indeed, CD-ROM may well have a better user interface; facilities such as pull-down menus and windows are already available. Graphics and sound can also be provided so that, for instance, a music catalogue on CD-ROM could include sound extracts from the works indexed. Nimbus already market a compact disc catalogue of classical music with such extracts. And the technology is not standing still; new retrieval techniques such as Hypertext are being developed and CD-ROM is fast becoming a 'multimedia' medium. There is also the possibility of a 'seamless' interface between the CD-ROM drive and the computer's hard disc, so that the user can switch from CD-ROM to online for newer titles.

Admittedly, CD-ROM is slow compared with online retrieval but this is unlikely to cause many problems in a library catalogue situation. Where speed is concerned, and indeed other aspects of catalogue use, the comparison should not perhaps be between CD-ROM and online but between CD-ROM and the earlier forms of catalogue such as card. There can be little doubt where the great advantage lies.

Akeroyd concludes that: 'CD-ROM provides opportunities for providing online catalogues which in many ways are analogous to COM microfiche. They should prove to be compact, easily handled, reliable and require little technical insight or know-how. They may be limited by currency but they provide the most extensive subject-retrieval facilities yet seen in the majority of general libraries. They are capable of providing both sophistication and user cordiality together with reliability. Couple this with the flexibility to adapt to new developments at a pace unknown to current OPACs, and CD-ROMs begin to measure up as a viable catalogue alternative'.[1]

Most of the currently available products are North American. Bibliographic utilities such as OLCL, UTLAS and WLN provide a CD-ROM cataloguing facility (see p.200) and commercial suppliers include Brodart's Le Pac and Pendragon's SearchMe. One of the first library suppliers to provide a CD-ROM product was CLSI and its CD-CAT was the first such system to become available in the United Kingdom.[2]

Mention must also be made of the many other CD-ROM products which act as aids to cataloguers, some of which have already been cited in this work, e.g.: the Library of Congress *CDMARC bibliographic*, *CDMARC names* and *CDMARC subjects* and the British Library's *BNB on CD-ROM* and *The general catalogue of printed books to 1975*.

---

[1] CD-ROM as an online public access catalogue / John Akeroyd, *Electronic library* 6 (2) Apr 1988 120-4.
[2] CD-CAT : catalogue output on CD-ROM / Mary Rowbottom, *Vine* (72) Nov 1988 3-7.

Sample screens from WLN's, US, CD-ROM catalogue — LaserCat
(1) Search screen showing search on keyword 'northwest'

Sample screens from WLN's, US, CD-ROM catalogue — LaserCat
(2) Title index display

```
        Timberland Regional Lib.     WLN LaserCat V3.31         Brief Record Display
                                                                    Record 1 of 3
    ->‹      Title: 50 hiking trails : Portland & northwest Oregon /
            Author: Lowe, Don.
         Publ Info: Touchstone Press, c1986. [86-210901]
           Call f: 917.9504 LOWE

       ‹      Title: Northwest adventures [videorecording] : a video guide to
                     Northwest trails /
         Publ Info: Tempest Productions, c1986. [wln87-052764]

       ‹      Title: Northwest outdoor vacation guide /
            Author: Spring, Ira.
         Publ Info: Writing Works, [1981?] [81-052031]
           Call f: 917.9504 SPRING






    TITLE     KEYWORD "northwest"                                  - End -
    PgUp PgDn Home
    F6-Full F7-Holdings F8-Complete              F10-Print Bib     ESC-New Search
```

Sample screens from WLN's, US, CD-ROM catalogue – LaserCat
(3) Brief record display

```
        Timberland Regional Lib.     WLN LaserCat V3.31            Full Display
                                                                    Page 1
    ->‹      Title: 50 hiking trails : Portland & northwest Oregon /
       ‹    Author: Lowe, Don.
         Publisher: Touchstone Press, c1986.
          Descript.: 128 p. :
       ‹   Subject: Hiking—Oregon—Guide-books.
       ‹   Subject: Hiking—Oregon—Portland Region—Guide-books.
       ‹   Subject: Hiking—Cascade Range—Guide-books.
       ‹   Subject: Oregon—Description and travel--1981- --Guide-books.
       ‹   Subject: Portland Region (Or.)—Description and travel—Guide-books.
       ‹   Subject: Cascade Range—Description and travel—Guide-books.
      ‹Add Author: Lowe, Roberta,
      ‹ Add Title: Fifty hiking trails.
      ‹ Add Title: Portland & northwest Oregon.
      ‹ Add Title: Portland and northwest Oregon.
            ISBN: 0911518703 (pbk.) :
            LCCN: 86-210901
            Date: 1986          Lang: eng            Lrge:
            Type: Book          Govt:                Juvn:
           Call f: 917.9504 LOWE

    TITLE     KEYWORD "northwest"                                  - End -
    PgUp PgDn Home
            F7-Holdings F8-Complete    F9-Search Hdgs F10-Print Rec   ESC-New Search
```

Sample screens from WLN's, US, CD-ROM catalogue – LaserCat
(4) Full record display

Chapter 12
Searching

If the physical form of output is in hard copy, e.g. card or printed book format, then the search methodology for the computer-produced catalogue will be exactly the same as when the catalogue is produced in some other way. 'Conventional' classified and dictionary arrangements may be used as illustrated on pp.55, 78 and 82.

A similar situation exists where output is via microform, which is, in effect, a printed form very much reduced in size. However, the size factor is important because, as previously indicated, it makes possible the provision of additional access points which, with computer production, can quite easily be generated.

Apart from classified and dictionary formats, the computer can be used to produce other 'inner' forms of catalogues and indexes. A keyword from title list, for instance, as indicated on p.68, may require no intellectual effort to produce. Entries are automatically generated for all title words apart from those on 'stoplists'. An example is reproduced on the following page. A 'back of the book'-type index can also be produced using the computer, as described on p.276.

Whilst it is still necessary, at this moment in time, to consider such approaches as those described above, two facts can be stated with some certainty:

1 The printed book-, card- or microform-computer-produced catalogues are interim forms only. All will eventually be replaced by online systems.
2 Traditional classified/dictionary arrangements, in the context of online access, are redundant. Online searching offers much more flexible and exciting possibilities.

F

Permuted keyword from title (KWIC) index from Online review *13 (4)*
Aug 1989 Supplement. The last entry under 'Fax' is also indexed under
'CD-ROM', 'Shared', 'Reference' and 'Resources'

159

FOTHERINGHAM :	AMERICAN GOVERNMENT AND POLITICS	[320.473
FALKUS : THE SPANISH	ARMADA	[942.05
PUNNETT :	BRITISH GOVERNMENT AND POLITICS	[320.442
CLIFTON :	BUSINESS DATA SYSTEMS	[658.4032
	CLIFTON : BUSINESS DATA SYSTEMS	[658.4032
CLIFTON : BUSINESS	DATA SYSTEMS	[659.4032
WOOD : INSHORE	DINGHY FISHING	[799.1
	FALKUS : THE SPANISH ARMADA	[942.05
WOOD : INSHORE DINGHY	FISHING	[799.1
	FOTHERINGHAM : AMERICAN GOVERNMENT AND POLITICS	[320.473
FOTHERINGHAM : AMERICAN	GOVERNMENT AND POLITICS	[320.473
PUNNETT : BRITISH	GOVERNMENT AND POLITICS	[320.442
WOOD :	INSHORE DINGHY FISHING	[799.1
FOTHERINGHAM : AMERICAN GOVERNMENT AND	POLITICS	[320.473
PUNNETT : BRITISH GOVERNMENT AND	POLITICS	[320.442
	PUNNETT : BRITISH GOVERNMENT AND POLITICS	[320.442
FALKUS : THE	SPANISH ARMADA	[942.05
CLIFTON : BUSINESS DATA	SYSTEMS	[658.4032
	WOOD : INSHORE DINGHY FISHING	[799.1

AKWIC (Author and Key Word In Context) computer-produced index (generated, in this instance, by means of a program written by G. B. Moersdorf at Ohio State University). Entries under unwanted key word, e.g. 'The', 'And', etc. are automatically suppressed by means of a 'stoplist

---

```
ELECTRICAL ENGINEERING      621.3
ENGINEERING      620
HARDWOODS
     BUILDING MATERIALS      691.1
     TIMBER INDUSTRIES      674
     TREES
          FORESTRY      634.976
HARRIER
     MILITARY AIRCRAFT      623.746047
LECLERC, GENERAL
     FRENCH ARMY
          WORLD WAR II      940.5412
RADIO
     ELECTRICAL ENGINEERING      621.3841
THERMIONIC VALVES
     RADIO ENGINEERING      621.384132
```

*Selected entries from the 1990 edition of the Dorset County Library (UK) printed Subject index. This is not a pure 'chain' index but many of the entries reflect a chain structure; examine the entries under 'Thermionic valves', 'Radio', 'Electrical engineering' and 'Engineering'. The 'relative' nature of the index can be seen in the entries under 'Hardwoods'. In the actual index, ** indicates numbers used most recently but these asterisks have been omitted here. The index is also used by Cheshire County Library*

Searching in an online system

Essentially, online searching will feature one of three basic approaches: *menu* (including *form-filling*), *command* or *free text*.

The *menu* approach provides the user with a series of options which will be displayed on the screen of the VDU, e.g.:

```
DO YOU WISH TO SEARCH UNDER
  1 AUTHOR
  2 TITLE
  3 SUBJECT
ENTER APPROPRIATE NUMBER AND
  THEN PRESS RETURN KEY
```

A mnemonic feature can be introduced by replacing the numbers with letters, e.g.:

```
A AUTHOR
T TITLE
S SUBJECT
```

After the user has selected an option more guidance may be given, for example, if option 'A' is chosen:

```
ENTER THE AUTHOR THAT YOU REQUIRE
SURNAME FIRST FOLLOWED BY A SPACE
AND THEN THE INITIALS EXCLUDING
PUNCTUATION MARKS
```

Although the menu approach could be described as 'user-friendly', it can become slow and tedious once one is familiar with search methodology, especially if a series of menus and submenus, which may be irrelevant to the particular enquiry, have to be worked through.

A method different to that described above but one which still might be considered a 'menu' type of approach is the 'form filling' technique where the complete record format is displayed on the screen. The user selects the required option by moving the cursor to the relevant field and then typing in the search term in a manner similar to that illustrated on p.143, e.g.:

```
┌─────────────────────────────────────────────────────────────┐
│ ┌─────────────────────────────────────────────────────────┐ │
│ │                                                         │ │
│ │  AUTHOR_SURNAME: .TROMBETTA. . . . . . . . . . . . . . . │ │
│ │  AUTHOR_INITIALS (EXCLUDE PUNCTUATION AND SPACES): .M. . │ │
│ │  TITLE . . . . . . . . . . . . . . . . . . . . . . . . . │ │
│ │  . . . . . . . . . . . . . . . . . . . . . . . . . . . . │ │
│ │  PUBLISHER: . . . . . . . . . . . . . . . . DATE: . . . .│ │
│ │  SUBJECT: . . . . . . . . . . . . . . . . . . . . . . . .│ │
│ │  CLASS: . . . . . . . . . . . . . . . . . . . . . . . . .│ │
│ │      ENTER REQUIRED SEARCH TERM(S) IN APPROPRIATE       │ │
│ │              FIELD AND PRESS SEND                        │ │
│ └─────────────────────────────────────────────────────────┘ │
└─────────────────────────────────────────────────────────────┘
```

With the *command* approach, the user types instructions to the computer, e.g.:

FIND AUTHOR SHAKESPEARE

Unfortunately, there is no consistency or standardization of command languages and there may well be no explanation of the available commands given on the screen. The user must obtain these from some other source, e.g. an adjacent explanatory chart, leaflet, or manual.

Some catalogues do incorporate screen explanation, e.g.:

TO SEARCH FOR AN AUTHOR TYPE
  FIND AUTHOR
FOLLOWED BY THE AUTHOR'S SURNAME, E.G.
  FIND AUTHOR SALTER

It is possible to abbreviate commands in many systems, e.g.:

F A SALTER

The command mode can become complex and the user may have to be provided with detailed instructions. Simple commands such as FIND may be easy to understand but others, e.g. BACKUP (to return to a previous search result after a modification), are more difficult.

In either menu or command mode, the facility of stringsearching may be available. An example might be:

FIND TITLE CONTAINS TREES
or F T CT TREES

which would find any title which contained the term 'trees'. Stringsearching is a very useful facility. It enables a search to be made for a string of characters which is contained within a larger string. One form is the 'keyword'-from-title type of search shown above but it is also possible to search the whole of a record as in free text searching.

162

Free text searching, in some ways, is the most user-friendly of the various approaches because all that the user is required to do is to enter a search term. No menus are necessary, nor does the search term need to be preceded by a command such as FIND. A multiple field search is automatically generated.

For example, the user could type in the search term

TITANIC

and the following record might be retrieved and displayed:

KENNETT, FRANCES

THE GREATEST DISASTERS OF THE 20TH CENTURY

MARSHALL CAVENDISH, 1975

24 MAJOR CATASTROPHES INCLUDING THE SAN FRANCISCO EARTHQUAKE, THE TITANIC, THE HINDENBERG AND R101, HURRICANE FIFI AND ABERFAN

The search term appears only in the abstract but this makes no difference; relevant records will be retrieved no matter where the search term occurs.

Stringsearching, although extremely useful, can sometimes be slow (depending upon the system) and expensive, especially when searching through complex records in large files.

Qualifiers may be employed in some free text systems as limit factors to restrict the search. This can assist the user to define the requirement more clearly and may result in a faster response. For example, a search on

WHITING

would yield some items by or about persons of that name and also items on the subject as a type of fish. Inserting a qualifier, e.g.:

WHITING (AU)

would restrict the search to relevant *authors*.

Possible qualification parameters, which can be of general use, include language, type of publication and date of publication.

163

MELVYL™
Catalog
Guide

University of California, Santa Cruz 11/88

6. How to display your search results.

For a list of books with call numbers, type **d**

For one-line listings (most per screen), type **d rev**

For most information for each item, type **d long**

For some of the books, type **d 1-3 6 8**

For subject headings, type **d su**

For a continuous list, type **d con**

7. How to find periodical titles.

Exact periodical titles
To find periodicals by their exact titles, use **f xpe**
Example: f xpe journal of social issues

Periodical title words
To find periodicals by key words, use **f pe**
Example: f pe alcohol studies

To display periodical search results, type **d**
Then to see call numbers and holdings, type **d short**
To see holdings at all campuses, type **d all**

Limit periodical search results by location
You can limit periodical results only by campus
Example: f xpe landscape at ucsc

8. Additional help

The MELVYL system has hundreds of helpscreens,
available during your search.
To get help, type **help (h)**
   or type **explain (e)**
To get more specific help, type **e <term>**
Examples: **e date   e subject**

Look at the flipguides near many MELVYL terminals.

Ask for help at the Reference Desks. x2801, x2886.

9. Four common problems.

The large size of the Melvyl Catalog and its ability
to find every distinctive word in every title and
subject heading sometimes create problems but
usually reward inventive searching.
Be persistent and try the following solutions.

9a. Zero results?

- Check your typing
- Check your spelling
- Use fewer terms
- Use more general terms
- Use terms in another index, eg: su - tw , xt - pe
- Find other terms in LCSH

9b. Too few results?

- Use fewer terms
- Use more general terms
- Use terms in another index, eg: xs - su, su - tw,
- Link alternate terms with or
- Use truncation, eg:-f tw   sport# injur#
- Use other sources, eg:-
   - periodical & newspaper indexes
   - government publications

9c. Too large results?

- Use more terms
- Use more specific terms
- Do exact searches - xt, xs, xpe
- Use language and date limits
- Link useful terms with and

9d. "Long Search"?

- Use more terms
- Use more specific terms
- Do exact searches
- Omit and
- Don't use or
- Keep searches simple - use only one index

When in doubt, ask for help at the
Reference Desks. x2801, x2886.

The University of California, Santa Cruz MELVYL Catalog guide (Note the command language)

164

1. What is in the MELVYL Catalog?

The MELVYL Catalog consists of 3 separate files:

Book Catalog

- lists over 9 million books at libraries on 9 UC campuses;
- lists more than 98% of the books at UCSC;
- is constantly growing;
- is accessible in COMMAND mode and LOOKUP mode;
- contains information about books, not periodicals;
- lists many but not all scores, recordings and videotapes.

For complete UCSC holdings, consult microfiche Catalog.

Periodicals List

- lists over a million periodical titles;
- shows holdings of over 30 campuses;
- -- UC (9), CSU (19), Stanford, USC, & other libraries;
- is infrequently updated;
- often contains incomplete information;
- is accessible only in COMMAND mode.

For current information, consult the UCSC Serials List.

MEDLINE/MELVYL database

- indexes over 900,000 articles in the health sciences

About 500 journals indexed in MEDLINE are at UCSC.

2. How to use the terminal.

Always wait for the prompt arrow (>) before typing.

Press return key to send your request to the computer.

To start	Type start
To enter COMMAND mode	Type start command
To erase a mistake	Press backspace key
To cancel a request	Press break key
To end a session	Type end

3. Use the Command Mode.

Use the command mode, not the lookup mode.
The command mode is more powerful, more flexible and takes only a few minutes to learn.

This guide covers the essentials of the command mode.

4. How to use the command mode

Each search consists of the following 3 parts:
find f)*findex* *search words
then to see results, type   display (d)

4a. To find titles

Exact titles   [xt index]
If you know the exact title, always use f xt
Example: f xt oliver twist

If the search result is zero, try:

Title words   [tw index]
If you know some words of the title, use f tw
Use important words, not common words.
Example: f tw fall roman empire

4b. To find authors

Personal authors   [pa index]
To find books by a personal author, use f pa
Last name, comma, first name is quicker.
Example: f pa Irving, John

Corporate authors [ca index]
To find books by an organization, use f ca
Example: f ca ibm

4c. To find subjects

Subject terms [xs index, su index]
Only subject terms in Library of Congress Subject Headings (LCSH) and the Medical Subject Headings (MeSH) are used in the subject indexes: xs, su

If you know the exact subject heading, use f xs
Example: f xs new criticism

If xs retrieves zero or too few, use f su
Example: f su television sports
xs is quicker and more precise than su

If su retrieves zero or too few, try f tw
Titles contain many terms not in LCSH or MeSH.
Example: f tw american dream
Then to see subject headings assigned to the books you found, type d su

5. How to refine your search results.

Since the MELVYL Catalog is very large, you may often retrieve far more titles than you need. Fortunately, the command mode allows you to refine results by location, language, date of publication, or by modifying your original search with additional terms.

5a. By library location

To limit your results to the local campus library, use at
Example: f xt industrial revolution at ucsc
then: f xt industrial revolution
or: at ucsc ucb

5b. By publication date

To limit to the last 10 years, use and date recent
To limit to the last 3 years, use and date current
To limit to a given year (pre-1960), use and date <year>
Example: f xs ddt and date current
or: f pa orwell, george
then: and date 1949

5c. By language

To limit to books in English, use and lan eng
To limit to books in French, use and lan fre
Example: f xs mann, thomas and lan eng
or: f pa dickens, charles
then: and lan fre

5d. With additional terms

To reduce your results, use   and
Example: f xs navajo and xs ethnobotany
or: f xs navajo
then: and xs ethnobotany

To increase your results, use or
Example: f xs navajo or xs hopi
or: f xs navajo
then: or xs hopi

To exclude some results, use and not
Example: f su california plants and not su power plants
or: f su california plants
then: and not su power plants

The University of California, Santa Cruz MELVYL Catalog guide (Note the command language)

When a record is located, the computer will respond in different ways, dependent upon the system design, e.g.:

1 The retrieved record will be displayed immediately. If several records match the search term, these may be displayed together and 'scrolled' if screen capacity is exceeded. Alternatively they may be displayed and examined a screen at a time or a record at a time (see also pp.174, 176 and 180).

   In some systems the retrieved records are displayed initially in brief form, usually one-line entries, and the user may select any particular record and request a fuller display if required (see also pp.174, 177 and 186).

2 That portion of the catalogue sequence nearest to the search term will be displayed and the user may then select the record that he/she requires and perhaps request more detail relating to that particular item.

   It may also be possible to browse forwards or backwards through the catalogue sequence, from this position, by entering, for example, 'F' or 'B' (see also p.177).

3 The computer will respond with

   FOUND

   or something similar (or NOT FOUND if no relevant items are retrieved) and the user must then enter a command such as

   SHOW

   or DISPLAY

   to display the record on the screen.

   When the number of records relevant to a particular search could be large, it may be necessary to provide an indication of the number of 'hits', e.g.:

   23 RECORDS FOUND

   The user may then need to refine the search. Alternatively, it may be possible to display a sample of the retrieved records, e.g.:

   SHOW 3

   to display the first three (see also MELVYL catalog example on p.187).

When a system is not directly related to a sequential file but merely checks for records or fields which contain the search term, then it is, of course, difficult to provide a 'browse' mechanism as indicated in (2) above.

Various levels of detail can sometimes be selected for display, e.g. title only, title, author and publisher, etc., and it may also be possible to select the order in which these elements are to appear (see also examples on pp.179 and 186−7).

Some systems provide a full MARC display complete with tags, indicators, subfields, etc. Such a display is complex, can easily take up more than one screen, and is unsuitable for public consumption.

The various approaches are not mutually exclusive and dividing lines can sometimes be obscure. Some systems use a combination of the menu and command modes; others offer a choice between the two, and free text will still require a command language for the display of records once retrieved.

Whatever the approach, one or more of certain other features may also be provided for.

Truncation, for instance, enables the user to enter only part of a search term. This helps to compensate for the lack of a scan facility. For example, if the user does not know whether a required author's surname is spelled MILLIGAN or MILLIGEN, the truncation of MILLIG can be searched for. Similarly, a search on the stem COMPUT will retrieve COMPUTER, COMPUTERS, COMPUTERIZATION, COMPUTING, etc. The truncation may be indicated by a symbol of some sort, e.g.:

COMPUT:
or COMPUT#

or it may be implicit.

It is possible to use truncation on classification numbers, e.g.:

72   All works on architecture
726   All works on buildings for religious purposes
726.6   All works on cathedrals

Some systems allow front truncation as well as back truncation. For example, if the user is not sure whether an author is spelled ELIOTT OR ELLIOTT, then a search on

#LIOTT

would yield items indexed under either spelling.

'Wild card' characters can cater for searches which involve variant spellings, plurals, etc. ORGANI#ATION will search for ORGANISATION or ORGANIZATION; M#N will search for MAN and MEN.

It is often possible to link search terms by means of the logical operators 'AND', 'OR' and 'NOT' (see also p.95).

A search on

GLASS AND CRYSTAL

would yield all items indexed under *both* these terms.

A search on

GLASS OR CRYSTAL

would yield all items indexed under *either* of the two terms.

A search on

GLASS NOT CRYSTAL

would yield all items indexed under GLASS but *not* those indexed under CRYSTAL.

Such logic may be used to help refine searches. For example, a search on

EDUCATION

might yield

SET 1: 500 RECORDS FOUND

A search on

COMPUTERS

might yield

SET 2: 700 RECORDS FOUND

and finally, a search on

LIBRARIANSHIP

might yield

SET 3: 200 RECORDS FOUND

The three searches could then be linked, e.g.:

SET 1 AND SET 2 AND SET 3

or

1 AND 2 AND 3

and the resultant yield, in terms of the number of items found, will obviously be considerably reduced to more manageable proportions.

Terms may also be linked by relational operators such as 'greater than', 'less than', or 'equal to', usually symbolized by $>$, $<$, or $=$ respectively. For example:

FIND SUBJECT MOON AND DATE >1984

would yield all items on the subject of the moon with a date later than 1984.

Proximity, or 'position' operators are sometimes employed in free text searching to enable the searcher to specify the position of search terms relative to one another. For example:

FIND WALL W2 DEATH

would retrieve 'Wall of death' (W2 meaning within two words). This can be helpful, especially if such a phrase appears, for example, in an abstract and the word 'of' is included on a stoplist and not indexed.

'Approximation' searching allows for spelling errors in user input.

In some systems, it may be possible to examine the thesaurus of indexing terms online. For example, the thesaurus entry shown on p.99 might be displayed on the screen thus:

```
                    THESAURUS BROWSE
        TERM    EXPENSES
        BROADER    —  FINANCIAL BENEFITS
                   —
                   —
        NARROWER   —  FAMILY ALLOWANCES
                      (PROVIDED BY FIRM)
                   —  TRAVEL ALLOWANCES
                   —
                   —
        RELATED    —  COMPENSATION
                   —  GRANTS
                   —  GRATUITIES
                   —  LOANS
        USE FOR    —  ALLOWANCES
                   —
                   —
                   —
```

In an online system, it is not unusual for a user to find him/herself in a position of not knowing what to do next. It is therefore useful to have a 'help' feature to cater for this situation. The user can type in

HELP

at any time and guidance will be given (see also pp.178, 182-4 and 185).

With the various facilities as detailed above, it is clear that online searching can be very flexible. It is easy for the computer to handle searches which would be extremely difficult, if not impossible, in a manual system, e.g.:

'What tape/slide presentations on the computer, published later than 1983, are available which are suitable for eleven-year-olds?'
or 'What works on Liverpool have been published in Liverpool?'

It is also possible to provide a multi-lingual capability, allowing the searcher to select the language in which he/she wishes menus, instructions, etc. to appear (see pp.188−9).

Chapter 13
Searching the online public-access catalogue (OPAC)

The search methodologies described in the preceding section relate to online systems in general; for example, the BLAISE-LINE service (see p.214) offers free text searching, Boolean logic, truncation and qualifiers. They do not relate specifically to online *public*-access catalogues. Indeed, certain OPACs may have limited facilities only: they may not, for instance, provide free text, Boolean logic, truncation, or qualifiers, but merely rely on other, simpler means of access.

When some writers describe online public-access catalogues, they do so in terms of those systems that are in use in large academic or public libraries. However, it must be borne in mind that it is possible to implement an OPAC in even the smallest library. Such a library may not have the financial means to join a cooperative or purchase an expensive package, but the use of one or more microcomputers (either as standalone machines or networked together) and a general database management system such as dBase IV (cost c.£500) or a dedicated library system such as Library Catalogue (cost c.£30) may be feasible (see also p.254).

Thus there are a great number of systems in use and a wide variety of search methodologies and facilities. In general terms, either the menu, form-filling, command or free-text mode may be employed and the major approaches will be via:

1 AUTHOR
2 TITLE

Where the author approach is concerned, various systems may use the full author, e.g. MOORE, PETER, the surname only, e.g. MOORE, or a derived search key, e.g. MOOR,PET,G (in this instance a '4,3,1' code is applied to the author's name).

Instead of displaying retrieved records immediately, some OPACs will show the appropriate alphabetical section of the author index and the user will select the specific author that is required from this index.

Where the title approach is concerned, various systems may use the full title, the first words of the title only, keywords from the title, or a derived acronymic key, e.g. WAROFTW (in this case a 3,2,1,1 code is used for *War of the worlds.*

It may be possible to link authors and titles with search 'keys', e.g. JORDAN/WELFARE to search for William Jordan's *Freedom and the welfare state*, or WELLWAROFTW as an acronymic key to search for H. G. Wells' *War of the worlds.*

The third major approach is:

3 SUBJECT

The keyword from title caters for subject access to some degree but there are problems with this approach, as indicated on p.68. Some, but not all, systems go further and cater for searches via subject-index terms, or subject headings, or classification numbers.

In certain systems searching by alphabetical subject terms merely provides a class number which must subsequently be entered as a search term.

Thus the three major approaches − author, title and subject − are provided in different ways and to varying degrees, with the subject approach not always being available, despite the fact that one of the major findings of the CLR-sponsored survey referred to on p.267 was that there is a need for such a feature.

What Hildreth refers to as third-generation OPACs,[1] would permit access via phrases and searches expressed in ordinary language. Some OPACs have already attempted to provide such features. In the early 1980s, for example, the National Library of Medicine's CITE public-access catalogue introduced the unusual feature of entry of subject queries in plain English, e.g.:

: community health services for the elderly and the handicapped[2]

CITE retrieves and displays related textwords, subject headings and subheadings and the user selects from this list the terms most relevant to the search, ranked in their order of importance, or types in ALL if every term is required. The combinatorial search technique used in CITE is substantially the same as that of Okapi (the online public-access catalogue developed at the Polytechnic of Central London with funding from the British Library and the Department of Trade and Industry).[3]

---

[1] Pursuing the ideal : generations of online catalogs / Charles R. Hildreth *In Online catalogs, online reference − converging trends : proceedings of a LITA Preconference, 23−4 June 1983, Los Angeles.* — Chicago : American Library Association, 1984, 31−56.

[2] CITE/NLM : natural language searching in an online catalog / Tamas E. Doszkocs, *Information technology and libraries* 2 (4) Dec 1983 364−80.

[3] *Designing an online public access catalogue : Okapi, a catalogue on a local area network* / Nathalie Nadia Mitev, Gillian M. Venner, Stephen Walker. — London : British Library, 1985.

Various aspects of the subject approach are dealt with in *Subject control in online catalogs.*[1]

As well as author, title and subject, it may also be possible to search under other access points, e.g. publisher, or date. 'Global', 'all field' searches can be undertaken on some systems and facilities such as Boolean logic and truncation may be available.

One access point that has not yet been mentioned is the control number, e.g. the International Standard Book Number (ISBN). Such a facility may be available to the public but it is scarcely likely to receive heavy use.

The samples reproduced on the following pages are illustrative of screen displays on typical OPAC systems. Most of these screens have been recorded online and reproduced directly without editing. Any minor textual errors were caused by faulty transmission over the network.

---

[1] *Subject control in online catalogs* / edited by Robert P. Holley. — New York : Haworth Press, 1990.

```
         29 NOV 90              STIRLING UNIVERSITY LIBRARY           02.37pm
                                  PUBLIC ACCESS MODULE


                            Welcome to the online catalogue.
                            Select one of the searches below:

                             1.    Title words
                             2.    Title Alphabetical list
                             3.    Author
                             4.    Subject words
                             5.    Series
                             6.    Class mark (Shelf mark)
                             7.       Reserve Book Room
                             8.    Review Patron Record
                             9.    Quit searching



         Enter your selection (1-9) and press <Return> :
         Commands:  ? = Help, BB = Bulletin Board
```

Stirling University Library, UK — OPAC (Dynix)
Welcome Menu
Note the feature for patrons to review their own borrowing record and note also
that the available commands are listed and explained at the foot of each screen

```
         29 NOV 90              STIRLING UNIVERSITY LIBRARY           02:39pm
                                  PUBLIC ACCESS MODULE

         Your search:  HUNTER E
            AUTHOR (May be truncated)                               Titles
           1.   Hunter, Doreen                                        1

           2.   Hunter, Doreen M.                                     1

        > 3.   Hunter, Elizabeth                                      2

           4.   Hunter, Eric J.                                       1

           5.   Hunter, Eric Joseph                                   5

           6.   Hunter, Eveline                                       2

           7.   Hunter, Floyd                                         1


         Enter a line number :
         Commands:  SO = Start Over, B = Back, P = Previous Screen,
                        <Return> = Next Screen, ? = Help
```

Stirling University Library, UK — OPAC (Dynix)
Result of author search for Hunter E

```
29 NOV 90              STIRLING UNIVERSITY LIBRARY              02:40pm
                           PUBLIC ACCESS MODULE

       Your search: Hunter, Elizabeth
         AUTHOR                      TITLE (truncated)           PUB  DATE
       1.  Amidon, Edmund           Improving teaching: the analysis of 1966
       2.  Hunter, Elizabeth        Reading skills: a systematic approa 1977
                                    - - - -2 titles, End of List - - - -




       Enter a title number for more detail :
       Commands:  SO = Start Over, B = Back, ? = Help
```

Stirling University Library, UK — OPAC (Dynix)
Result of choosing 3 from previous screen

```
29 NOV 90              STIRLING UNIVERSITY LIBRARY              02:41pm
                           PUBLIC ACCESS MODULE

    Shelved at: KC 4.31 HUN
    Author,ed.           Hunter, Elizabeth

        TITLE   Reading skills: a systematic approach. - Elizabeth Hunter. -
                London: Council for Educational Technology for the United Kingdom
                Distributed by Councils and Educational Press, 1977. - 74p

        SERIES     Guidelines (Council for Educational Technology for the United
                   Kingdom). - 3. -
    SUBJECT(S)     1) Reading
                   2) Schools—curriculum subjects—reading—teaching




    Press <Return> to see Copy status :
    Commands:  SO = Start Over, B = Back, RW = Related Works, S = Select
       ? = Help
```

Stirling University Library, UK — OPAC (Dynix)
Result of choosing 2 from previous screen giving greater detail relating to chosen item

```
########################################################
#                                                      #
#        HULL UNIVERSITY - INFORMATION SERVICE         #
#        -------------------------------------         #
#        WELCOME TO THE BYNMOR JONES LIBRARY GEAC 9000  #
#           This network service gives access to the   #
#         Library Catalogue and to other information systems. #
#                                                      #
#  Terminal/network faults: Call Computer Centre, ext 5685 #
#  Other queries: Call GEAC Computer Room, ext 6203    #
########################################################

         1. Look for a Library Book ( or T for Title, S for Subject, etc.)
         2. Look at record of own Loans and Reservations.
         3. Look at Bibliographies, Reading Lists and other catalogues.
         4. Look at Careers Vacancy Bulletin.
         5. Look at Stores catalogues.
         6. GEMS - Geac Electronic Message System (BJL).
         7. Connect to other Academic Library Catalogues.
         8. Look at Library & University Information.
         E. END SESSION AT ANY STAGE AND RETURN TO THE NETWORK
     Enter here:
```

Hull University Library, UK — OPAC (Geac)
Title screen — Opening Menu
(Note the services additional to the library catalogue)

```
                    Brynmor Jones Library Catalogue
                    ``````````````````````````````````

     Q Quick author/title search   S Subject search

     T Title search   P Periodicals search

     A Author search   L Lecturers' reading lists

     K Keyword in Title search   R Record/Poetry library

     C Classmark search   H Help

     N Keyword in Author search   X - return to main menu

     How do you wish to search? :
```

*Hull University Library, UK — OPAC (Geac)*
*Catalogue Menu after choosing 1 from previous screen*

175
```

Hull University Library, UK — OP.AC (Geac)
Explanation of quick search

Hull University Library, UK — OPAC (Geac)
Result of searching for JONES/BANKING

```
28-11-90   15:00     LIBRARY CATALOGUE            AUTHOR SEARCH
----------------------------------------------------------------------
1. AUTHOR: Dickens, C.
   TITLE | Letters #e2nd ed                       MULTIVOLUME

2. AUTHOR: Dickens, C.
   TITLE | The life and adventures of Martin Churzlewit.    DATE: 1869

3. AUTHOR: Dickens, C.
   TITLE | The life and advetures of Martin Chuzzlewit.     DATE: 1906

4. AUTHOR: Dickens, C.
   TITLE | The life and adventures of Nicholas Nickleby.    DATE: 1000

5. AUTHOR: Dickens,C
   TITLE | Mr. and Mrs.Charles Dickens: his letter to her   DATE: 1935

----------------------------------------------------------------------
Enter number (1-5), type one of the following OR input another search.
F Forwards.  B Backwards.  K Keyword.   T Title.  A Author.      S Subject
Q Quick.     C Classmark.  H Help.      X eXit.   N Author Keyword. O Stoplist

ENTER HERE:
```

Hull University Library, UK — OPAC (Geac)
Result of searching for an author when a number of hits occur

```
          Newcastle University Information Service

                1.   Library catalogue

                2.   Library information

                3.   Computing service

                4.   General information.

                5.   About this service ...


     Enter option number then press RETURN   (STOP to finish)
```

Newcastle University Library, UK — OPAC (Cambridge University CATS system)
Main Menu
This system is available on the University campus and over the JANET network.
An OCLC LS/2000 OPAC is available within the library buildings.
These systems may well be replaced when the University installs a new
mainframe computer in 1992

```
              NETWORK ONLINE CATALOGUE -- NEWCASTLE


         Newcastle University Library - Network Catalogue

                    1. ALL INDEX search
                    2. AUTHOR with TITLE
                    3. AUTHOR only
                    4. TITLE  only
                    5. SUBJECT only
                    6. FORMAT setting
                    7. CONCISE mode of searching
                    8. HELP
                    9. Finish searching session

        Type number of option, and ress RETURN
```

Newcastle University Library, UK – OPAC (Cambridge University CATS system)
Catalogue menu

```
    ALL INDEX search
    For help and an example type H
    Keyword>


    This searches Author, Title and Subject indexes
    for a given keyword. It is useful as a first attempt at
    subject search, and may show useful entries which may be
    missed by looking in the wrong index

       * do not be too specific
       * give only one keyword (for a first attempt)
       * do not give qualifiers, author initials, etc

    Example:
    To find all index entries for the word "coppei "

        Keyword>  COPPER

    For more information please select item 8 from main
    list of options.  Press RETURN to continue
```

Newcastle University Library, UK – OPAC (Cambridge University CATS system)
Help screen for ALL INDEX search

178

```
AUTHOR + TITLE search
For help and an example type H
Author surname
hildreth
Title significant words
legislation
Estimated number of answers is 1, (maximum)

    1  Theory of legislation, by Jeremy Bentham ; translated from the French of
       Etienne Dumont by R. Hildreth
       LAW             340.1-BEN

End of list.

Press RETUN to continue, R to restart, C to change format, Q to quit
```

Newcastle University Library, UK — OPAC (Cambridge University CATS system
Author/title search for Hildreth and 'legislation' as a keyword from the title

```
Options (1) Short (2) Medium (3) Long  ...
1
Please type item number from which to restart  ...
1

   1 Theory of legislation, by Jeremy Bentham ; transla ... LAW: 340.1-BEN

End of list.

Press RETURN to continue, R to restart, C to change format, Q to quit
c
Options (1) Short (2) Medium (3) Long  ...
```

Newcastle University Library, UK — OPAC (Cambridge University CATS system)
Use of C to change format from previous screen and result of choosing (1) Short

179

```
Item 1,

Author:          Bentham, Jeremy, 1748-1832
Title:           Theory of legislation, by Jeremy Bentham ; translated from
                 the French of Etienne Dumont by R. Hildreth
                 [3rd ed.]
                 London: Trubner, 1876
                 xv, 472 p.; 20 cm code.--Principles of the penal code
Subjects:        Law--Philosophy
                 Criminal law
                 Civil law
                 Utilitarianism
Other entries:   Dumont, Etienne, 1759-1829
                 Hildreth, Richard, 1807-1865

Location:        Shelfmark:
LAW              340.1-BEN
Press RETURN to continue, R to restart, C to change format, Q to quit
```

Newcastle University Library, UK – OPAC (Cambridge University CATS system)
Long format

```
SUBJECT (LCSH) SEARCH
For persons as subjects, us AUTHOR search.
For help and an example type H
LCSH subject words
swimming
Estimated number of answers is 18, (maximum)

Item 1,

Author:          Counsilman, James E
Title:           The science of swimming, [by] James E. Counsilman
                 Englewood Cliffs, N.J.: Prentice-Hall, [1968]
                 xiii, 457 p: illus; 24 cm
Subjects:        Swimming

Location:        Shelfmark:
MAIN             375.7972-COU

Press RETURN to continue, R to restart, C to change format, Q to quit
```

Newcastle University Library, UK – OPAC (Cambridge University CATS system)
Search under subject 'Swimming' as Library of Congress subject heading

```
TITLE ONLY search
For help and an example type H
Title significant words
#EXAIAA
Estimated number of answers is 3, (maximum)
  1  Examples illustrating Anglo-American cataloguing ru ... MAIN: Quarto 025.3-

End of list.


Press RETURN to continue, R to restart, C to change format, Q to quit
```

Newcastle University Library, UK – OPAC (Cambridge University CATS system)
Searching using an acronymic or derived key, in this case a title search on a 3,1,1,1
coded key. Thus EXAIAA gives 'EXAmples Illustrating Anglo-American
cataloguing rules'

```
                    ONLINE LIBRARY CATALOGUE
                    ~~~~~~~~~~~~~~~~~~~~~~~~~~
                Files updated weekly Thursday night

    T    Title search                 A    Author search

    Q    Brief author/title search    C    Class number search

    L    Information and library news  S    Subject index

    H    HELP!                         K    Keyword search

                ~~~~~~~~~~~~~~~~~~~~~~~~~~~~~
    Please remember when you have finished using OPAC, that you must
    return to THIS page to exit. At this point you should press CTRL
    and P, followed by A. At the PAD prompt > Type in CLR and return.
                    ~~~~~~~~~~~~~~
        PLEASE ENTER YOUR SEARCH OPTION AND PRESS RETURN
```

Leicester Polytechnic Library, UK – OPAC (BLCMP)
Catalogue menu

```
                 HOW  TO  USE  THE  CATALOGUE
                 ~~~~~~~~~~~~~~~~~~~~~~~~~~~~~~
    The online catalogue lists items held in the Polytechnic
    libraries. It will help you to find which items are in stock,
    where they are in the library, and whether they are on loan.
    The following pages will give you some help in using the
    catalogue. If you are not sure what to do, try looking up the
    examples given for title search, brief author/title search and
    subject search. Each kind of search has its own instructions
    and a help screen to guide you.

    If in doubt, or if you encounter any prblems, PLEASE ASK a
    member of the library staff, who will help you. On the
    following pages you will find information on:

            Looking for a book
            Looking for a subject
            Finding material in the library
            What if it's not in the catalogue?
            Future developments and ....
            HELP for problems with OPAC on the network

N next page    P previous page    E end enquiry           PRESS RETURN
```

Leicester Polytechnic Library, UK — OPAC (BLCMP)
Help Screen 1 — How to use the catalogue

```
                      LOOKING FOR A BOOK
                      ~~~~~~~~~~~~~~~~~~~~

    If you know the title of a particular item, you can look
    it up on TITLE SEARCH. If you know both author and tite,
    you can use BRIEF AUTHOR/TITLE SEARCH.

    When you enter information (andl PRESS RETURN) the computer
    will either display a single record - which should be the
    item you want - or an index list in alphabetical order. You
    can scroll this index forwards or backwards, and can call up
    any of the records listed, to find out where a particular
    item is, and if it is on loan.

    If you have any problems, please ask a member of the library
    staff.




N next page    P previous page    E end enquiry           PRESS RETURN
```

Leicester Polytechnic Library, UK — OPAC (BLCMP)
Help Screen 2 — Looking for a book

```
┌─────────────────────────────────────────────────────────────────┐
│  ┌────────────────────────────────────────────────────────────┐  │
│  │                    LOOKING FOR A SUBJECT                    │  │
│  │                    ~~~~~~~~~~~~~~~~~~~~~                     │  │
│  │                                                            │  │
│  │   If you want to find out what material the library has on a │  │
│  │   particular subject, you can use SUBJECT SEARCH. First look up │  │
│  │   the subject in the subject index, and then enter the      │  │
│  │   classmark given beside it. Try to look for the most specific │  │
│  │   term you need, e.g. don't look up PHYSICS (530) if what you │  │
│  │   really want is THERMODYNAMICS (536.7).                     │  │
│  │                                                            │  │
│  │   When you enter the number (and PRESS RETURN) the computer will │  │
│  │   display an index list, this time in classmark order, ranked by │  │
│  │   date of publication. You can scroll this index backwards or │  │
│  │   forwards, or call up individual records listed.            │  │
│  │                                                            │  │
│  │   If you have any problems with SUBJECT SEARCH, please ask a │  │
│  │   member of the library staff.                              │  │
│  │                                                            │  │
│  │                                                            │  │
│  │  N next page    P previous page    E end enquiry       PRESS RETURN │  │
│  └────────────────────────────────────────────────────────────┘  │
└─────────────────────────────────────────────────────────────────┘
```

Leicester Polytechnic Library, UK − OPAC (BLCMP)
Help Screen 3 − Looking for a subject

```
┌─────────────────────────────────────────────────────────────────┐
│  ┌────────────────────────────────────────────────────────────┐  │
│  │                      KEYWORD SEARCH                         │  │
│  │                      ~~~~~~~~~~~~~~                         │  │
│  │                                                            │  │
│  │   Keyword search allows you to find a item by a word appearing │  │
│  │   anywhere in the title. If you have not used this type of search │  │
│  │   before please read the HELP screen that accompanies this search │  │
│  │                                                            │  │
│  │   Please enter the most specific word that describes the subject │  │
│  │   you wish to search for e.g. ALGEBRA not MATHEMATICS.       │  │
│  │                                                            │  │
│  │                                                            │  │
│  │   H for help                    X display the keyword index │  │
│  │                                 E end your search           │  │
│  │                                      PRESS RETURN           │  │
│  └────────────────────────────────────────────────────────────┘  │
└─────────────────────────────────────────────────────────────────┘
```

Leicester Polytechnic Library, UK − OPAC (BLCMP)
Instruction for keyword search

```
                 SUBJECT INDEX SEARCH
                 ~~~~~~~~~~~~~~~~~~~~~

     Subject index search allows you to find the classmarks of books
     on a particular subject.

     Enter the most specific word that describes your subject




         Enter H for HELP!
         Enter E to end your enqury          PRESS RETURN
```

Leicester Polytechnic Library, UK — OPAC (BLCMP)
Instruction for subject index search

```
 1   LIBRARIES IN SOCIETY  --------------------------------- 021

 2   LIBRARIES: ADMINISTRATION  ---------------------------- 025.1

 3   LIBRARIES: ARCHITECTURE  ------------------------------ 727.8

 4   LIBRARIES: EVALUATION  -------------------------------- 021

 5   LIBRARIES: FINANCE  ----------------------------------- 025.11

 6   LIBRARIES: GUIDES  ------------------------------------ 021.0025

 7   LIBRARIES: HIGHER EDUCATION  -------------------------- 027.7

 8   LIBRARIES: SPECIAL COLLECTIONS  ----------------------- 026

 9   LIBRARIES: SYSTEMS THEORY  ---------------------------- 021


     Select a line number to see books with this classmark

 N next screen in the index              E end your enquiry
 P previous screen in the index          PRESS RETURN
```

Leicester Polytechnic Library, UK — OPAC (BLCMP)
Result of a subject index search for libraries

```
Welcome to Lookup mode.

You can search for books by:
    the name of the person who wrote the book      (Personal Author)
    by the title of the book                       (Title)
    or by the Subject headings assigned to the book  (Subject)
------------------------------------------------------------------------
    Type...      for one of the following choices:

    PA           Personal Author search
    SU           Subject search
    TI           Title search

    HELP         More information on choices

    END          End your session.
```

University of California, US − OPAC (MELVYL* catalog)
Lookup search prompt screen

*MELVYL is a registered trade mark of The Regents of the University of California

```
Please choose one of the following search indexes.

 PA index - to find all the books in the catalog by a particular person,
   e.g., the books by Ernest Hemingway.

 TI index - to find a book when you know its title, e.g., For Whom the
   Bell Tolls. Also use the TI index to find books when you know two or
   three significant words in the title, e.g., LOCH NESS MONSTER.

 SU index - to find books on a particular topic. Books are indexed by
   Library of Congress Subject Headings. A reference librarian can assist
   you in finding the appropriate headings to search under, e.g., SEA
   MONSTERS, SEA SERPENT, LOCH NESS MONSTER.
---------------------------------------------------------------------
 Type... for one of the following choices,  or type END to end your session.

 PA      Personal Author search
 SU      Subject search
 TI      Title search
```

University of California, US − OPAC (MELVYL catalog)
Explanation display if user types HELP from previous screen

```
User: DISPLAY  or  DISPLAY SHORT

MELVYL Catalog:

Search request: FIND SU IMAGINATION CHILDREN
Search result:  24 records at all libraries

Type HELP for other display options.

1. Armstrong, Michael.
      Closely observed children : the diary of a primary classroom / Michael
   Armstrong. London [England] : Writers and Readers in association with
   Chameleon, 1980.
      Series title: Chameleon books.
         UCLA  Ed/Psych  LB 1062 A75 1980
         UCR   Rivera    LA633 .A75

2. Bausinger, Hermann.
      Marchen, Phantasie und Wirklichkeit / Hermann Bausinger.  1. Aufl.
   Frankfurt am Main : Dipa-Verlag, 1987.
      Series title: Jugend und Medien ; Bd. 13.
         UCSB  Library    PT1021 .B38 1987
```

University of California, US – OPAC (MELVYL catalog)
Result of search FIND SU IMAGINATION CHILDREN using DISPLAY SHORT
Note the command mode methodology

```
User: DISPLAY REVIEW

MELVYL Catalog:

Search request: FIND SU IMAGINATION CHILDREN
Search result:  24 records at all libraries

Type HELP for other display options.

 1. ARMSTRONG, Michael.                Closely observed children : the... 1980
 2. BAUSINGER, Hermann.                Marchen, Phantasie und Wirklichkeit. 1987
 3. BUHLER, Charlotte...               Das Marchen und die Phantasie des... 1961
 4. COBB, Edith, 1895-1977.            The ecology of imagination in... 1977
 5. Curiosity, imagination, and play : on the development of... 1987
 6. DAVIDSON, Audrey, 1916-            Phantasy in childhood,. 1952
 7. The Development of children's imaginative writing. 1983
 8. The Development of children's imaginative writing. 1984
 9. EGAN, Kieran.                      Teaching as story telling : an... 1986
10. EGAN, Kieran.                      Teaching as story telling : an... 1989
11. EGAN, Kieran.                      Teaching as story telling : an... 1988
12. ERIKSON, Erik H. 1902-            A way of looking at things :... 1987
13. FARRAR-HARTMAN, Dorathea, 1942-
       The differential effects of radio and television... 1984. DISSERTATION
14. FEIN, Greta G.                     Cognitive and social dimensions of... 1976
15. GRIFFITHS, Ruth.                   A study of imagination in early... 1970
```

University of California, US – OPAC (MELVYL catalog)
Result of search FIND SU IMAGINATION CHILDREN using DISPLAY REVIEW

```
User:  DISPLAY 12 LONG

MELVYL Catalog:

Search request: FIND SU IMAGINATION CHILDREN
Search result: 24 records at all libraries

Type HELP for other display options.

12.
Author:        Erikson, Erik H. (Erik Homburger), 1902-
Title:         A way of looking at things : selected papers from 1930 to 1980 /
               Erik H. Erikson ; edited by Stephen Schlein. 1st ed. New York
               : Norton, c1987.
Description:   xxvi, 782 p. : ill. ; 24 cm.

Notes:         Includes index.
               "Bibliography, the complete writings of Erik H. Erikson
               (1930-1985)": p. 749-755.

Subjects:      Psychoanalysis.
               Imagination in children.

Other entries: Schlein, Stephen.

Call numbers:  UCB    Ed/Psych   BF173 .E6541 1987
               UCB    S.Welfare  BF173 .E6541 1987 Desk
               UCD    Main Lib   BF173 .E654 1987
               UCI    Main Lib   BF173 .E654 1987
               UCLA   Biomed     WM 460 E68w 1987
               UCLA   College    BF 173 E654 1987
               UCLA   Ed/Psych   BF 173 E654 1987
               UCR    Rivera     BF173 .E654 1987
               UCSC   McHenry    BF173 .E654 1987
               UCSD   Central    BF173 .E654 1987
```

University of California, US — OPAC (MELVYL catalog)
Result of search FIND SU IMAGINATION CHILDREN using DISPLAY 12 LONG

```
User:  BROWSE SU IMAGINATION CHILDREN

MELVYL Catalog:

Browse request: BROWSE SU IMAGINATION CHILDREN
Browse result:  3 subject headings found

Type SHOW SEARCH to see other results available for DISPLAY.

1.    Imagination in children.
2.    Imagination in children -- Addresses, essays, lectures.
3.    Imagination in children -- Congresses.
```

University of California, US — OPAC (MELVYL catalog)
Looking at available subject headings using the command BROWSE SU

```
UCW Aberystwyth                    LIBERTAS Library Management System 4.0


          Code
          1   CATALOGUE ENQUIRIES
          2   YOUR OWN USE OF THE LIBRARY

          3   SET LANGUAGE CODE

          ?   Help



Enter code and press RETURN:
```

University College, Wales — OPAC (LIBERTAS)
Main menu

```
      Set Language Code

           The language codes currently defined are as follows:

                 1   English
                 3   Welsh

                 2   French      6   Italian
                 7   German      8   Spanish

             Enter language code :
```

University College, Wales — OPAC (LIBERTAS)
Result of selecting 3 (Set language codes) from previous screen

```
MEN\ F\R KATALOGANFRAGEN


        Code
         1   Detaillierte Anfrage nach AUTOR/TITEL
         2   Schnellanfrage nach AUTOR/TITEL
         3   TITELanfrage
         4   FACHGEBIETSanfrage
         5   NAMENanfrage

         6   Alphabetische AUTORENliste

         8   KLASSIFIZIERUNGSanfrage
         /   Ruckkehr zum Hauptmenu

         ?   Hilfe


Code eingeben und RETURN drucken:
```

University College, Wales — OPAC (LIBERTAS)
Search menu in German after selecting 7 from previous screen

189

Chapter 14
Networks (General)

The definition of a 'network', in its original context of electrical engineering, is, according to *Chambers's technical dictionary*: 'A group of electrical elements connected together for the purpose of satisfying specified requirements'.

If the words 'electrical elements' are deleted and 'libraries and/or information service points' substituted, then the following workable definition of a library network is obtained: 'A group of libraries and/or information service points connected together for the purpose of satisfying specified requirements'.

Although very simple, this definition does suffice as a basis for understanding the meaning of the term. It also enables simple pictorial, diagrammatic representations of networks to be drawn. The following is an example:

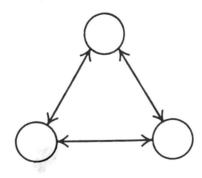

Diagram of a 'network' in which a number of libraries agree to interlend their stocks. The arrows indicate the direction of flow of material or bibliographic data

Centralized and cooperative cataloguing

'Network' is a comparatively recent addition to the terminology of librarianship but the definition given above would, in fact, also include those centralized and cooperative systems which for many years have been reducing the workload of individual libraries.

The former involves the creation of a central authority which assumes responsibility for the cataloguing and classification of material and which then makes this cataloguing information available to any library which may require it. (Centralized cataloguing can also refer to the cataloguing by a central department of all material added to the stock of a single library system.)

The Library of Congress

The Library of Congress provides an outstanding example of such a service. Since 1901 it has made available printed cards containing cataloguing data, classification numbers (LC and DC) and subject headings. Each item is allocated a Library of Congress number (LCCN) which is included in the major United States trade bibliographies. This facilitates the ordering of card sets. On offer are more than 9.4 million MARC, non-MARC, and CIP (Cataloging In Publication) records from 1898 to the present. Each card set contains eight copies of the LC main entry card.

Tremendous demands have been made upon this service. It was inevitable that mechanization would have to be introduced. In the early 1970s, methods such as direct optical scanning to sort orders according to card stock numbers and the automatic printing of cards were used. Currently, cards are printed from MARC records on demand and the Library of Congress also operates an 'Alert Service'. A participating library establishes a profile consisting of the subject areas that are of interest. Then, when the LC enters a bibliographic record that matches this profile into its MARC database, a catalogue card is automatically printed for despatch to the library that same week.

Printed catalogue cards are not the only media for the distribution of cataloguing data. The advent of computerization led to the centralized production and distribution of such data in machine-readable format which can then be manipulated and processed by the individual library to produce a catalogue of any required form. As noted on p.136, the Library of Congress developed a MARC (MAchine Readable Cataloguing) format and began MARC Distribution Service in the mid-1960s. Today, the MARC databases can be accessed online and CD-ROM services are also available. CDMARC Subjects contains the entire Library of Congress subject authority file of about 182,000 records. CDMARC Names provides nearly 2.4 million Library of Congress name authority records on three CD-ROM discs. Announced as 'coming shortly'[1] in 1990 was CDMARC Bibliographic, the complete LC bibliographic file on seven compact discs. This will be a major new resource for cataloguing, reference, and retrospective conversion.

---

[1] *Access CDS 1990* / Library of Congress Cataloging Distribution Service. LC, 1990, 27.

Where records prior to MARC are concerned, work continues on the upgrading of the Pre-MARC file (which is also related to REMARC — see p.258). This project is expected to take 'at least sixteen years but the file as it currently exists, with all its inconsistencies, provides the Library with much-needed machine-readable access to its older collections'.[1]

British National Bibliography

The United Kingdom was half a century behind the United States in providing a centralized service similar to that of the Library of Congress. The British National Bibliography, which is now part of the National Bibliographic Service of the British Library, was established in 1950. Originally based upon the books received by legal deposit in the British Museum and later upon those received by the Agency for the Copyright Libraries, the *British national bibliography* consists of a weekly printed list with entries classified and arranged by the Dewey Decimal Classification. Author/title and subject indexes are provided (see pp.66 and 243). There are now two four-monthly cumulations per annum, followed by an annual volume. From 1991, the classified section of the *BNB* is in two parts. The first part consists of 'Forthcoming titles', arranged by the 12th abridged edition of Dewey, and 'Titles recently received on legal deposit', arranged by the 20th edition of Dewey.

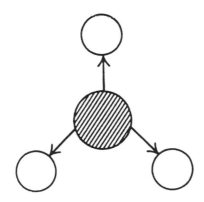

Diagram of BNB printed card service. The central base (in this case the BNB) from which the data flows is shaded

---

[1] *LC information bulletin*, 31 Jul 1989 271.

The *BNB* was initially intended to be a national bibliography rather than a cataloguing aid, although the first issues were printed upon one side only so that entries could be cut out and pasted upon catalogue cards. However, a printed card service began in 1956. Cards could be purchased using the *BNB* serial number and later the ISBN for ordering. The stencils from which the cards were printed were mechanically produced from the initial machine-readable format of the bibliography. Sheaf slips were also produced at one time but this service was discontinued in 1969.

BNB cards were delivered by return of post but the waiting time for Library of Congress cards could be some weeks. However, the Library of Congress service provided a much wider coverage. BNB cards were esentially a by-product of a *national* bibliography and, in addition, this bibliography omits some categories of materials such as maps and certain government publications. Library of Congress cards are based upon the library's *acquisitions*, which are vast and which include a great deal of foreign material.

As from early 1978, the BNB card service was taken over by BLCMP but the service has now almost ceased (see p.217).

The British Library National Bibliographic Service issues a number of other bibliographies and bibliographic aids in addition to the *BNB*. These include a *UKMARC manual*,[1] a *Name authority list* (on microfiche)[2] and *Cataloguing practice notes for UKMARC records*[3] (see also pp.214 – 5). The *BNB* is also available on CD-ROM as two distinct products, a backfile covering 1950 – 85 (over 900,000 records on two compact discs) and a current file for records from 1986 on.

A MARC distribution service began in the United Kingdom in 1969 and currently some 200 United Kingdom libraries and other institutions use BLMARC records for local cataloguing and housekeeping purposes.

The British Library introduced a new 'Licence to Use BL Records' in 1986 in an attempt to take the lead in easing restrictions on bibliographic record supply within the EEC.[4] All organizations intending to use BL records in machine-readable form require this licence, which entitles them to obtain BLMARC records from within the network of licensees, using whichever supply method is most convenient to them. It also permits them to distribute BL records to any other licensee without restriction.

---

[1] *UKMARC manual*. — 3rd ed. — London : British Library, 1989-90. — 2 pts.

[2] *Name authority list*. — London : British Library. — Microfiche cumulating monthly.

[3] *Cataloguing practice notes for UKMARC records*. — 3 sets. — Set 1 Notes 1-20 — Set 2 Notes 21-30 — Set 3 NOtes 31-40. — Each note is individually numbered and separately printed on A4 paper.

[4] Licence to use British Library MARC records *British Library Bibliographic Services Division newsletter* (38) Oct 1985 3-4.

42   English Language

428

Merson, Alick James
     A simpler English course. Book 1. Longmans, Green, 2/6.
Jan 1950. viii,85p. 18¼cm. Lp.   (50-5)

428

Merson, Alick James
     A simpler English course. Book 2. Longmans, Green, 2/10.
Jan 1950. vi,106p. 18¼cm. Lp.   (50-6)

428

Merson, Alick James
     A simpler English course. Book 3. Longmans, Green, 3/-.
Jan 1950. v,138p. 18¼cm. Lp.   (50-7)

428

Moon, Arthur Reginald, and **McKay, George Harry**
     English exercises for grammar schools. Longmans, Green, 5/-.
Jan 1950. viii,207p. 19cm.   (50-8)
     First published 1936 as *New English exercises for School Certificate.*

51   Mathematics

511

Francis, Edward Carey
     Highway arithmetics. Book 8. Longmans, Green, 1/6. Jan
1950. 112p. diagrs. 18¼cm. Sd.   (50-9)

53   Physics

532.5

Richardson, Edward Gick
     Dynamics of real fluids. Edward Arnold, 21/-. 1950. vii,144p.
illus., 2 plates, diagrs., tables. 22cm.   (50-10)
     Published Dec 1949.

Extract from the classified sequence of the first issue of the British National
Bibliography. *Actual size was 8½ × 5½ inches*

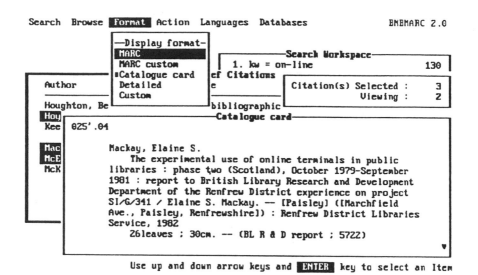

—Display format—
MARC
MARC custom
Catalogue card
Detailed
Custom

——Search Workspace——
1. kw = on-line   130

Author
——————
Houghton, Be

Citation(s) Selected :   3
                Viewing :   2

Hou
Kee   025'.04

Mac
McE
McK

Mackay, Elaine S.
          The experimental use of online terminals in public
     libraries : phase two (Scotland), October 1979-September
     1981 : report to British Library Research and Development
     Department of the Renfrew District experience on project
     SI/G/341 / Elaine S. Mackay. — [Paisley] ([Marchfield
     Ave., Paisley, Renfrewshire]) : Renfrew District Libraries
     Service, 1982
          26leaves ; 30cm. — (BL R & D report ; 5722)

Use up and down arrow keys and **ENTER** key to select an Item

*Screen from the British National Bibliography on CD-ROM
illustrating use of pull-down menus and windows, reproduced from*
Program, *23 (4), Oct 1989*

*Along the top of the screen is a 'menu-bar' where possible options, e.g. Search,
Browse, Format, etc. are displayed. Selecting an option is done by using the cursor
or 'arrow' keys to move to the option required, e.g. Format, and pressing the Enter
key. The relevant menu, e.g. MARC, MARC custom, etc., is then 'pulled-down' and
in a 'window'. A 'window' is a separate area of the screen in which information
can be displayed. Windows are also used in the above example for other purposes,
e.g. the 'Catalogue card' format is displayed in an 'overlaid' window.*

Bye, A. E. (Arthur Edwin)
    Art into landscape, landscape into art / A.E. Bye. — 2nd ed.
— Mesa, Ariz. : PDA Publishers Corp., c1988.

    xiv, 186 p. : ill. (some col.) ; 28 cm.

    Bibliography: p. 182-185.
    ISBN 0-914886-43-6

    1. Bye, A. E. (Arthur Edwin)   2. Landscape architecture—United States—
Pictorial works.   3. Landscape architecture—Pictorial works.   I. Title.

SB470.B93A3   1988   89-100077
                        712'.0973'022—dc20
                                            AACR 2   MARC

Library of Congress

                                CATALOGING IN PUBLICATION 04/90
    Larousse gardens and gardening / Pierre Anglade, editor. — New
    York, N.Y. : Facts On File, 1990.

            p.   cm.

        ISBN 0-8160-2242-9

    1. Gardens.   2. Gardening.   I. Anglade, Pierre.
    SB450.97.L37   1990   635.9—dc20   89-45612
                                            AACR 2   MARC CIP 4/90

    Library of Congress

*Library of Congress printed cards — the second example shows a CIP
(Cataloging In Publication) entry*

*The first part of the card consists of the AACR 2 entry. At the bottom of the card
is a 'tracing', i.e. an indication of the headings under which added entries should
be made. Those preceded by Arabic numerals are subject-added entries and those
preceded by Roman numerals are author/title-, etc., added entries. Following the
tracing is the Library of Congress book or call number (i.e. SB470.B93A3 1988),
the Library of Congress card number (i.e. 89-100077) and the Dewey Decimal
Classification (20th ed.) number. Note that the Library of Congress book number
includes the Library of Congress classification number and a numeric code which
is used to represent the alphabetical author/title main entry heading. Such codes
are also used to represent alphabetical subdivision at certain places within the Library
of Congress classification scheme. A note on codes for alphabetical subdivision
appears on the opposite page*

There are a number of codes used to represent names alphabetically.

The Library of Congress, because of its size, has developed its own system and it is one that is now used by many libraries. The following are examples from the LC tables.

For names beginning with a consonant followed by a vowel:-

Second letter	a	e	i	o	r	u	y	e.g. Baker would be B3
Number	3	4	5	6	7	8	9	Crogan would be C7
								Fuller would be F8

For names beginning with a vowel followed by a consonant:-

Second letter	b	d	l, m	n	p	r	s, t	e.g. Arnold	= A7
Number	2	3	4	5	6	7	8	Esterman	= E8
								Ibsen	= I2

When an additional number is wanted.

for the third letter: a-d e-h i-l m m-q r-t u-w x-z
use number: 2* 3 45 6 7 8 9
(* optional for the third letter a or b)

	e.g. Cabot	.C3
	Cannon	.C36
	Cazalas	.C39

Interpolation and decimal expansion provides for letters or combinations not listed in these tables, when there are no existing conflicting entries in the shelf list. Thus:-

The book number for Oliver Bell's *America's changing population* would be:

HB 3505 (LC class no. for population of U.S.)
.B4 (Code for Bell)

Bell's code would not necessarily be B4 for all of his books. It will vary depending upon authors in other areas.

In many places within the Library of Congress classification an alphabetical subdivision is prescribed which utilizes a similar method to that described above,

e.g.   e.g. Volcanoes

QE 522 General works
QE 523 Individual, A-Z

therefore QE 522.E8 Etna
          QE 523.K5 Kilauea

e.g. Botany
     History of botany

QK15 General works
QK21 Local. By county or region A-Z

therefore QK21.G7 History of botany in Great Britain

Alphabetical subdivision in the Library of Congress

Cooperative cataloguing

Cooperative cataloguing, as the name implies, involves an agreement between a number of libraries to *share* the work. A natural result of such cooperation is often the production of a union catalogue, which will contain entries and locations relating to the stock of more than one library.

The prime example of cooperative cataloguing is probably that of the *National union catalog*. This originated in 1901 when Herbert Putnam, Librarian of Congress, authorized the exchange of Library of Congress printed cards for cards printed by other libraries.

In 1983 publication of NUC in 48× microfiche began. This contains bibliographic data for items catalogued by the Library of Congress and cataloguing contributed by some 1,000 United States and Canadian libraries.

In the United Kingdom, in 1988, the Librarians of the six copyright deposit libraries agreed to proceed with a Shared Cataloguing Programme for the cooperative creation of bibliographic records of British books for the British National Bibliographic Service and for their own catalogues. A pilot project commenced in 1989 with a 1991 target date for a full operational programme.[1] Each of the libraries has undertaken to be responsible for a particular section of UK publishing output, and has agreed to apply AACR 2 1988 revision and the *UKMARC manual*, 3rd edition.

In Europe, a consortium of seven national libraries (Denmark, France, Federal Republic of Germany, Italy, the Netherlands, Portugal and the United Kingdom) has been formed to cooperate on a two-year project, starting in 1990, which will develop common approaches to enable the libraries to exchange their bibliographic records on CD-ROM.[2] The project is being coordinated and managed by the British Library and it follows the publication of several European national bibliographies on CD-ROM and the cooperation of the British Library and the Bibliothèque Nationale on a joint pilot project.

Contemporary networks

Although all of the systems described above may be thought of as networks according to our definition, today the term 'network' more accurately refers only to those systems which contain elements of computerization, with machine-readable databases capable of being accessed either offline or online. However, the concepts of centralized cataloguing, cooperative cataloguing and union catalogues must obviously still be considered as having an important part to play within such frameworks.

---

[1] Copyright libraries and shared cataloguing *British Library Bibliographic Services newsletter* (48) Feb 1989 2.

[2] *European national libraries to create CD-ROM 'Single market' for bibliographic records* British Library press release 20 March 1990.

The objectives of the modern network may perhaps be stated as being:
1 to reveal the contents of a large number of libraries or a large number of publications
2 to make the resources thus revealed available to individual libraries and individual users *when* and *where* they may need them
3 to share the expense or the work involved in making these resources available so as to reduce the rate of increase in cost to individual libraries and users.

As regards (1), it must be stressed that most networks are, at present, bibliographic rather than textual. That is to say that citations which pinpoint possible information sources are indicated rather than the information itself retrieved. From this point of view, the term 'information retrieval' is a misnomer; although, in many cases, *abstracts* of relevant sources may be searched and retrieved. 'Non-bibliographic' databases, from which actual information is provided upon demand are, however, becoming much more prevalent.

The words 'when' and 'where' in objective (2) bring into focus the two great advantages that the computer offers. First, the great speed with which databases can be searched and, second, the fact that a user does not necessarily need to be within the physical confines of a library environment. Computer terminals provide the facility of remote access, the only requirement being the availability of a telephone. The terminal is plugged in, via the telephone, to the normal public telecommunication system and a telephone number is dialled in the usual way to call up a database. Alternatively, networks can use dedicated terminals and lines.

Objective (3) implies that the databases which lie at the heart of computerized networks may be built up in one of two different ways:
a The *work* is shared: participating libraries contribute records to centralized databases
b The *cost* is shared: here the work is done by an individual organization and users of the service pay for access to the resultant data.

There may, of course, be elements of both (a) and (b) involved in particular networks. An example of (a), for instance, is the OCLC system described below but access is also allowed to subscribers who do not contribute in any way other than financially. An example of (b) is the MEDLARS system which is also described below.

Records in databases may also be of two types. They may consist, as does OCLC, of information relating to documents held in the stocks of libraries; or they may consist, as does MEDLARS, of indexes and abstracts of the *contents* of such documents. The latter is analogous to analytical cataloguing. Searches of both types of base will produce bibliographical details relating to relevant sources and they may, therefore, in the cataloguing context, be considered together.

Chapter 15

Networks of the United States

The United States led the world in networking; bibliographic utilities such as OCLC and services such as MEDLARS were the forerunners of many other systems. As regards the former, the major networks are OCLC, RLIN and WLN. The UTLAS system must also be considered for, although based in Canada, its products are available in the United States.

OCLC, UTLAS and RLIN (Research Libraries Information Network) offer their services to all types of library and are nationwide (i.e. North America and Canada) in scope, with the latter concentrating, not surprisingly, on research libraries. WLN is also concerned with all types of library but has confined its growth to the north-west region. OCLC, RLIN and WLN operate on a non-profit basis. UTLAS, which developed out of library automation activities at the University of Toronto, was subsequently acquired by the International Thomson Organisation and now operates as a for-profit company.

The utilities are similar in many respects; all offer online access to large databases of cataloguing records with local holdings information; all include MARC records in their databases; all provide printed cards which can be produced to individual library specifications; all offer some form of retrospective conversion service; all provide online access to the Library of Congress name authority and subject authority files; all provide an interlibrary loan subsystem. However, there are differences: for example, not all utilities have a subject search facility or provide microform catalogues. The WLN system has built-in authority control; name and subject headings are checked against Library of Congress forms and automatically changed where necessary.

The utilities are also active in the provision of distributed standalone facilities. In the 1970s special terminals were developed for communication with the various systems but these are now being replaced by microcomputer-based workstations that support both online access and local information processing. In addition, the advent of CD-ROM has led to services such as OCLC's CAT CD450, UTLAS's CD-CATSS and the WLN LaserCat.

200

The first computerized cataloguing network, the pacemaker for those that were to follow, was OCLC.

OCLC (Online Computer Library Center Inc.)

Established in 1967 as the Ohio College Library Center, the first computerized service became operational in 1970, with a batch-processed MARC-based monograph cataloguing system. This was replaced in 1971 by an online remote-access system which led to considerable expansion. The organization changed its name to OCLC Inc. in 1977 to reflect nationwide growth to libraries all over the United States and Canada. The name was changed again in 1981.

OCLC provides various cataloguing services. Records can be searched for online and modified to meet local needs. Customized cards, sheaf slips, COMfiche, magnetic tapes, spine labels and accession lists can be supplied. There is online access to the LC Name Authority and Subject Authority files. Retrospective conversion and reclassification of local catalogues can be handled. Use of the cataloguing subsystem can be complemented by the Micro Enhancer software package which runs on OCLC M300 and M310 work-stations or IBM PC AT or XT compatibles. This allows batch searching and downloading of records, with offline editing and printing. A standalone local library (LS2000) system and a CD-ROM cataloguing (CAT CD450) system are available and OCLC also provides for an Interlibary Loan Subsystem.

One of the major drawing cards of OCLC continues to be its size in terms of the number of records in the central online union catalogue (over 22 million in 1989, with nearly 2 million records being added each year, and with over 330 million location listings);[1] the largest database of its kind in the world. Most libraries achieve a cataloguing 'hit rate' of upwards of 90%. In December 1982, OCLC decided to copyright its database, claiming that this action recognized its growing value to the information community of this unique international resource.[2] A selective Record Supply Service allows libraries to extract and make use of OCLC records without requiring any input in return.

OCLC has over 10 thousand participating libraries using its various services and a similar number of dedicated terminals/workstations online. In 1988/9 the network handled an average 2.5 million transactions per day.[3] More than 25 countries outside the United States utilize its products. There is an OCLC Europe located in Birmingham, UK. In the United Kingdom, something approaching 30 libraries use the shared cataloguing service and a number of additional libraries take other services. Through an agreement between OCLC and the British Library, access to the union catalogue is provided via the BLAISE Record Supply Service (see p.215).

---

[1] *OCLC annual report, 1988/9.* — Dublin : OCLC, 1989. 3.
[2] Library networking in the United States, 1982 / Glyn T. Evans *In Bowker annual of library & book trade information.* — 28th ed., 1983. — New York : Bowker, 1983. 70-6.
[3] *OCLC annual report, 1988/9.* — Dublin : OCLC, 1989. Inside cover.

OCLC provides reference as well as cataloguing services. Various databases are provided on CD-ROM through the Search CD450 system and there is a new online service, EPIC. This service features subject access to a variety of databases and is implemented on OCLC's new online system (utilizing Tandem hardware) which is replacing the system that has been in use for some 15 years. A modern, state-of-the-art, packet-switched network will provide a more flexible telecommunications environment. It will have improved capabilities for cataloguing, searching and authority control and will permit, among other improvements, facsimile transmission and linking with other systems and networks.[1]

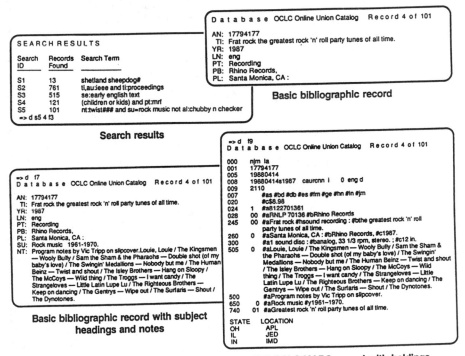

Searching the OCLC Online Union Catalog using the EPIC service

---

[1] ibid. (i.e. ref. 3 previous page) 1.

The OCLC M300 workstation, an IBM personal computer to which OCLC has added special hardware and software features to allow the OCLC online system to be accessed more efficiently. The M300 was introduced in 1984 and the later M310 workstation in 1987. More than 1,000 of the latter have since been installed

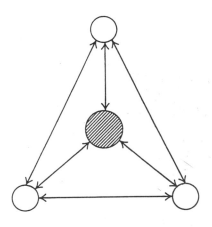

Diagram of a network such as OCLC. The participating institution both extracts and inputs data to the system and also exchanges data or material with other participants

WLN

WLN dates back to 1967 when the Washington State Library assumed responsibility for developing the network. Ten libraries participated in a batch pilot system in 1972; an 'early' online system was developed in 1975 and became fully operational in 1977. By this time WLN computer services were being made available to libraries outside the State of Washington but WLN is still essentially a regional system, restricted to western North America. Currently (1989) some 550 libraries are WLN users,[1] geographically dispersed between Arizona and Alaska, with approximately 40% of subscribers located in the state of Washington. To reflect the client base more accurately, the name was changed from Washington to Western Library Network in 1985 but, from 1990, the network is known simply as WLN.

WLN members constitute different types of participant, which may be broadly categorized as those who add records to the central database and those who do not. Contributing members may be online or offline users, the latter typically using the WLN system for retrospective conversion.[2]

WLN provides its members with shared cataloguing and catalogue maintenance, and offers an automated acquisitions facility. The central database contains approximately 5 million records and also acts as a union catalogue with over 14 million holdings recorded as at March 1990.[3] An agreement with RLIN to exchange records enhances the breadth and depth of the base.

One of the significant features of the WLN system is its authority control. In addition to catalogue records and holdings information, the database contains more than 5 million authority records, accompanied by cross-references and notes. This file is used by participants to verify existing and establish new headings. LC name authority records are transferred to WLN electronically via the Linked Systems Project and subject authority records on magnetic tape are received from LC and other sources.

A new database upgrade service known as MARS (MARC Record Service) was offered to libraries nationwide from May 1990. Authority tapes with cross references as well as a wide range of related bibliographic conversion services are available. Finished products include customized CD-ROM catalogues using LaserCat software and microform products.[4]

---

[1] *System overview* / Western Library Network. — Washington : Washington State Library, [1989?]. 1.

[2] Six bibliographic utilities : a survey of cataloging support and other services / William Saffady, *Library technology reports* 24 (6) Nov-Dec 1988 723-839.

[3] *WLN participant* 9 (2) Mar/Apr 1990 16.

[4] ibid. 1.

The WLN CD-ROM LaserCat system was introduced in 1987. It contains more than 2 million records from the WLN database, including the holdings of 250 libraries, on three compact disks and is suitable for current cataloguing or retrospective conversion. The disks are updated quarterly (see also pp. 156–7).

RLIN (Research Libraries Information Network)

The RLG (Research Libraries Group), which is responsible for RLIN, is a consortium of research libraries dedicated to resolving common problems in collection development, management, access and preservation. In early 1978 RLG announced its intention to utilize BALLOTS (Bibliographic Automation of Large Library Operations using a Timesharing System), which was based on Stanford University in California. BALLOTS was an online system combining some of the features of OCLC, some of Lockheed/SDC (see p.210) and some features not available on either of the other two systems. It has a subject capability; searches can be made using classification numbers and subject headings.

When it became the system selected by RLG, BALLOTS adopted the name RLIN.

RLIN's central files are divided into segments that correspond to the eight types of library materials recognized by MARC formats, namely books, serials, music, sound recordings, visual materials, maps, computer files, and archives and manuscripts. The books file is by far the largest, containing 80% of the records. Overall the database contains some 30 million records but this includes numerous duplicates and variants.[1] The base acts as an online union catalogue of the holdings of the system's participants. If required, subscribers can have their online records converted to MARC-format magnetic tapes for input to a local in-house system. Alternatively printed cards or book-form catalogues can be supplied.

Like other utilities, RLIN supports both original cataloguing and cataloguing obtained from source files or contributed by other RLIN participants. To facilitate cataloguing decisions, RLIN provides online search-only access to the Library of Congress name authority and subject authority files.

Other services available from RLIN include online acquisition and interlibrary loan subsystems. The latter makes it possible for a user to search the database and immediately request a required item online from the library holding it.

---

[1] Six bibliographic utilities : a survey of cataloging support and other services / William Saffady, *Library technology reports* 24 (6) Nov-Dec 1988 723-839.
Library networks, cooperation and resource sharing in 1987 / JoAn S. Segal *In The Bowker annual of library and book trade information.* — 33rd ed., 1988. — New York : Bowker, 1988. 22-42.

RLIN offers online access not only to its own database but to certain other bases such as the Avery Index (citations from architectural periodicals) and ESTC (the Eighteenth Century Short Title Catalogue).

UTLAS International (formerly University of Toronto Library Automation System)

This is a Canadian bibliographic utility which has been supplying computer-based systems, services, and products in both English and French since 1973. More recently, UTLAS has won clients in countries outside Canada, including the United States and Japan. With regard to the latter, the first high-speed data communications link between Canada and Japan was established in 1982. This allowed the Maruzen Company (one of Japan's largest book companies) and the International Christian University to connect online to UTLAS in Toronto.[1] Today UTLAS is used by more than 20 Japanese libraries.

UTLAS is now a 'for-profit' organization and currently serves more than 2,500 institutions in Canada and the United States. More than 70% of Canadian university and research libraries are UTLAS customers. A variety of services are offered, including online cataloguing and online public-access catalogues, acquisition control, retrospective conversion, and serials control. UTLAS also claims that it has 'the best online fully integrated authority facilities available in the market place'.[2] Book, card and COM catalogues can be supplied, as well as machine-readable records on magnetic tape. Customers may opt to maintain a strictly private file on the system but must subscribe to a shared-data concept in which copies of records created by them, minus local data, are added to the pool of cataloguing information available to users. The Cataloging Support Service (CATSS) database now contains well over 50 million records. This makes UTLAS the largest utility measured in terms of the number of records available online but it should be noted that the size of the database is inflated by the storage of duplicate and variant cataloguing records derived or contributed by individual libraries. The number of unique records available online is nearer 10 million.[3]

The CATSS database contains the following Canadian source files: CANMARC; the MARC Québecoise database produced by the Bibliothèque Nationale in Québec; the Centrale des Bibliothèques database of records for monographs and audiovisual materials; and the Canadian Institute for Historical Microreproduction CIHM database. In addition LCMARC, UKMARC, Bibliothèque Nationale and US National Library of Medicine files are also available online.

---

[1] Cataloguing in Canada, *International cataloguing* 11 (3) Jul/Sep 1982 28-32.
[2] *Utlas.* — Toronto : Utlas International, [1989]. — Publicity leaflet.
[3] Six bibliographic utilities : a survey of cataloging support and other services / William Saffady, *Library technology reports* 24 (6) Nov/Dec 1988 723-839.

UTLAS provides batch mode access to the REMARC database which contains 4.5 million records with imprint dates ranging from 1897 to 1978 and which includes records for items published prior to the inception of the MARC program.[1] The REMARC database was created in the late 1970s and early 1980s by Carrollton Press, a company subsequently acquired by International Thomson and merged with UTLAS International.

UTLAS was one of the first library-oriented vendors to experiment with optical storage technology, and CD-ROM products based upon CATSS are also available. CD-CATSS offers a complete 'current multilingual cataloguing system combining CD-ROM technology and easy-to-use software on a stand-alone or online basis'.[2]

Other utilities, services and local networking

Although space does not permit a detailed examination, there are other bibliographic utilities, e.g. the AGILE II system operated by Auto-Graphics Inc. and the Interactive Access System, operated by Brodart. Mention should also be made of the many regional organizations, most of which currently depend upon utilities such as OCLC or other services for their computerized systems. Examples are SOLINET (South Eastern Library Network) and DALNET (Detroit Area Library Network). The latter Wayne State University-based group share a NOTIS system containing nearly 2 million bibliographic records that tells users if a member library owns a particular title, where a copy of the title is in the system and whether it is available for loan.[3] Many regional networks are moving into CD-ROM; for example, SOLINET has become a designated authorized distributor of SilverPlatter CD-ROM databases.[4]

The role of the Library of Congress

It was probably inevitable, if perhaps unfortunate, that network progress, in the context of the bibliographic utilities, should have been made in a piecemeal way with no overall national system. However, the Library of Congress has assumed the role of 'coordinator'.

---

[1] Six bibliographic utilities : a survey of cataloging support and other services / William Saffady, *Library technology reports* 24 (6) Nov/Dec 1988 723-839.

[2] *Utlas*. — Toronto : Utlas International, [1989]. — Publicity leaflet.

[3] Library networking in 1988 / JoAn S. Segal *In Bowker annual library and book trade almanac*. — 34th ed., 1989-90. — New York : Bowker, 1989. 26-50.

[4] ibid.

LC's involvement in networking goes back a long way. As previously indicated, it began a card service in 1901 and, more recently, began work on the MARC project and the subsequent MARC Distribution Service in 1965. In the mid-1970s, LC responded to a suggestion that it should assume the role of network coordinator by establishing a Network Development Office and by calling the first meeting of the Network Advisory Committee in 1976. Representatives of the major network organizations were invited to attend this meeting to discuss networking activities and to explore ways in which a more cohesive nationwide system might be developed. A preliminary edition of the Committee's first planning paper was published in 1977.[1]

A study commissioned by the Network Development Office and funded by NCLIS (National Commission on Libraries and Information Science) was published in 1978[2] and this supported LC's role as coordinator and stated that the requirement for machine-readable records would be largely satisfied if LC continued and expanded its MARC services and made the data available both on and offline.

The Library of Congress began to establish a core bibliographic base for a national system, using MARC as a cornerstone, in 1969. By 1989 the MARC (Books) database had grown to over 2.75 million records. Within LC there have been several automation projects designed to facilitate access to and manipulation of this base. These include MUMS (MUltiple Use MARC System) for online interrogation and correction of MARC data; APIF (Automated Process Information File), designed to determine whether an item is in stock and to speed up and improve processing techniques; and SCORPIO (Subject Content Oriented Retriever for Processing Information Online), a general purpose retrieval system designed for use with MARC databases and other files.

MARC bibliographic record distribution services are handled by the Cataloguing Distribution Service of LC. 'The growth of local processing does not seem to be lessening the dependence of American libraries on LC cataloguing'.[3]

The Library of Congress has participated in various cooperative programmes.

---

[1] *Towards a national library and information science network : the library bibliographic component* / Network Advisory Group. — Prelim. ed. — Library of Congress, 1977. [The Network Advisory Group changed its name to the Network Advisory Committee in 1977].

[2] *The role of the Library of Congress in the evolving national network* / Lawrence F. Buckland. — Library of Congress, 1978.

[3] Online public access to library files in North America / Alan Seal, *Vine* (53) Apr 1984 33-7.

The CONSER (Cooperative ONline SERials) program is an effort by LC, together with other selected US libraries, the National Library of Canada and OCLC, to build a machine-readable database of quality serials cataloguing information. Libraries participating in CONSER can upgrade their records and add information to the OCLC Online Union Catalogue in accordance with CONSER bibliographic standards and agreed-upon conventions. The National Library of Canada publishes *CONSER microfiche*, which includes all of the records authenticated by participants, and the Library of Congress issues a *CONSER editing guide*, a comprehensive tool for the cataloguing of serials in an online environment.

The Linked Systems Project, initiated in 1980, is a movement towards a national network based upon a diversity of systems linked by a standard interface, so that a subscriber to one service or bibliographic utility can search the database of other services or utilities without having to learn the search procedures of those systems. The participants are the Library of Congress, the National Library of Canada, UTLAS, OCLC, RLIN, WLN and library automation vendors such as Geac. The Authorities Implementation, the first of the LSP applications, was introduced in 1981 as the Name Authority File Service (NAFS). In 1984 NAFS became NACO (the Name Authority COoperative) and currently NACO/LSP enables the Library of Congress and its partners, the RLG/RLIN and OCLC, to contribute records to and receive records from the national authority file using the Standard Network Interconnection (SNI), the telecommunications component of LSP. Records contributed by LSP libraries are also available to subscribers to MARC tapes.

A series of *Network planning papers* is available from LC and provides historical as well as recent information on important topics for the networking community of the United States. The papers include the proceedings of the Network Advisory Committee. The Committee has recently been focusing attention on the growing importance of non-bibliographic databases and the necessity of extending networks to accommodate such data.[1]

Indexing and abstracting services

The central databases of networks such as OCLC and RLIN consist of records of documents. There are other networks, e.g. MEDLARS, which provide records of the *contents* of such documents. The latter is analogous to analytical cataloguing. A detailed discussion of these bases is outside the scope of this text; nevertheless they cannot be completely ignored in the cataloguing context for they require similar indexing techniques and the end result of searching in them is similar to the result of searching a catalogue − the production of a bibliographic citation or citations.

---

[1] *Information bulletin* / Library of Congress 48 (2) 10 Jul 1989.

MEDLARS (MEDical Literature Analysis and Retrieval System)/ MEDLINE

In common with many other databases, MEDLARS was primarily an offshoot from a printed indexing service. The database, which contains references from some 3,000 biomedical journals published throughtout the world, is the same as that used to create *Index medicus*, *Index to dental literature* and *International nursing index*.

At first, such databases were 'batch' processed; that is, an enquiry was sent off, processed, and two to three weeks later a computer print-out listing relevant references would be received by the enquirer. He or she could then obtain copies of required articles through the usual library channels.

Now, however, the MEDLARS service, which is provided by the National Library of Medicine (US), is online (MEDLINE), is arguably the world's foremost database of its type and there are now more than 20,000 user codes[1] (see also pp.214−5). MEDLINE is also available in CD-ROM format.

There are a great many online 'indexing and abstracting' services of which MEDLARS was the pioneer. Here are just a few examples:

COMPENDEX (COMPuterized ENgineering inDEX) PLUS
Abstracted information from the world's significant engineering and technological literature

ERIC (Educational Resources Information Center)
File of educational materials: research projects, projects, and journal articles

NTIS (National Technical Information Service)
Database consisting of government-sponsored research, development, and engineering plus analyses prepared by federal agencies and others

PSYCHINFO (formerly Psychological Abstracts)
Psychology and related social science areas.

DIALOG and SDC

At one time, databases were accessed separately but subsequently large networks of bases such as those first introduced by Lockheed (now DIALOG Information Services, Inc.) and the System Development Corporation (SDC), with its ORBIT retrieval system, were set up in an attempt to standardize access languages. Unfortunately, these two organizations went their own individual ways and the result was that there are now two major access programs. However, each of these programs provides one search methodology for accessing a large number of databases and this makes the job of the searcher considerably easier. Once having got into the system, he or she can switch from database to database at will. DIALOG Information Services, for

---

[1] National Library of Medicine / Robert B. Mehnert. *In Bowker annual library and book book almanac*. — 34th ed., 1989-90. — New York : Bowker, 1989. 136-9.

example, which has been operational since 1972, now has over 350 databases from a broad scope of disciplines available on the system.[1] These databases contain in excess of 200 million records.

Such networks contain not only databases of the abstracting and indexing type but also some others. DIALOG, for instance, provides access to bibliographic files such as LCMARC — BOOKS and REMARC (see p.258).

In addition, there are now a great number of non-bibliographic bases which provide actual information or the complete text of journal articles, etc., rather than references to sources. Examples are:

CENDATA
Selected statistical data, press releases and product information from the Bureau of the Census, US Department of Commerce

DISCLOSURE DATABASE
In-depth financial information on over 12,500 companies

MARQUIS WHO'S WHO
Detailed biographies of over 77,000 individuals

MICROCOMPUTER SOFTWARE GUIDE
Information on virtually every microcomputer software program and hardware system available or produced in the United States

NEWSWIRE ASAP
Complete text and comprehensive indexing of news releases and wire stories from four news organizations

POLYMER ONLINE
Online version of the 2nd edition of Wiley's *Encyclopedia of polymer science and engineering*

The full text collection of databases on DIALOG has grown dramatically during the past two years. There are also 'offline' services, including various CD-ROM products — databases on compact disc which contain the same information that is available online.

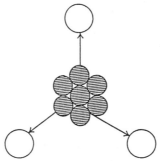

Diagram of the DIALOG type of network with a number of databases in the nucleus

[1] *DIALOG database catalog, 1990.* — Palo Alto, CA : DIALOG Information Services, 1990. 1.

DIALOG

The Basic Search Process

Retrieving information on DIALOG involves a conversation between you and the computer. In response to the system prompt (a question mark), you enter a command telling the computer what to do and then press the ENTER key to send the command to DIALOG. The system responds to the command, and sends you a prompt for the next instruction.

Once you are connected to DIALOG, your online search usually will follow a sequence similar to that shown below and in the sample search on the next page. The commands that you would enter are shown in bold face type in the sample search. The basic search process, the commands used, and their abbreviations are described below.

Search Process	Command Examples
① * Connect to a specific database with BEGIN n (where n is the File number). Also use BEGIN n to change databases; the sets in your previous search will be erased. (Refer to the *Database Catalog* for file numbers.)	BEGIN 48 B 48
② Search for records by SELECTing search terms and combining them (or the sets that contain them) with logical or proximity operators (see p. 8).	SELECT AEROBIC? S SHOE? OR FOOTWEAR S S1 AND S2
③ Look at some or all of your results at your terminal with TYPE. Enter the set number, the format number, and the records you wish to view (see page 10).	TYPE S3/6/1-2 T S3/5/1 T S3/3/1,6-8,12
④ Request that the results be PRINTed offline and mailed to you. Enter set/format/records after the command (see page 10).	PRINT S3/5/ALL PR S3/7/1-10
⑤ Change databases with BEGIN, or disconnect your equipment from DIALOG with LOGOFF. You will receive an estimated cost for your search session.	LOGOFF

* A special DIALOG feature called OneSearch℠ allows you to conduct your search in more than one database at a time by entering more than one file number after BEGIN, e.g., BEGIN 50,53.

Extracts from DIALOG basics : a brief introductory guide to searching. — Palo Alto, Ca. : DIALOG Information Services, 1988

TOPIC: Find information on aerobics shoes. (The SPORT (File 48) database is used in this example; you might also look at the business databases for information about the sales and marketing of aerobic shoes, the medical files for more information on injury prevention, or at the patent files to identify patents for athletic footwear.)

(1) ? begin 48
         08sep88 12:26:27 User053951
              $0.12   0.004 Hrs File1
      $0.12 Estimated cost File1
      $0.12 Estimated cost this search
      $0.12 Estimated total session cost   0.004 Hrs.

    File 48:SPORT DATABASE 1977- Aug 88
          (COPR. SIRC 1988)

          Set Items Description
          --- ----- -----------
(2) ? select aerobic(w)exercise? or aerobic(w)dance or aerobics
          4263   AEROBIC
         20369   EXERCISE?
           185   AEROBIC(W)EXERCISE?   *The ? specifies truncation and*
          4263   AEROBIC   *the (w) that terms be adjacent*
          2694   DANCE
           378   AEROBIC(W)DANCE
           170   AEROBICS
     S1   664   AEROBIC(W)EXERCISE? OR AEROBIC(W)DANCE OR AEROBICS
    ? select shoe? or footwear
          1827   SHOE?
            92   FOOTWEAR
     S2   1849   SHOE? OR FOOTWEAR
    ? select s1 and s2
           664   S1
          1849   S2
     S3   26   S1 AND S2
(3) ? type s3/6/1-2

    3/6/1
    0219460
    Choosing the right shoe for you. What you need to know when buying shoes
       for running, walking, court sports, aerobics and fitness.

    3/6/2
    0219446
    On your feet: aerobic shoes.

    ? type s3/5/1

    3/5/1
    0219460
    Choosing the right shoe for you. What you need to know when buying shoes
       for running, walking, court sports, aerobics and fitness.
    Australian fitness & training annual (Sydney, Aust.), 1988, 64-76
    LANGUAGE(S): English DOCUMENT TYPE: Journal article
    COUNTRY OF PUBL.: Australia
    LEVEL: Basic
    SECTION HEADING: 905340 Clothing - Shoes
    KEYWORDS: shoes; selection; evaluation

(4) ? print s3/5/all
    P087: PRINT S3/5/ALL   (items 1-26) est. cost of $7.80

(5) ? logoff
         08sep88 12:27:43 User053951
              $1.47   0.021 Hrs File48
              $0.25   1 Types in Format 5
              $0.00   ? Types in Format 6
              $0.25   Types
              $7.80 26 Prints in Format 5
              $7.80   1 Print transaction(s)
      $9.52 Estimated cost File48
      $9.52 Estimated cost this search
      $9.64 Estimated total session cost   0.024 Hrs.
    Logoff: level 17.8.10 C 12:27:46

DIALOG basics (contd)

Chapter 16

Networks of the United Kingdom

Although the United Kingdom tended to lag behind the United States in the development of online networks, over the past 20 years there have been some major developments on a national and regional scale.

BLAISE (British Library Automated Information SErvice)
BLAISE became operational in early 1977 and has since established itself as one of the world's largest networks. It has taken a number of significant steps in its efforts to improve its services.

As early as 1981, for example, CORTEX was introduced. This was a microcomputer-based cataloguing and information-retrieval software package designed for a multiplicity of uses involving data preparation and derived cataloguing from, and local storage of, centrally produced records available online from BLAISE.

In 1982, the BLAISE online service was separated to form two new services: BLAISE-LINK and BLAISE-LINE. Currently there are three online services offered:

BLAISE-LINK
BLAISE-LINE
BLAISE-RECORDS

BLAISE-LINK is operated in collaboration with the US National Library of Medicine and offers access to the biomedical and toxicological information on major databases such as MEDLINE, TOXLINE, RTECS, etc. Other files, e.g. CATLINE and SERLINE, provide records of books and serials held by the NLM.

November 1989 saw the launch of 'what is probably the most important enhancement ever made to the BLAISE-LINK service'. This is a microcomputer based software package which provides an extremely user-friendly interface to all the databases on BLAISE-LINK. There is no need to learn a complex search language; the search terms are simply entered offline and the package does the rest. The program was developed by staff at the NLM and has been in use in North America since 1987. Modifications have been made for use in the United Kingdom. The package is known as GRATEFUL MED (chosen as a result of a competition run by NLM).[1]

BLAISE-LINE is the British Library's own online service offering bibliographic data in all subject areas. The service offers full details of British publishing and books published throughout the world in English and other languages. It provides some 10 million records of items from the beginning of printing to publications of the present day. Databases include the catalogues of the collections of the British Library and the holdings of the US Library of Congress and the University of London. Other databases provide details of official publications, conferences, grey literature, serials, maps, music, AV materials and antiquarian material. The databases currently offered (1990) are: BNBMARC; Whitaker (produced by J. Whitaker and Sons); BLISS (British Library Information Sciences Service); British Library Catalogue Preview (entries converted so far in the British Library Catalogue Conversion Project); Document Supply Centre Catalogue; Humanities and Social Sciences Catalogue; Science Reference and Information Service Catalogue; LCMARC; University of London Catalogue; AVMARC;. Cartographic Materials; HELPIS (database of audio-visual materials produced by the British Universities Film and Video Council); Music Library Catalogue; Conference Proceedings Index; SIGLE (records for 'grey' literature such as scientific and research reports, theses, technical notes and working papers); HMSO; NSDC (United Kingdom National Serials Data Centre); ESTC (Eighteenth Century Short Title Catalogue); and Register of Preservation Microforms.

In May 1989 a multifile search facility was introduced to BLAISE-LINE which, as the name suggests, permits the user to enter a search strategy once and run it against several files. The system automatically connects to each file in turn and runs the search. This facility had also been introduced to BLAISE-LINK some months previously.

BLAISE-LINE is now connected to JANET (the UK Joint Academic Network — see p.222) which makes access to the service cheaper and more convenient for academic users.

BLAISE-RECORDS offers record supply facilities from the BLAISE-LINE database backed up by OCLC. Records are supplied via downloading or on magnetic tape. Any failure to find a match on the British Library files can be searched for in the OCLC database. These combined databases offer a very high 'hit rate'. Records from BLAISE-LINE are supplied in UKMARC format but OCLC records are in OCLCMARC which corresponds to LCMARC. However, the BL offers a service whereby users can select and order records and have them delivered on tape in UKMARC format. Downloaded records remain in OCLC format. Currently there is no subject search facility for OCLC as there is with BLAISE.

---

[1] *BLAISE services newsletter* (101) Nov/Dec 1989 6.

Records selected via BLAISE-RECORDS may also be added to a LOCAS masterfile. LOCAS (LOcal CAtaloguing Service) was first introduced in 1974 for those libraries who wished to take advantage of a centralized service for the production of catalogues from data preparation to final output. LOCAS maintained a local MARC-based catalogue file for each participant and libraries specified the kind of catalogue required. LOCAS ceased to be a mainstream BL service in 1988 but, with certain conditions, it has continued to be available to existing customers until they could/can make alternative arrangements. At its peak in 1983, nearly 80 libraries were receiving LOCAS catalogues but batch-processed services such as LOCAS have been steadily overtaken both economically and technically.[1]

The BLAISE RECORDER is designed to connect an IBM personal computer to the BLAISE-RECORDS service and other online facilities. Additional features allow the most efficient use of online time. Searches can be prepared before connection, so that error-free searches can be transmitted at high speed and costs are kept to a minimum. A downloading facility offers data capture so that records are available immediately for use in the local library system.

BLCMP Library Services Ltd

BLCMP began life in 1969 as the Birmingham Libraries Cooperative Mechanization Project. The first cooperative automated cataloguing service in the United Kingdom, its membership consisted originally of three libraries only (the Universities of Aston and Birmingham and Birmingham Public Libraries). These three libraries were joined later by Birmingham Polytechnic. Today, BLCMP provides services to a large number of libraries of all types and sizes throughout the United Kingdom and claims to be the leading UK supplier of library systems.

BLCMP has designed and implemented a computer system which utilizes the UK and USMARC databases and also produces records locally in the MARC format. The latter category produces over 140,000 records a year to add to a database which currently contains 6 million MARC records.[2] Whitaker's *Books in print* is included in the base. A Selective Record Service is offered and BOSS, the BLCMP Online Support Service, supports comprehensive online cataloguing, access and acquisition facilities. There are also online circulation and serials control modules, and a management information package. The various modules are becoming increasingly integrated and most utilize data drawn from the union cataloguing database. Offline output may be on cards, in book form or in microform, the most frequently chosen medium being microfiche.

---

[1] *BL Bibliographic Services newsletter* (41) Oct 1986 2

[2] *BLCMP Library Services Limited*. — Birmingham : BLCMP, [1990?]. — Publicity brochure.

BLCMP supplies standalone as well as shared systems and OPACs are now widely installed among BLCMP members. The OPAC system is designed to integrate closely with the standalone circulation control system (CIRCO) and all standalone systems may be linked by telecommunications to BLCMP's computers, enabling immediate access to the central database. Networking capacity between libraries is also available and access to and from local systems can be provided using networks such as JANET (see p.222).[1]

In 1978 BLCMP became responsible, under contract to the British Library, for BNB printed cards but, by 1990, BLCMP had ceased the BL card service. Card production is now a very minor aspect of the BLCMP service.[2]

BLCMP's aim is to secure for its members the benefits of the latest technology, whilst at the same time introducing increased individual library control over bibliographic information. The maintenance and development of bibliographic standards is regarded as very important and is actively pursued on a variety of fronts.[3]

```
                            528 JAS
JASPERT, JULIE

   THINKING OF SMALL CHILDREN : ACCESS, PROVISION
   AND PLAY / RESEARCHED AND WRITTEN BY JULIE
   JASPERT, SUE CAVANAGH AND JANE DEBONO. -
   LONDON : WE WELCOME SMALL CHILDREN CAMPAIGN,
   WOMEN'S DESIGN SERVICE AND LONDON BOROUGH OF
   CAMDEN, C1988
   Y8443659

   KL    88.17634    CI/SFB    528 JAS
```

BLCMP card produced for Kingston Polytechnic.
As noted above, card production is now a very minor part of BLCMP services

---

[1] ibid. (i.e. ref. 2 previous page)
[2] Letter to the author from BLCMP dated 12 Jun 1990.
[3] ibid.

LASER (London and South-Eastern Library Region)

LASER originated in the 1930s as SERLS (the South-Eastern Regional Library System). The original functions of such regional systems were to facilitate the interlending of books among libraries in their area and via the National Central Library, to act as centres of bibliographic information and to maintain union catalogues. The LASER network as it is known today, however, dates from 1970 and has an involvement not only with interlending but also with cataloguing services and with other technology such as viewdata systems.

The LASER union catalogue database contains well over one million bibliographic records which represent the 57 member libraries' stock of more than 40 million volumes. All members are located within the LASER geographic area.

LASER pioneered a form of union catalogue which is now used in other British regions, a microform cataloguing listing ISBNs or *BNB* serial numbers with locations.

It was from work done by LASER, with the British National Bibliography, that the retrospective UKMARC database extending back to 1950 was born. LASER also has a post-1900 retrospective extra-MARC database. LASER records have been used by an increasing number of public libraries — both members and non-members — as the basis of their files.

In 1987, it was agreed that all public library and major non-public LASER members should be brought online to the VISCOUNT interlending network, which had been under development since 1985.[1] VISCOUNT (Viewdata and Interlibrary Systems Communications Network) became operational within LASER in April 1988, providing an online search, retrieval, location find and messaging (i.e. electronic mail) facility.

Between 1987 and 1989 work proceeded on testing the feasibility of extending the VISCOUNT system to other regions. 'The interlibrary loan system in the UK is probably the most organised and developed in the world, offering all library users access to materials held within the UK and abroad through the regional and national interlending services'.[2] The project attempts to build on this well established network. The database has been so designed that the holdings of the particular region will always be displayed first, together with those of the BLDSC (British Library Document Supply Centre) — one of the objectives is to reduce the load on this Centre. A second-stage search will display holdings in other participating regions. Once a required item has been located, electronic mail will be used to request a loan.

The present design of VISCOUNT is adequate in the short term but will require further upgrades in order to fully implement a nationwide system.[3] Links with other networks such as JANET (see p.222) are also planned.

---

[1] *List of members and annual report, 1988-9* / London and South-Eastern Region (LASER). — London : LASER, 1989. 2.

[2] The VISCOUNT project at LASER / Peter Smith, *Vine* (68) Nov 1987 11-18.

[3] *List of members and annual report, 1988-9*. ibid. 2.

SLS (Information systems)

Like BLCMP, SLS began in 1969, as SWALCAP (South-West Academic Libraries Cooperative Automation Project). Financial support came from OSTI (the Office for Scientific and Technical Information, later the British Library Research and Development Department). From its university roots SLS has grown into a leading developer and supplier of automated library systems.

Flagship of the Company's information products is LIBERTAS − a comprehensive library management system, with particular emphasis on public access through networking. LIBERTAS caters for acquisition, cataloguing, circulation and serials control but it is claimed that the systems and software go beyond this to transform the library into an online information service.[1]

The SLS database, maintained since 1976, contains 2.5 million records in addition to half a million records in the University of London libraries which chose LIBERTAS for use in the federated catalogues.[2]

SLS also continues to operate its computer bureau service. Computer terminals in participating libraries access the service via a private telecommunications network.

SCOLCAP (SCOttish Libraries Cooperative Automation Project)

The development of SCOLCAP began in 1973 when a group of Scottish librarians decided to investigate the advantages of library automation and the opportunities it offered for cooperation among Scottish libraries. Activities began in 1976, when funds were made available by the British Library Research and Development Department.

From the start there were problems and, in 1984, it was reported that: 'The SCOLCAP project's history over the past five years is proof, if proof were needed, that the path of automation is full of pitfalls ... development and full implementation of the system has been hung up on a succession of contractual difficulties.'[3] The contractual position was resolved and the projected SCOLCAP package, providing for online acquisitions, cataloguing, information retrieval and management information, was scheduled for late 1984. 'Though it reached a certain level of acceptance, this system was never fully implemented and was not seen as a satisfactory vehicle for continuing development'[4] and, in 1987/8, the decision was taken to acquire the Virginia Tech Library System, popularly known as VTLS, to run cataloguing and acquisitions for monographs and serials and to provide online public access to SCOLCAP's catalogue records. Alas, 'the irresistible move away from cooperative systems towards standalone systems proved too much'.[5]

---

[1] *SLS information systems and software.* − Bristol : SLS, [1989].

[2] ibid. 6.

[3] SCOLCAP, *Vine* (54), June 1984, 21.

[4] The introduction of VTLS at SCOLCAP / Bernard Gallivan and Fred Guy, *Vine* (70) May 1988 15-19.

[5] Letter to the author from Bernard Gallivan, 9 May 1990.

Unlike other bibliographic utilities, which developed their own local systems, SCOLCAP never did, or perhaps more accurately was never given the opportunity to do so, and the last of the shared users acquired its own local system (Dynix) in late 1989/early 1990. Thus SCOLCAP ceased to exist after a lifespan of some 14 years.

Other networks and developments in the United Kingdom

Those networks described above are the ones of particular interest to cataloguers in Britain but there are other services of relevance. For example, there is ISIS (a merging of the previous systems Pearl and Isis), which is a serials acquisition and control system from Blackwell/Computer Design Systems. Basically, this is a standalone single or multi-user system with online public display but it is of interest from the network point of view because it offers facilities such as record capture and downloading and online ordering and claiming. Where downloading is concerned, an increasing number of systems provide for downloading bibliographic records online, rather than loading them from tape.

Services such as DIALOG are well used in the UK but there are also other DIALOG-type networks such as Pergamon Financial Data Services. This service provides access to upwards of 30 bases containing news files and information on companies, financial intelligence, trade marks and standards, etc. Two networks which are also much used in the UK but which are not actually UK-based are ESA-IRS and DataStar. The former is the information-retrieval service of the European Space Agency, based in Frascati, near Rome, and the UK National Centre is IRS-Dialtech. IRS-Dialtech became part of the British Library on 1 Oct 1990. DataStar (Data Storage and Retrieval) is owned by Radio-Suisse and is marketed worldwide by D-S Marketing of London, with agents in France, West Germany and Japan. This service specializes in business, chemical, biomedical and engineering information.

Other developments of direct relevance are the activities of the Cooperative Automation Group; the setting up of the JANET network and the establishment of the UK Office for Library Networking. These are described more fully below.

Cooperative Automation Group

It was clearly desirable to have some means of coordinating the work of the main networks in the UK, with a view to planned development, and in 1980 the Cooperative Automation Group (CAG) was formed under the auspices of the British Library. The membership of CAG comprises representatives from the British Library, all of the major networks, and nominees from Aslib, the Library Association, SCONUL (Standing Conference of National and University Libraries) and COPOL (Council of Polytechnic Librarians). The general aim of CAG was to ensure the most effective articulation of the services provided by the British Library and the library cooperatives in the interests of the library community at large.

At an early stage, the Group decided to focus upon the possibility of creating a common database which would enable users in the UK to have access to a much larger file of catalogue records than any of the participants could offer individually — a UK Library Database System (UKLDS).

UKLDS

It was envisaged that the UK Library Database System as recommended by CAG would have two principal applications: first, to make bibliographic records available for cataloguing purposes; second, to provide locations for reference or interlending use. There were two major problems, the first relating to technical and operational difficulties and the second to the conflict that must inevitably exist within a particular cooperative between the interests of its own members and those of a wider library community. In an attempt to overcome the financial implications of the latter whilst at the same time solving the former, support was sought from the Office of Arts and Libraries to facilitate the technical enhancement of the various systems to provide the necessary interfaces. However, no government money could be made available and CAG found it necessary to evaluate other options. In a press release issued in July 1984, CAG concluded that:

> It is no longer a realistic objective to pursue the establishment of UKLDS in the way that was originally conceived. Instead, what is envisaged is a loose series of networking arrangements, resulting in the exchange of data between different parties on mutually agreed terms and conditions. In this way the cooperatives and the British Library will be free to make arrangements at their own pace with priorities that match their organisational objectives. CAG will thus formally cease to have as its objective the structured development of UKLDS, although it is expected that the networking arrangements will go a long way towards fulfilling one of the major aims of UKLDS, that of improving the sharing and accessibility of bibliographic records.

CAG continued to exist with the same members and terms of reference but the main force at work shifted to a Steering Group, in which representatives of the British Library and the cooperatives continued to meet, thus providing a forum for the discussion of issues of common interest. One area of particular concern is the development and use of common standards and CAG has achieved a great deal in this area.

The CAG Standing Group on Bibliographic Standards produced its proposal for a recommended input standard for UKLDS in 1983. Following public comment on these proposals the CAG Group embarked on a programme of work to extend the standard, which was then concerned only with printed monographs, in order to make provision for other kinds of material. In view of the demise of the UKLDS project, the standard was also rewritten in the more general context of systems for record exchange between libraries. A first revision of the standard, covering the requirements of printed monographs, audiovisual material, music, cartographic material and serials, listed in terms of the UKMARC format, was published in late 1984.[1]

JANET (Joint Academic NETwork)

JANET is not presently a coherent information service but merely a private network connecting together computers in the academic and research community within the UK. It was inaugurated in 1984 and combined the functions of several previous networks. It is now fully established and provides communication links between users of computing facilities in over 100 universities, polytechnics, research establishments and other institutions. About 1,000 computers are presently (1990) connected to the network. In addition JANET permits access through gateways to EARN (European Academic Research Network), to the US Internet, and to the public packet-switched systems.

The following network services are available:

electronic mail
interactive access
file transfer
job transfer

JANET operates 24 hours a day, 7 days a week.

Of specific interest to cataloguers is the fact that there are currently (1990) over 50 library online public-access catalogues (OPACs) that can be accessed via the network.[2] Thus remote access to the catalogues of some of the largest library collections in the UK is now possible.

UK Office for Library Networking

'Current networking developments such as wide-spread networks and OSI (Open Systems Interconnection) are becoming vitally important to libraries. Many librarians feel a sense of frustration at the scale of the issues involved. They find it difficult to keep abreast of technical and organisational initiatives and the many developments at a national and international level. There is a need for the library community to be involved in decision-making, to influence current services and future information policy.'

The above extract is taken from a British Library press release[3] which announced that, to help librarians cope with the problems as outlined, the UK Office for Library Networking had been inaugurated on 1 November

---

[1] Proposals for a recommended input standard / Cooperative Automation Group, *Catalogue and index* (75) Winter 1984 1-7.
[2] *JANET starter card.* — [Abingdon] : Joint Network Team, [1990].
[3] *UK Office for Library Networking established at Bath University.* — London : British Library, 1989. — Press release.

1989. This Office, although funded by the British Library, is based at the University of Bath and will work closely with the existing Centre for Bibliographic Management (see p.264).

The aims of the Office are:

1 to represent the needs of libraries to the computing and telecommunication industry

2 to promote effective use of existing and developing networking infrastructure in the United Kingdom and abroad.

Chapter 17
Networks outside the USA and UK

Although the brevity of this work precludes the detailing of developments worldwide, it must be stressed that networking is not confined to North America and the United Kingdom. The following examples are included in order to illustrate more general trends.

ABN (Australian Bibliographic Network)
ABN serves as a national bibliographic utility for shared cataloguing; it 'combines in effect the functions of an on-line cataloguing network, a national database, and a national union catalogue'.[1] It is administered from the National Library in Canberra and became operational in 1983. 'It has participants in every State and Territory of Australia, and provides services to libraries of all types'.[2]

ABN makes use of the WLN software, which was purchased by the Australian government in 1979 after a comparative study of available systems. The WLN LCMARC-based file was retrospectively acquired and to this were added the National Library's AUSMARC and selected UK and CANMARC records. This formed the basis of a bibliographic file which now contains over 4 million records. Cataloguing information for material other than books, including audiovisual materials, is being added.

Online searches are command driven and a number of access points are provided, including author, title or subject. Right-hand truncation is possible and there is some Boolean capability. There are five levels of display, from brief entries to full MARC format.

---

[1] ABN : a national cataloguing network / Judith Baskin, Warwick Cathro, Diana Dack, *Vine* (53) Apr 1984 4-12.
[2] The Australian bibliographic network / Warren Horton, *International cataloguing* 16 (1) Jan/Mar 1987 8-10.

A participating library, after finding a relevant record in the database, can opt to accept it and simply add a holdings statement or to amend the record first before adding the statement. Before the advent of ABN, libraries were mostly cataloguing through in-house systems or through regional co-operatives or commercial vendors.

Starting with six full participants (ie libraries who add records and location statements to the database), after six years of operation, in 1988, there were 137 full participants and 572 dial-up customers.[1]

The National Library also maintains in-house automated cataloguing for Australiana and Australian published materials. This separate system facilitates the production of the Australian National Bibliography, or ANB.[2] The AUSMARC format was originally developed for this in-house system. 'with minor differences it relates closely to USMARC.[3]

Many US vendors, such as CLSI, GEAC, Carlyle, VTLS and DYNIX have installed systems in Australia. In addition there is URICA, which was developed in Australia. 'Certainly it can be said that ABN has been responsible for tremendous growth in the area of cooperative and in-house ILS systems, since many of the records used in these systems come from the ABN database.'[4]

PICA (Project for Integrated Cataloguing Automation) – Netherlands

PICA, the Dutch academic library network, provides a joint national shared cataloguing database together with a package of local systems. The former may be used by participating institutions for cataloguing, interlibrary loans (networked messaging is available) and information retrieval. The base includes LC and UKMARC records and locations are given, thus making it a national union catalogue. To ensure compatibility of entries in the database, extensive thesauri of name and subject headings are maintained. The local systems provide circulation control, book ordering, online public-access catalogues and word processing.[5]

Members include the Royal Library, university libraries, the Dutch National Bibliography and the Dutch Documentation Centre. This last organization provides certain services, such as the production of catalogue cards, for public libraries.

[1] The Australian scene 4 : Living together in the Australian Bibliographic Network : a member's view / Tom Cochrane, *International cataloguing and bibliographic control* 17 (4) Oct/Dec 1988 51-3.

[2] Australia : The ABN, ANB, AUSMARC and the National Library / Curt E. Conklin, *Cataloging and classification quarterly* 8 (3/4) Oct/Dec 1988 51-3.

[3] ibid.

[4] ibid.

[5] The relationship between central and local PICA systems / L. Costers *et al. PICA-Mededilingen* 10 (4) Nov 1987 4-8.

Some university libraries make use of in-house systems but mutually beneficial agreements can still be made with PICA. The Utrecht University Library, for example, installed a Geac system in 1980 but shares its cataloguing records with the PICA database. It therefore provides an interesting 'study of the potentially conflicting demands of belonging to a shared "national" system and meeting local needs via a local system'.[1] The library sees the main benefits of PICA 'not in its use as a shared cataloguing resource but in its interlending potential'.[2] In recent years the need for efficiency, improved response time and greater flexibility has rendered less clear-cut the previous division of certain computer routines into fully centralized or local departmental systems.

Whilst PICA links Dutch academic libraries to the national union cataloguing database, SURFnet provides an automated communications network for Dutch institutes of higher education and research. In 1987, PICA and SURFnet signed an agreement to enable SURF users to access the PICA database.[3] Through SURF it will eventually be possible to exchange data between libraries throughout Europe.[4]

The OSI (Open Systems Interconnection, which has been adopted by the Library of Congress, OCLC, etc.) is designed to enable users to link systems from several manufacturers. The International Standards Organisation (ISO) initiated a program to develop standards for OSI and PICA is being further developed according to the OSI model in order to link libraries and information systems at all levels.[5]

NACSIS (National Center for Science Information System) – Japan

In 1973, a proposal was made for improvements in the methods of distribution of scientific information and in 1976 a Research Center for Library and Information Science was set up at the University of Tokyo. Further investigations and reports followed and The Center for Bibliographic Information was established, also at the University of Tokyo, in 1983. A cataloguing system was subsequently developed at the Center and it became an inter-university facility in 1984. The Center was abolished in 1986 when NACSIS (then the National Inter-University Research Institute) was established. The purpose of NACSIS is to gather, organize and provide scholarly information as well as to carry out research and development in that area. Among its

---

[1] Dutch and Belgium library systems : a compendium / Derek Law, *Vine* (53) 1984 38-42.

[2] ibid.

[3] Opportunities and problems with creating networks / M. Dekkers, *PICA-Mededelingen* 11 (1) Mar 1988 2-4.

[4] Data communication : Groningen University Library's SURF-link to PICA in the Hague / A. C. Klugkist, *Open* 20 (7/8) Jul/Aug 1988 248-50.

[5] Opportunities and problems with creating networks. *op.cit.*

activities are the development of an automated union catalogue of library materials; the provision of bibliographic and other information; and the promotion of database construction.

NACSIS is now the nucleus of a nationwide network which links university libraries and other computer and information processing centres. A database potentially consisting of 140 million books and 1.9 million journals held at 460 universities and institutions is being constructed.[1] This database is the product of joint cataloguing input by participating libraries. Ninety-one university libraries were connected online as at April 1989.

Currently (1990) some 23 databases are offered via the network, including bases produced outside Japan (e.g. Compendex, Scisearch and LCMARC) and those compiled by NACSIS itself (e.g. a full-text base of articles appearing in academic journals in the field of chemistry, and union catalogues of Japanese books, foreign books, Japanese serials and foreign serials).[2] The NACSIS books databases contain over 800,000 records (of which 250,000 relate to Japanese books) and 1,600,000 holdings. Also available is Japan MARC, compiled by the National Diet Library. This is a national bibliography of books published in Japan from 1969 onwards and currently consists of 800,000 records. It is also available on CD-ROM as J-BISC (Japan-MARC on disc).

LIBRIS (LIBRary Information System) and BUMS (Bibliotekstjänst, Utlåningosch Mediakontroll System) — Sweden

There are two predominant computerized library networks in Sweden, the LIBRIS system for the state-financed research libraries and the BUMS system for the municipal public libraries. Insofar as housekeeping and bibliographic control are concerned, for many years there was scarcely any computerization that was not connected with these networks, although some movement towards local systems appears to be changing this situation. Both networks maintain a common database of holdings of the participating libraries in what is, basically, a MARC format. These databases, however, have been created in different ways.

LIBRIS, centred upon the Royal Library, has probably been the major of the two projects. It began in 1972 and was primarily designed to meet the needs of Sweden research libraries. There are currently (1990) 33 libraries permanently attached to LIBRIS,[3] adding records to the base, which contains about 2.3 million records,[4] and another 400 libraries which use the base only

---

[1] *National Center for Science Information System (NACSIS) 1989-90.* — Tokyo : NACSIS, 1989. 4.

[2] ibid.

[3] *LIBRIS — a computer-based information system for the Swedish research libraries.* — Stockholm : The Royal Library, 1990. — Publicity leaflet.

[4] The Swedish bibliographic scene / Ingrid Cantwell, *International cataloguing and bibliographic control* 19 (2) Apr/Jun 1990 19-22.

227

for searching and to a certain extent for interlibrary loans.[1] LIBRIS was, from the beginning, an online system; participating libraries could search and update the base via remote terminals of which, presently, there are around 1,000. It is a true cooperative system; the cataloguing of an item is done at the library which first acquires it and the input is immediately available for online retrieval at all the libraries in the network. The central base also contains LCMARC and UKMARC records.

The principal purpose of the LIBRIS system is to aid in the cataloguing function of the participating libraries and to serve as a national union catalogue and interlibrary lending mechanism in the research library area. It is also used for producing the Swedish national bibliography and for the provision of catalogue cards, lists of newly acquired literature, and so on.

Many of the libraries that input records to LIBRIS now also have their own local library systems and OPACs.[2] They continue to participate because there is an appreciation of the importance of a central database. The local OPAC and LIBRIS are accessed from the same terminal.

In 1988, the Royal Library took over full responsibility for the operation and development of LIBRIS, and LIBRIS became a department of its own within the library. Current projects include the conversion of LIBRIS records to CD-ROM, the indexing of subject headings within the base, authority control, and the development of a conversion program for records in UNIMARC format.[3]

BUMS was primarily intended as a circulation control system. It was developed by Bibliotekstjänst, the Swedish libraries' central service organization. However, the central database, which was compiled by Bibliotekstjänst (the owner) from the holdings of the participating libraries, also acts as a union catalogue. A library can order specialized lists from data stored in the central files (BURK), e.g. lists of recent acquisitions, books in various foreign languages, books in local collections, etc.

Currently catalogues are also generated on CD-ROM (CD-KAT). Each CD-KAT disc contains the catalogues of a region comprising several counties. It serves as a local public catalogue, complete with holdings and other local data. The disc may also be used by library staff, with a different set of search and display screens, as a union catalogue for the region. The CD-ROM catalogue makes it possible for printed lists such as those noted above to be produced locally. The CD-KAT system with more than 1,000 installed workstations is the largest CD-ROM application in Sweden.[4]

---

[1] ibid. (i.e. ref. 4 previous page)
[2] ibid.
[3] LIBRIS satsar pa utveckling [LIBRIS of today and in the future] / Mayre Lehtila-Olsson, *LIBRIS-meddelanden* May 1990 4-7.
[4] Information supplied by Bibliotekstjänst.

A turnkey, Unix-based, local library system (BTJ2000) is now also available from Bibliotekstjänst. This system allows the use of the central database BURK and a CD-ROM catalogue is offered as a useful complement to the local online catalogue.[1]

BUMS is confined entirely to Sweden and 80 public library systems make use of the service.[2]

Although LIBRIS and BUMS comprise two separate automated systems, over recent years collaboration has intensified. The translation of AACR 2 and the revision of the Swedish classification scheme were joint ventures.[3]

The European Community and EURONET/DIANE

The EURONET, European host network, concept had its beginnings in 1971 when the Council of Ministers of the European Community passed a resolution with a view to 'coordinating the action of the Member States regarding scientific and technical information and documentation'. The initial intent of the overall EURONET plan, which grew out of this resolution, was to utilize the international, national and specialized systems already in existence and bring them together under the control of one European agency. This was an ambitious project; the system took some time to develop, eventually becoming operational in 1980. Progress then quickened; for example, in late 1980 there were 16 hosts offering upwards of 100 databases and by 1983 there were about 40 hosts with approximately 400 bases. The service was then referred to as EURONET/DIANE; DIANE (Direct Information Access Network for Europe) was the name given to the ensemble of available information services and the name EURONET was reserved for the telecommunications network.

Various DIANE centres continue to exist but EURONET has gone. It was replaced by bilateral agreements between post and telephone authorities in 1986.[4]

The Council of Europe

In late 1987, the Committee of Ministers of the Council of Europe adopted a recommendation for the guidance of member countries with major implications for cooperation among libraries all over the world. Specific points included are facilitation of the exchange of data, promotion of interconnection,

---

[1] Information supplied by Bibliotekstjänst
[2] ibid.
[3] The Swedish bibliographic scene / Ingrid Cantwell, *International cataloguing and bibliographic control* 19 (2) Apr/Jun 1990 19-22.
[4] *Online*, Jan 1987.

data transfer and unrestricted access; development and promotion of standards; encouragement of service to users; cooperation in collection development; support for cataloguing of all materials; preservation action; exchange of library staff and education of librarians in cooperation; and consideration of a permanent cooperative organization.[1]

---

[1] Cooperation among research libraries in Europe, *Information retrieval and library automation* 24 (8) Jan 1989 5-6.
Cited in: Library networking in 1988 / JoAn S. Segal, *In Bowker annual library and book trade almanac.* — 34th ed., 1989-90. — New York : Bowker, 1989. 26-50.

Chapter 18

The management of cataloguing

In previous chapters the principles of cataloguing have been described and discussed. The essence of good management lies in the application of these principles in such a way as to provide the most effective catalogue for a library and its users. Correct decisions must be made on such matters as the fullness of cataloguing required; whether to use a conventional classified or alphabetical subject catalogue or some other system; the method to be used for establishing subject headings or subject index entries; what filing system to use; policy with regard to analysis and annotation; the physical form of catalogue; and the extent to which CIP (Cataloguing-in-Publication) information, centralized services and/or the computer are used.

With regard to centralized services, writers such as Foster maintain that 'To process books efficiently, every library, large and small, must have a good portion of its cataloging performed by an outside source'.[1] If a centralized service is utilized, some decisions may, of course, be taken out of the individual cataloguing agency's hands.

Cataloguing needs may vary, not only in different kinds of library but also within the same library system. In some special libraries the major demand may be for current subject information and more use may be made of a subject-based retrieval system than of an author catalogue constructed according to AACR 2. In others, such as the library of a professional organization sending many items on postal loan, there may be a strong case for detailed cataloguing under author and subject. Within any library system the fullness of cataloguing may vary according to the kind of material — some audio-visual materials may lack 'browsability' and so be given more detailed cataloguing than books, and books which are on the open shelves may be catalogued less fully than those which are not.

---

[1] *Managing the cataloging department* / Donald L. Foster. — 2nd ed. — Metuchen, NJ : Scarecrow Press, 1982. 39.

Management techniques

Whatever the kind of library, there are certain management techniques which can be applied to the cataloguing process. There is a bewildering number of techniques, 'more than 250 of them being described in Finch's excellent guide',[1] but it must be remembered that they are only a means to an end — *aids* to decision-making or problem solving. Just as cataloguers should not become so immersed in their cataloguing rules or methods that they overlook the overriding purpose of the catalogue — to help users of the library to find what they want — so managers should avoid becoming so immersed in a particular technique that they forget its purpose — to improve or optimize performance, to measure value or to rectify faults.

MBO (Management by objectives)

Foster, in his *Managing the cataloging department*, cites 'management by objectives' (MBO) as 'typical of the more innovative management concepts (that is to say tools) found in libraries today'.[2] Currently, 'MBO is so much a part of everyday normal management behaviour that the term is rarely used'[3] but it is still very relevant to cataloguing as 'an approach to assessing performance by reference to the achievement of results'.[4] MBO involves formulating *objectives* (e.g. to ensure that library materials reach the public for whom they have been acquired with a minimum of delay); setting *targets* to allow these objectives to be met (e.g. cataloguing x number of items per day); and removing any *obstacles* to the achievement of these targets.

Before becoming part of Humberside Libraries, Kingston upon Hull City Libraries published three editions of its statement on the application of MBO to the library service.[5] The cataloguing objective was defined as 'to ensure the maximum usefulness of the catalogue' by (a) surveying the use of the COM catalogues; (b) reviewing the information required (i.e. considering the application of MARC and the latest edition of the Dewey Decimal Classification to new stock and old stock); and (c) considering new applications for the catalogue database (organizing input and retrieving data to provide stock revision information, booklists on a subject and new accessions lists).

---

[1] *A concise encyclopaedia of management techniques* / F. A. Finch. — London : Heinemann, 1976 *cited in Managing user-centred libraries and information services* / K. G. B. Bakewell. — London : Mansell, 1990. 44.

[2] *Managing the catalog department, op. cit.* 220.

[3] *Makers of management : men and women who changed the business world* / David Clutterbuck and Stuart Crainer. — London : Macmillan, 1990. 63.

[4] *The ABC of management : a handbook of management terms and concepts* / John Blake and Peter Lawrence. — London : Cassell, 1989. 15.

[5] *What, why & how : MbO in the library service.* — 3rd ed. — Kingston upon Hull : Kingston upon Hull City Libraries, 1973.

The specimen objective on cataloguing in the American Library Association's 1980 planning manual for public libraries was concerned specifically with automation: 'to automate the acquisitions, cataloging, and circulation functions within the five year period' with a view to lowering the elapsed time from receipt of materials to shelf to 20 days.[1]

At New South Wales Institute of Technology the objectives of the cataloguing department were defined as 'to carry out the cataloguing and classification of all monographs, A/V and serials needed by the staff and students of the Institute' and the method of achieving these objectives reflected the underlying philosophy of the library: 'that the use of technological advances and resources sharing among libraries is the only effective and rational way of operating in these days of economic stringency'.[2]

Standards

In order to set targets it is necessary to have some generally accepted standards. In cataloguing, there are adequate standards of technique or practice but there are no generally accepted standards of timing or performance — inevitably, perhaps, in view of the different kinds of material to be catalogued, the variation in difficulty of this material, and the differing amounts of information on catalogue entries.

For example, it was reported in 1970 that at Bebington, a small UK borough with a population of 57,000 (then independent but now part of Wirral Libraries), one cataloguer, who deputized on occasion as a readers' adviser, catalogued approximately 9,000 books per annum — roughly the same number as were dealt with by a fairly large staff in Birmingham Public Libraries' cataloguing department.[3] The difference was that, whereas Birmingham's cataloguing department dealt largely with reference material, much of it difficult to handle, roughly half of Bebington's stock was fiction and most of the rest was covered by BNB cards.

A study at Cornell Law Library, using the OCLC database, showed that the average cataloguing time was 8−9 minutes per record[4] and, in a survey of members of the OCLC network, 91% of the libraries surveyed reported that the time required to catalogue items had been reduced by online cataloguing.[5]

---

[1] *A planning process for public libraries* / Vernon E. Palmour, Marcia C. Bellassai, Nancy V. De Wath. — Chicago : American Library Association, 1980. 250.

[2] Administration of a cataloguing department / the N.S.W.I.T. experience / Keir Kirkby, *Cataloguing Australia* 6 (1) Jan-Mar 1980 13-16.

[3] Planning for cataloguing / K. Bakewell, *Catalogue & index* (20) Oct 1970 8-9.

[4] The quality of OCLC bibliographic records : the Cornell Law Library experience / Christian M. Boissonnas, *Law library journal* 72 (1) Winter 1979 80-5.

[5] The impact of OCLC / Joe A. Hewitt, *American libraries* 7 (5) May 1976 268-75.

4 and 5 are cited in: Cataloging and catalogs : a handbook for library management / by David F. Kohl. — Santa Barbara : ABC-CLIO, 1986. 98, 106-7.

A small study at Bath University Library showed that the *cataloguing* of 160 items took only 293 minutes, or an average of just under two minutes per item, but it must be borne in mind that this involved very brief catalogue entries. The average time taken to *classify* 148 items was just under five minutes per item, and classification normally forms part of the cataloguing process.[1]

It should be possible for each library to determine its own standards and to see that these are adhered to. The Centre for Library and Information Management (CLAIM) at Loughborough University, United Kingdom (now The Library and Information Statistics Unit) has shown how this can be done using the 'diary' technique, with each member of staff keeping an accurate record of the time spent on every activity.[2] A study by CLAIM's predecessor, the Library Management Research Unit, of four libraries serving schools, colleges and institutes of a university, showed that one library spent an average of 8 minutes cataloguing each item, two spent an average of 10 minutes per item and one (dealing with difficult medical material) spent an average of 16 minutes per item.[3] The four libraries were commensurate in size and staff involvement.

At La Trobe University, Melbourne, Australia, cataloguers kept detailed monthly statistics of the time spent on each operation. They did not object to the establishment of minimum output figures; rather, they requested such figures because they provided a target and a basis for assessing their performance.[4] It should be borne in mind, however, that all human beings are different: they are not machines, and some people will inevitably perform tasks more quickly and efficiently than others.

Interlibrary comparisons

A library may well find it helpful to compare its own activities and costs with those of other libraries in the same group, and published comparative statistics are useful from this point of view.

In the UK, for example, the Centre for Interfirm Comparison (CIFC), after its formation in 1959, carried out many comparisons of performance data in industry, showing that such comparisons can be a valuable management tool to help in the establishment of standards and in the evaluation of activities and procedures.

---

[1] The cost of classification : a note / Maurice B. Line, *Catalogue & index* (16) Oct. 1969 4.

[2] *Administrative effectiveness* / Centre for Library and Information Management, Department of Library and Information Studies, Loughborough University. — Loughborough : CLAIM, 1980.

[3] *Work measurement techniques and library management : methods of data collection* / Lesley Gilder, J. L. Schofield. — Loughborough : Library Management Research Unit, 1978. 35.

[4] Cataloguing work performance / Helene Hoffmann, *Cataloguing Australia* 4 (3-4) Jul-Dec 1978. 40-5.

In 1978/9, CIFC, with the financial support of the British Library, undertook an interlibrary comparison of 27 public libraries[1] and this was followed, in the early 1980s, by a similar study of academic libraries (12 university and 8 polytechnic).[2] Where cataloguing is concerned, data was provided on such matters as relative numbers of staff and the cost of cataloguing.

Having studied this data, polytechnic library B might, for instance, wish to investigate why its cataloguing staff costs per item catalogued (£6.38) were very much higher than those of other similar polytechnic libraries, e.g. library F staff costs per item were only £1.47.

Workflow

A smooth workflow will help to streamline the cataloguing process, the various operations being performed in a reasonable chronological sequence and the layout of the cataloguing department being such that no member of staff has to exert himself more than necessary when carrying out his particular tasks. This is an example of *ergonomics* (or *human engineering*, as the Americans call it) — the relationship between the worker, his environment, and the equipment he uses. Ergonomics is a technique which is sometimes overlooked in librarianship.

A restructuring and reorganization of the workflow at La Trobe University, Melbourne, Australia, led to an increase of 55.1% in the number of titles catalogued annually over a five-year period. The staff of the Technical Services Division increased by 8% (31 to 33.5), but there was no increase in the cataloguing staff. The number of titles catalogued per hour rose from 4.5 to 6.6 (a decrease from 13 minutes to 9 minutes per item).[3] The restructuring involved moving the orders section from acquisitions to a new technical services division consisting of the orders, precataloguing and end-processes sections. The reorganization of the workflow included the sharing by orders and precataloguing of a bibliographic searching area, with clerical staff verifying requests before orders were placed.

Network analysis can be of value in planning and controlling cataloguing operations, particularly those concerned with recataloguing or retrospective conversion. There are several network planning techniques, the best known being PERT (Program Evaluation and Review Technique) and CPM (Critical Path Method). The time required for the activities and the sequence in which

---

[1] *Inter-library comparisons : pilot comparison with public libraries*, Centre for Interfirm Comparisons. — London : British Library, 1981.

[2] *Inter-library comparisons in academic libraries* / Centre for Interfirm Comparisons. — London : British Library, 1984.

[3] Cataloguing work performance / Helene Hoffmann, *Cataloguing Australia* 4 (3-4) Jul-Dec 1978 40-5.

they should be performed are analysed and represented in the form of a diagram known as a 'network'; the activities forming the 'critical path' are then identified to enable the project to be completed in the shortest possible time. Marian Orgain has described the use of network planning in reorganizing the library of the *Houston chronicle* (Texas), and cataloguing was identified as one of the jobs forming the critical path.[1]

Cost and cost-benefit analysis

Another management technique applicable to cataloguing is cost-benefit analysis which, as its name implies, involves weighing the cost of an activity against the benefits accruing from that activity. It may be costly to make a lot of analytical entries, but is the cost justified by the time saved on searching for information and improved service to readers? Conversely, is the cost of full cataloguing justified if few readers use the catalogue or if the majority simply want to locate an item and are not interested in publication details or physical description? Helene Hoffmann has said, 'The work performance of a cataloguing department is judged not only by the way in which the department keeps up with the current intake of material and its annual throughput but also by the ease for the user in finding material in the catalogue and on the shelves'.[2]

Items to be considered in costing include the cost of labour and materials, subscriptions to outside services, maintenance and depreciation costs, and overheads such as heating and lighting. Factors affecting costs include:

a   *cataloguing policy*, such as fullness of cataloguing, the rules to be used and the extent of analysis and annotation

b   the *methods employed*; for example, computerizing the catalogue

c   the *proper use of staff*; for example, it may be cheaper to use clerical staff for routine cataloguing and checking

d   the extent to which cataloguing is *coordinated with other operations*.

Whatever decisions are made, the *benefit* part of the cost-benefit equation should not be ignored. Where (d) is concerned, for example, a major advantage of computerization is that it allows one record to be used for many purposes, including ordering, cataloguing, circulation control, interlibrary loans, preparation of reading lists and production of management information.

In a survey of OCLC members, 80% of the libraries surveyed reported that their primary objectives had been met. For some libraries the primary objective was reduced costs, whilst for others it was faster cataloguing or

---

[1] Problems of reorganizing a newspaper library / Marian Orgain, *Special libraries* 53 (12) Dec 1962 586-9.

[2] Cataloguing work performance / Helene Hoffmann, *Cataloguing Australia* 4 (3-4) Jul-Dec 1978 45.

improved interlibrary loans.[1] Thus both cost *and* efficiency benefits had accrued from membership.

Surprisingly, although the number of catalogue cards produced for members by OCLC is decreasing, it was still 106 million in 1988−9![2] Cost-benefit analysis can be applied here by considering not only the cost of such cards but also the speed with which they can be acquired and filed in the catalogue. In 1974 a study at the Denison Memorial Library, University of Colorado Medical Center compared the cost and effectiveness of producing catalogue cards in-house with the cost and effectiveness of purchasing cards from the National Library of Medicine. The cost of in-house production was slightly higher but considerably more effective in that books were available to users much more quickly (an average of 16.07 days, compared with 26.97 days when purchasing cards) and the cards were filed in the catalogue more quickly (19.88 days compared with 34.11 days).[3] No doubt these results would be different today as methods of card production and delivery have improved greatly but, nevertheless, this study still serves as an interesting example.

A study by the Bath University Programme of Catalogue Research (now the Centre for Bibliographic Management − see p.264), undertaken in 1979 to establish the size and distribution of the market for automated cataloguing services, produced a considerable amount of data relating to the *cost* of cataloguing.[4] Unfortunately, the report did not relate these figures to the kind of cataloguing or the value of the catalogue to the user − in other words the *cost-benefit* element was missing.

AACR 2 and cataloguing management

Whether (and how) to change to AACR 2 (or to any other code of cataloguing rules) is a major management decision. How many headings in the catalogue will need to be changed? How costly will the change be and, more important, how cost effective? Will it result in a better catalogue or allow more effective use of networks?

A study at La Trobe University Library, Melbourne, indicated that the time spent on cataloguing might rise by 2.3% as a result of introducing

---

[1] The impact of OCLC / Joe A. Hewitt, *American libraries*, 7 (5), May 1976, 268-75 *Cited in: Cataloging and catalogs : a handbook for library management* / David F. Kohl. — Santa Barbara : ABC-CLIO, 1986.

[2] *OCLC annual report, 1988-9.* — Dublin : OCLC, 1989. Inside cover.

[3] Cost-performance analysis of cataloging and card reproduction in a medical center library / Margaret Butkovich and Robert M. Braude, *Bulletin of the Medical Library Association* 63 (1) Jan 1975 29-34.

[4] *Cataloguing costs in the U.K. : an analysis of the market for automated cataloguing services* / C. Mary Overton, Alan Seal. — Bath : Bath University Library, 1979.

AACR 2.[1] Training would be an additional cost, though a 'one-off' cost which would need to be absorbed during a brief period of time. 'All in all', concluded George Stecher, 'the adoption of AACR 2 . . . is not likely to cause financial disaster to libraries with up to date practices'.

Five possible methods of implementing a change to AACR 2 are:

1 starting a new catalogue for all items *acquired* after a specified date (which the University of Liverpool Library did when it adopted AACR 1 in 1968)[2]

2 starting a new catalogue for all items *published* after a specified date (which the National Library of Scotland did when it first adopted AACR 1, though it later merged the two sequences.[2] The Bibliothèque Nationale's online catalogue is a continuation of the existing printed catalogues as well as three card catalogues)

3 'superimposition' (i.e. adopting new headings only when they do not conflict with headings already in the catalogue)

4 changing the old headings as required

5 interfiling the new entries with the old ones and linking as necessary with *see also* references, e.g.:

SMITH (W.H.) & SONS *see also* W.H. SMITH & SONS
W.H. SMITH & SONS *see also* SMITH (W.H.) & SONS

Very large libraries are likely to opt for closure of the catalogue, but Rosenthal has pointed out that this step has implications for almost every library operation.[3] He has also emphasized the importance of very careful planning of any change and that the public relations aspects should not be ignored. Any system must be properly explained to noncataloguing staff and to the public.

If a library opts to automate and to make use of MARC records in some way, e.g. by subscribing to the BLAISE Records Service or by joining a bibliographic utility such as OCLC, the decision to change to AACR 2 becomes implicit.

It is claimed that the 1988 revision of AACR 2 'is a code supportive of the needs of library automation'.[4] Libraries of all sizes use automated systems and 'there is a greater reliance on, and indeed, a greater expectation of the availability of derived cataloguing copy'.[5] With such 'realities serving as a

---

[1] Projected cost estimates for introducing AACR 2 / George Stecher, *Cataloguing Australia* 5 (4) Oct-Dec 1979 26-35.

[2] Both the University of Liverpool and the National Library of Scotland now have automated systems (DOBIS/LIBIS and VTLS respectively).

[3] Planning for the catalogs : a managerial perspective / Joseph A. Rosenthal, *Journal of library automation* 11 (3) Sept 1978 192-205.

[4] *A brief guide to AACR 2, 1988 revision, and implications for automated systems* / Jean Weihs, Lynne Howarth. — Ottawa : Canadian Library Association, 1988. 47.

[5] ibid.

backdrop, and, with the urgings of ABACUS (Association of Bibliographic Agencies of Britain, Australia, Canada and the United States) to facilitate machine transfer of bibliographic information by further standardizing, in particular, the choice and form of authors, titles, and series, JSCAACR has developed a revision more conducive to automated environments . . . on the evolutionary scale of cataloguing codes, the 1988 revision of the *Anglo-American cataloguing rules* carries us one step closer to the goal of universal bibliographic control'.[1]

For those libraries maintaining non-MARC record-based systems there is more of an option to adopt AACR 2 or not. 'These non-MARC libraries must consider how *not* changing may effect exchange of information, or may impact on future plans for database or system conversion'.[2]

The claims made for AACR 2 cited above are sweeping claims which some librarians might consider debatable but nevertheless the fact remains that the AACR 2 1988 revision exists; it does form the basis of the MARC record, and therefore the majority of libraries in English-speaking countries and even elsewhere must be prepared to take decisions about its use.

CIP (Cataloguing-in-Publication)

For many years Ranganathan urged the inclusion of a catalogue entry in each book on publication — 'pre-natal cataloguing', as he called it. During 1958–9 the Library of Congress's 'Cataloging-in-Source' experiment attempted to establish the feasibility of this, in collaboration with publishers and with the assistance of a grant provided by the Council on Library Resources. At the end of the experiment it was decided that 'a permanent, full-scale Cataloging-in-Source program could not be justified from the viewpoint of financing, technical considerations, or utility'.[3]

In 1971, 'cataloging-in-source' was reborn in the United States as 'cataloging-in-publication', initially for a three-year experimental period, but it later became a permanent feature of Library of Congress record supply. For example, catalogue cards are printed from CIP records whenever full MARC cataloguing is not available. CIP entries differ from full MARC cataloguing in that records are shorter and references to pagination and size are omitted. An LC CIP printed card is reproduced on p.196.

Brazil implemented a cataloguing-in-publication programme in the same year as the United States (1971). CIP schemes now operate in many countries and they have become an integral part of bibliographic services.

---

[1] ibid. (i.e. ref. 4 previous page) 48.
[2] ibid. 51.
[3] *The cataloging-in-source experiment.* — Washington : Library of Congress, 1960.

In the United Kingdom, British Library Bibliographic Services began to provide brief catalogue entries on the verso of the title page of some British books in 1976 (dependent upon whether the publishers were collaborating in the scheme by supplying advance information). CIP entries began to appear in the *British national bibliography* and on MARC tapes in 1977. In January 1985, the first of a new-style CIP entry, conforming generally to AACR 2 Level 2 for description and containing full subject data, appeared in the *BNB*. Prior to 1985, the CIP entry was not intended to be definitive but the new programme was designed to realize the full potential of CIP as a major input source for the creation of permanent UKMARC records of both high quality and high currency. Thus the CIP record formed the actual basis of the 'definitive "national bibliographic" record'.[1] It was replaced by a new record only when comparison with the book, when eventually published, indicated that the publisher has made critical changes. This was a radical move away from the long-accepted principle of using the actual item as the primary source of cataloguing data. An essential requirement for an effective CIP programme is the fullest possible participation of publishers. By 1990 well over 1,000 British publishers were participating in the scheme.[2] 'It is a mutually advantageous service getting early information to libraries and offering increased marketing potential to participating publishers'.[3].

In 1988 the British Library entered into an agreement with Book Data Ltd, which was intended to lead to improvements in both the quality of data and the coverage of the CIP programme.[4] Book Data's declared objective is to serve publishers, booksellers and institutional buyers — including libraries, with particular emphasis on the acquisitions function — by creating a database of very full descriptive records about titles currently available or about to be published.[5] By 1990 the list of participating publishers included some 900 imprints accounting for more than 25,000 titles a year.

The British Library has stated that from April 1991 it will cease to create CIP records from advance information supplied by publishers.[6] In order to continue providing this service, however, the Library intends, as an interim arrangement, to continue to buy in CIP records from Book Data Ltd.

[1] Cataloguing in publication : the new programme set to take off, *British Library Bibliographic Services Division newsletter* (33) Apr 1984 1.
[2] *The British National Bibliographic Service : bibliographies and bibliographic aids.* — London : British Library, 1990. 1.
[3] *Introducing the British National Bibliographic Service.* — London : British Library. [1989].
[4] Developments in the UK CIP programme, *British Library Bibliographic Services newsletter* (45) Feb 1988 3.
[5] Book Data : a progress report / David Martin, *Vine*, (73), Dec 1988. 24-6.
[6] *A new look for the British National Bibliography.* [London : British Library, 1990]. Publicity leaflet.

These records will meet the minimum data requirement of AACR 2 Level 1 with some enhancement. They will include Book Data subject headings and will be classified according to Dewey Decimal Classification abridged edition. CIP records will continue to appear in *BNB* approximately six weeks before the expected date of publication. They will appear in a separate classified sequence (see also p.192).

As soon as the book has been published and received by the British Library Copyright Receipt Office a full authoritative record will be created which will then reappear in the main sequence of the *BNB*.

Whitaker is to supply CIP data to the British Library as from 1992.

Where Book Data is concerned, OCLC is also to mount a Book Data file as part of its EPIC Reference Service.

Various surveys have been undertaken in order to evaluate CIP programmes. In the United States, for example, the Council on Library Resources gave the Library of Congress a grant of $11,000 in 1980 to enable it to find out what use is made of CIP data and to identify its problems and benefits. A random sample of libraries of all types across the US were selected to participate and the usage and impact of CIP data examined for three areas of library operation: acquisitions, cataloguing and public services. The results of this survey were published in 1984[1] and the overwhelming response was that there should be more titles in the CIP programme and that more publishers should take part (currently some 2,000 US publishers participate). CIP was found to be used widely in cataloguing, to various degrees in acquisitions, and at a lower level in public services.[2]

---

[1] *Final report on a survey of a Cataloging in Publication Program to the Library of Congress Cataloging in Publication Division* / Kathryn Mendenhall. — Washington : LC, 1984.
[2] A conversation with Judy McDermott / J. McDermott and J. Dwyer, *Technicalities* 3 (1) Jan 1983 3-5.

British Library Cataloguing in Publication Data

Hunter, Eric J
    Cataloguing.—2nd, rev, and expanded ed.
    1. Cataloguing
    I. Title   II. Bakewell, K.G.B.
    025.3   Z693
    ISBN 0-85157-358-4

CIP entry *for the previous edition of* Cataloguing

303.4 — SOCIAL CHANGE

303.4 *(DC20)* — Social change
Vago, Steven
    Social change / Steven Vago. — 2nd ed. — Englewood Cliffs, N.J. :
    Prentice Hall ; London : Prentice Hall International, c1989. — x,438p ;
    24cm
    Previous ed.: London : Holt Rinehart and Winston, 1980. — Includes bibliographies and
    index
    ISBN 0-13-815507-0 : £38.50
    1.Ti   B90-11441

303.482 *(DC19)* — International relations. Policies of governments
*Tinbergen, Jan
    World security and equity / Jan Tinbergen. — Aldershot : Elgar, 1990. —
    [143]p : ill ; 22cm
    Includes index
    ISBN 1-85278-187-4 : £25.00 : CIP entry (Apr.)
    1.Ti   B90-00369

303.4824047 *(DC20)* — Western Europe. Cultural relations with Eastern
Europe
    Europe speaks to Europe : international information flows between east and
    west Europe / edited by Jörg Becker and Tamas Szecskö ; preface by Willy
    Brandt. — Oxford : Published for KomTech by Pergamon, 1989. —
    xx,445p ; 24cm
    Conference proceedings. — Includes index
    ISBN 0-08-036758-5 : £47.50 : CIP rev.
    Primary classification 303.4824704
    1.Becker, Jörg 2.Szecskö, Tamás, 1933-   B89-32017

Three consecutive entries from the British National Bibliography *1990 showing: (1)
entry produced from actual item; (2) CIP entry produced from advance publisher's
information; (3) CIP revised entry when examination of CIP entry following
publication of book indicates that this entry requires amendment in significant areas.
Compare with new-style entries opposite.*

242

760.044442843 *(DC20)*
Murray, Hugh, *1932-*
York through the eyes of the artist / Hugh Murray, Sarah Riddick and Richard Green. — York : York City Art Gallery, 1990. — 174p : ill(some col.),maps24cm
Published to accompany an exhibition at the York City Art Gallery, York, 1990. — Bibliography: p163. - Includes index
ISBN 0-903281-10-4 (pbk) : No price
1.Ti 2.Riddick, Sarah 3.Green, Richard 4.York City Art Gallery 5.*Graphic arts. Special subjects. Cities* 6.*England*   B91-07373

760.0446 *(DC20)*
Jackson, Steve, *1951-*
The fighting fantasy poster book / Steve Jackson, Ian Livingstone. — Fantail, 1990. — 32p
ISBN 0-14-090220-1 (pbk) : £6.99 : CIP rev.
1.Ti 2.Livingstone, Ian, 1949- 3.Sr: Fighting fant°°v 4.*Graphic arts. Special subjects. Fantasy (Arts)*   B90-49386

New-look BNB *entries (as from 1991). Note the disappearance of the verbal feature following the classification number and the inclusion of a subject tracing at the foot of the entry*

Nicholson, Michael
A measure of danger. — *Collins. £15.50 : CIP entry (Feb.)*
070.433092   Issue 2119   ISBN 0-00-215386-6
Nicholson, Robert
Ancient Egypt / Robert Nicholson and Claire Watts. — *Two-Can Publishing (pbk). £2.99 : CIP entry (Feb.)*
932   Issue 2123   ISBN 1-85434-057-3
Nicholson, Sir Robin
Science and technology in the United Kingdom / Sir Robin Nicholson and Catherine M. Cunningham. — *Longman. £85.00 : CIP entry (Mar.)*
509.41   Issue 2123   ISBN 0-582-90051-4
Nicky, 1 2 3 [Falwell, Cathryn]. — *Gollancz. £3.99 : CIP entry (Apr.)*
428.6   Issue 2121   ISBN 0-575-05071-3
Nicol, Mike
A Good looking corpse. — *Secker & Warburg. £17.99 : CIP entry (Apr.)*
968.05   Issue 2123   ISBN 0-436-30986-6
†**Nicolai, Helmut**
Helmut Nicolai and Nazi ideology / Martyn Housden. — *Macmillan. £35.00 : CIP entry (Aug.)*
943.085   Issue 2120   ISBN 0-333-54299-1
Nicolaides, Phedon
The evolution of Japanese direct investment in Europe / by Phedon Nicolaides and Stephen Thomsen. — *Harvester Wheatsheaf. £35.00 : CIP entry (Mar.)*
332.6735204   Issue 2123   ISBN 0-7450-1084-9
Nicole, Christopher *1930- See also* Cade, Robin, *1930- ;* Grange, Peter, *1930- ;* Gray, Caroline, *1930- ;* Logan, Mark, *1930- ;* McKay, Simon, *1930- ;* Nicolson, C. R., *1930- ;* Nicolson, Christina, *1930- ;* York, Andrew, *1930-*
Nicole, Christopher, *1930- See also* Cade, Robin, *1930- ;* Grange, Peter, *1930- ;* Gray, Caroline, *1930- ;* Logan, Mark, *1930- ;* McKay, Simon, *1930- ;* Nicholson, C. R., *1930- ;* Nicholson, Christina, *1930- ;* Savage, Alan; York, Andrew, *1930-*

†**Nijinsky, Vaslav**, *1890-1950*
Nijinsky and Romola / byTamara Nijinsky. — *Bachman & Turner. £19.95 : CIP entry (Jan.)*
792.80922   Issue 2121   ISBN 0-85974-138-9
Vaslav Nijinsky / Peter Ostwald. — *Robson. £14.95 : CIP entry (Mar.)*
792.8092   Issue 2120   ISBN 0-86051-711-x
Nijinsky and Romola : a biography / byTamara Nijinsky. — *Bachman & Turner. £19.95 : CIP entry (Jan.)*
792.80922   Issue 2121   ISBN 0-85974-138-9
Niles, Douglas
Viperhand. — *Penguin Books (pbk). No Price : CIP entry (Mar.)*
823[F]   Issue 2119   ISBN 0-14-014373-4
Nilsson, John A.
How to establish a business overseas. — *Published in association with the Institute of Directors [by] Director Books. £25.00 : CIP entry (Mar.)*
658.11094   Issue 2119   ISBN 1-87055-528-7
Nimmo, Claude
The Collins paperback French dictionary / [by Pierre-Henri Cousin ...[et al.] ; [contributors Claude Nimmo, Vivian Marr]. — American language ed. — *Collins (pbk). No price*
443.21   Issue 2120   ISBN 0-00-433576-7
Nin, Anaïs, *1903-1977*
Delta of Venus. — *Penguin (pbk). £3.99 : CIP entry (Dec.)*
823.914[F]   Issue 2119   ISBN 0-14-014664-4
Little birds / Anaïs Nin. — *Penguin (pbk). £3.50 : CIP entry (Dec.)*
813.52[F]   Issue 2119   ISBN 0-14-014663-6
Nineteen eighty-four / George Orwell. — *Longman (pbk). £3.50 : CIP entry (Jan.)*
823.912[F]   Issue 2119   ISBN 0-582-06018-4
Nineteenth century short title catalogue. — *Avero* Series 2
Phase 1: 1816-1870
Vol 21: Hunt-Jero. £230.00 : CIP entry (Feb.)
011.221   Issue 2120   ISBN 0-907977-38-3

Entries from the new-style BNB *author/title index with entries under authors, titles, series and names which are appearing as subjects.* Entries in this latter category are marked with a dagger (†) for easy identification. The above extracts are from issue no. 2123 30 Jan. 1991

Limited cataloguing

If necessary economies are not achieved by a more scientific approach to cataloguing, the library may resort to some form of 'limited cataloguing', an expedient useful also for reducing cataloguing arrears and speeding up the cataloguing process and for reducing the bulk of the catalogue by eliminating unnecessary entries. The term 'limited cataloguing' is a generic one covering *simplified cataloguing* and *selective cataloguing*.

The most usual form of simplified cataloguing is the reduction of the descriptive element of the catalogue, such as the omission of all or part of the publication area or physical description area. Other possibilities include the simplification of author headings (e.g. using initials instead of full forenames) and the elimination of certain added entries (perhaps making no title entries). These limitations apply to the whole of the library's stock, whereas selective cataloguing involves the use of a variant form of cataloguing, usually a simplified form, for certain items, and/or the omission of a catalogue entry for some items.

Most libraries can practice some form of selective cataloguing with little inconvenience to their readers. There seems little point in cataloguing standard specifications, especially if a library takes all of them, since they are easily retrievable via published indexes; alternatively they can be given a subject entry but not an author entry. Similarly, libraries which receive all government publications may rely on the official indexes rather than cataloguing each item – though the quality of cataloguing and subject indexing in the official lists may not be satisfactory for the library. Where UK official publications are concerned, a catalogue is also available on CD-ROM (UKOP). This provides over 180,000 bibliographic records for official publications published since 1980. Such materials as town guides, trade catalogues and annual reports need not usually be catalogued as they may be regarded as 'self-indexing'. Some public libraries do not catalogue fiction, though many would consider this to be an undesirable economy.

The Library of Congress adopted a limited cataloguing policy between 1951 and 1963 when, in order to deal with arrears which had accumulated over the years, accessions were divided into four groups: material of primary importance, given full cataloguing; material of secondary importance, catalogued individually but briefly; groups of documents considered primarily of interest as groups; and items given form entry only.

Care should be taken that the costs saved by adopting a limited cataloguing policy are not offset by greater inconvenience to library users because of reference and readers' advisory staff having to consult a large number of different sources for information. It is interesting that LC ended its limited cataloguing policy in August 1963 following comments from card subscribers and others. We are back to cost-benefit analysis.

In 1987, the British Library, as part of a plan for future development, identified certain categories of material to receive 'AACR 2 Level 1' treatment, i.e. 'minimal level' cataloguing. These categories included modern English fiction (15%), children's literature (10%), science and technology (25%), material with 32 pages or less (9%) and religion (4%). With overlaps, these categories cover 50% of *BNB* MARC annual output and it was estimated that overall savings in record creation of 10% would be made.[1]

Catalogue maintenance

Catalogue maintenance is an important part of a cataloguer's responsibility. It is essential that new and revised entries are filed regularly and correctly; superseded entries are withdrawn; worn cards or sheaf slips are replaced; filing errors and other inconsistencies are rectified; obsolete subject headings are replaced; and new subheadings are created when there are a large number of entries under one subject heading. Nowadays, simple instructions to the computer can often deal with these points.

Guiding and publicity

An important aspect of catalogue maintenance is ensuring that library users are:
  a   aware that a catalogue is available
  b   instructed in its use as required
  c   given guidance *within* the catalogue as necessary.
The catalogue is one of the most expensive commodities in the library, so we should surely do all we can to ensure that it is exploited to its full potential.

The first priority is to make the library user aware that a catalogue exists and where it may be found. This can be achieved by a general library plan, publicity leaflets, directional, e.g. hanging, guides, and the positioning of the catalogue in a prominent place. The space-eating card catalogue has, in some large libraries, been relegated to a separate catalogue room. Many librarians have, however, rejected the idea of a separate 'centre' for computer-based catalogues and indexes; the aim being to integrate machine-readable and eye-readable sources. The OPAC is itself a useful means of publicity.

External guides (instructions on how to use the catalogue) may take various forms; for example, a printed sheet or booklet either dealing with the catalogue alone or as part of a general library guide, a printed notice displayed near the catalogue or an introductory section in a book catalogue. The purpose of such guides is not to explain the niceties of cataloguing but to show the user how the catalogue can help him/her to find information. Professional jargon should be avoided and the judicious use of examples can be far more effective than verbose descriptions. The guidelines should be: keep it simple, make it clear, ensure that it is attractive and has impact.

It is important that the contents of microfiches, card catalogue drawers, etc., are clearly indicated *and* that labels are changed as reorganization of the catalogue takes place.

---

[1] *Currency with coverage : the future development of the British National Bibliographic Service* / British Library. Bibliographic Services; — London : British Library, 1987. 2-3.

Internal guides — such as cards with protruding tabs in a card catalogue and headings at appropriate points in a book catalogue — act as 'signposts' within the catalogue. A classified card catalogue is improved if 'feature headings' (i.e. verbal translations of the class numbers) are used, as in the examples of entries from the *BNB* on p.242. In a card catalogue, different coloured cards could be used for different kinds of entries, e.g. author, subject, analytics.

In an online public-access catalogue there may be an initial screen containing general instructions on the use of the catalogue and further help screens dealing with specific features may be available as required at the touch of a key or upon typing 'Help' (see p.169). Some online catalogues have more than one mode to provide for both the uninitiated and the more experienced user. The interactive nature of the online catalogue can be utilized to provide clear guidance to the user and thus make it easier for required material to be located. Online tutorials are also a possibility.

Staff management

Communication is an essential feature of good staff management; staff must be kept informed of what is happening and why. Wherever possible some form of participative management is desirable, staff being involved in the decision-making process. One useful technique to employ is *management by exception*, whereby matters are dealt with according to precise instructions or well defined objectives and only exceptional issues are referred to senior management.

The setting of objectives is an integral part of the MBO technique described on p.232 and there continues to be interest in MBO in British libraries, although the number of published references to its application has been on the decline.[1] In the United States, however, 'academic libraries appear to have abandoned MBO in favour of Management Review and Analysis Program (MRAP)',[2] an approach which relies very heavily on *staff participation*. MRAP was initially designed for use in large research libraries in the US in response to a perceived need to respond positively to the new economic, personnel and external pressures of the 1970s. The focus is placed firmly on *management functions*: planning, budgeting, management information, policies, organization, staff development, supervision and leadership, personnel and communication . . . for example . . . MRAP is *not* concerned with appraising or even developing a plan but with improving the *procedures* for planning.[3]

---

[1] *Management information and decision support systems in libraries* / Peter Brophy. — Aldershot : Gower, 1986. 15.

[2] *Academic library management research : an evaluative review* / J. R. Brockman. — Loughborough : Centre for Library and Information Management, 1984.

[3] The Management Review and Analysis Program / Buckland, M.K. *Journal of academic librarianship* 1 (6) Jan 1976 4-5.

[2] and [3] *above are cited in: Management information and decision support systems, op. cit.*

ANY SEARCH MUST BEGIN WITH THE SCREEN DISPLAY "SOMMAIRE", TO
OBTAIN THIS SCREEN DISPLAY, TYPE SOM, THEN STRIKE ENVOI

Search by author

When ? Use the search by author when you want to find the books
published by one author or a corporate body.
Administrations, business firms, learned societies,
associations, universities, research centres, museums, etc.
as well as congresses (colloquia, symposia, conferences)
are considered as authors.

How ? Type 2, then ENVOI on the screen SOMMAIRE ; or type AUT,
then ENVOI on any other screen.
You will be asked for the author's name as soon as the
following screen appears. For an individual author, type in
the surname and then the given name. For a collective or
corporate authorship, type in the correct name (be sure to
give exact spelling and word order). Then type ENVOI.

For the procedure to follow next, see paragraph ANSWERS.

Search by title

When ? Use the search by title when you know the title (or the
beginning of the title) of the book or the periodical you
are looking for.

How ? Type 1, then ENVOI on the screen SOMMAIRE ; or type TIT,
then ENVOI on any screen.
You will be asked for the title as soon as the following
screen appears. Type in the title omitting the first word
if it is an article (e.g. "le", "la", "a", "an", "the",
etc.) ; then strike ENVOI.

For the procedure to follow next, see paragraph ANSWERS.

Search by author and title

When ? Use the search by author and title when you know the name
of the author and the beginning of the title of the book
you are interested in. It is recommended to use the search
by author and title for an author who has published many
books or when the title is not "significant" (such as
Traité, Oeuvres complètes, Poésie).

How ? Type 3, then ENVOI on the screen SOMMAIRE ; or type A-T,
then ENVOI on any screen.
On the two following screens, you will be asked for the
author's name and the title. Type the author's name first,
then the first word of the title, then ENVOI.

For the procedure to follow next, see paragraph ANSWERS.

Extract from User's guide *to online catalogue of the Bibliothèque
Nationale (which uses a Geac system)*

The library catalogue contains details of all the books, pamphlets, videos and other materials which the library stocks. The library staff are still in the process of entering all this information onto the library's IBM 6151 computer but you may use one of the terminals near the counter to find out what books the library has and where to find them on the shelves.

This is the screen you will use to search the catalogue book index.

Before you start your search always ensure that the bottom right and left windows are clear. If there is any information contained in these windows, please press Function Key 2 (F2) at the top of the keyboard. This will clear your screen and allow you to begin your search.

Select a search point from one of the following: WORD IN BOOK TITLE, AUTHOR OR SUBJECT then press <RETURN>. Once you select an option the computer is waiting for you to key in a search item.

Type a single word request and press <RETURN>. The computer will search for and display that word and other alphabetically close terms in a window on the bottom right hand side of the screen.

Use the cursor keys to highlight your desired term and press <RETURN>. it will then be copied to the bottom left hand window and

will give you the number of books which match that term.

In order to have a look at the books which match your search term, choose DISPLAY BOOKS option (F1) option on the menu and the computer will display a short form listing of all the books found. This information contains the book classification number, author, short title, location and it will tell you whether the book is on the shelf (S) on order (O) or on loan (L). This information will allow you to find the book(s) on shelf if they are not on loan.

If you wish to look at the full catalogue record for any of the books chosen in your search, move the cursor to highlight the relevant record and press <RETURN>. The full record will then be revealed. Press F10 to return to the short form listing.

Press F10 to return to the menu screen and press F2 to clear before beginning a new search.

Extract from St Helens College, UK, library guide: Investigating your library

In more general terms, MRAP can be seen as a method of introducing participatory management into a library, for analysing the library's functions and for providing a new framework for decision-making.[1] MRAP 'has been used in a considerable number of American libraries with, it must be said, very mixed results' and 'does not seem to have caught on outside the United States'.[2]

Staff participation becomes absolutely essential when a library is implementing an automated system. In Norway, for example, the relevant trade union became interested in finding out what effect computerization had on personnel. After interviewing staff who had recently experienced automation in their libraries, one of the major findings was that adequate training is a very important requisite and this training should include *staff participation* at all stages as the system develops.[3]

Lovecy tells us that 'the most damaging element for staff morale is rumour and speculation'.[4] From the initial consideration of possible automation, it is important to involve members of staff in discussions. 'This makes sense from all points of view since no librarian really wants to make a decision on whether or not to computerize without someone to discuss it with . . . the more staff that can be drawn in to the discussion at this early stage the better.'[5]

Good staff management is helped by the use of a *procedure manual*, which should ensure consistency without endless repetition of verbal instructions.

[1] *Management information and decision support systems in libraries. op. cit.*
[2] ibid. 16.
[3] *Computerized cataloguing* / Eric J. Hunter. — London : Bingley, 1985. 161.
[4] *Automating library procedures : a survivor's manual* / Ian Lovecy. — London : Library Association, 1984. 149.
[5] ibid.

Chapter 19

The computer, networks and cataloguing management

Increased use of the computer, and of networks such as BLCMP and OCLC, is bound to have an effect on the management of cataloguing. The benefits of a computerized cataloguing system are indisputable but a decision to automate or not to automate the catalogue will depend upon a great many factors, including:

Size and type of library
Staffing levels
Financial support
Computer availability

Computerizing the catalogue might be difficult, for example, in a small one-person library with very restricted financial provision and no access to any sort of computer. It is appreciated that some small libraries, unfortunately, cannot afford even an adequate book stock, let alone consider automation. On the other hand, a large academic library with considerable resources and, in all probability, access to a large mainframe computer might find it difficult to resist automation.

It is not unknown, however, in the case of the small library, for things to change overnight and if, for instance, a chance were suddenly offered to purchase a microcomputer system, as might happen in a school or college library, then the possibility of automation would have to be reviewed.

This is not, of course, to imply that the larger library will always find it easy to automate. A number of sizeable libraries, such as Liverpool City Libraries, continue to have to manage with manual catalogues (although Liverpool is currently implementing a BLCMP automated system).

Before adopting an automated system it is necessary to carry out a process of systems analysis, which means that the existing method of operation must be examined in order to ascertain whether computerization might lead to an improvement. Initially, objectives must be defined and a *feasibility study* undertaken.

The feasibility study will examine the various ways that the defined objectives might be achieved and it will look at the costs that might be incurred in relation to the benefit accrued (cost-benefit analysis). It will also investigate cost effectiveness in terms of manpower. If, for instance, a feasibility study concluded, as it did in one Australian library, that the cost of continuing with a manual cataloguing system would be $5,000 more, over a five-year period, than a computer MARC-based system and would take some 17,500 extra man hours over the same period,[1] then the obvious recommendation would be an automated system.

There are several options which a library planning to automate its catalogue might choose from:

to develop a completely independent in-house system

to purchase a turnkey package

to join a bibliographic utility or cooperative network.

Whichever of the above is selected, it may be possible to make use of a centralized cataloguing service such as MARC in some way. Indeed, it may be obligatory to do so as in the case of the bibliographic utilities. Turnkey packages may not cater for the MARC format and for the importing of MARC records but many do and, in some instances, two approaches to the creation of the cataloguing database are offered — MARC and non-MARC.

It should also be noted that the bibliographic utilities usually offer some form of standalone turnkey system. This may also permit remote access to and interaction with the central database.

There may well be, therefore, some overlap between options.

Independent in-house systems

The 'go-it-alone', completely independent in-house system can vary from a single microcomputer configuration to a sophisticated set-up with large mainframe-computer support. If in-house development is chosen, care should be taken to ensure that on-going back-up and maintenance are available and that enhancement will be possible as and when necessary. It is not unknown for an in-house system to grind to a halt as it grows and develops, owing to the lack of such facilities.

One library which preferred to use its own independent automated system was Derbyshire, UK, because it provided control over what to accept or reject, control over standards, and priority of access.

The prime example of an in-house development is probably that of the University of California's MELVYL catalog system, which is recognized as one of the most sophisticated and advanced public online cataloguing systems in existence.

---

[1] Feasibility study for an automated cataloguing system / Peter James and Pam Ray, *LASIE* 9 (4) Jan/Feb 1979 34-41.

However, the development of suitable software can be a tedious, time-consuming and costly business and many libraries will prefer to purchase a ready-made solution.

Turnkey packages

The 'turnkey' package (as easy as turning a key in a lock — no prior knowledge necessary) is a complete system. This may run on specific hardware (i.e. specific computers) or on a range of machines. Geac, for instance, with their GLIS (Geac Library Information System), manufacture the computer, write the software, supply the training, make the conversion and provide the maintenance. Alternatively, Geac's Advance system runs on a range of machines, including microcomputers, using the Pick operating system.

There are a vast number of such packages, varying from systems for large libraries which offer fully integrated functions to systems for smaller libraries with not, perhaps, so many facilities. However, there are now several fully integrated comprehensive library systems available for microcomputers which are functionally comparable with those for the larger machines.

Among the suppliers of larger systems are firms such as CLSI (Libs 100), Databasix (Adlib), Dynix (Dynix), Geac (GLIS and Advance), IBM (Dobis/Libis), McDonnell Douglas (Urica) and SCSS (Bookshelf). Typically, many of these systems will be fully integrated real-time systems and will offer a number of functions including: acquisitions, cataloguing and online public-access catalogues, circulation control, and serials control. Some suppliers have 'consolidated their systems and are now looking at other areas, e.g. extending access to the system and developing further communications facilities, providing CD-ROM interfaces, and developing image-processing systems'.[1] 'One significant development has been the links between acquisitions modules on local systems with databases maintained by the book trade. This is not only for downloading new publications but also for electronic transfer of orders, invoices, etc.'[2]

Because of the need to enter the standalone market and with the competition from commercial firms, the bibliographic utilities have also had to develop viable turnkey systems. Examples are OCLC's LS2000 and BLCMP's BLS.

Among the smaller systems that are available, one example is IME's TINlib, which is a fully integrated relational database management system. It will run on single-user microcomputers, networks, and minicomputers. It offers not only cataloguing but also similar facilities to larger systems such as acquisitions, circulation control and serials management. There are also data-import and export facilities and integrated thesaurus management. This system has proved particularly successful in the special library management area.

---

[1] The turnkey systems marketplace : ten years on, *Vine* (76) Nov 1989 3-8.
[2] ibid.

Another example is the GMC Library System, which claims to offer a low-cost/user-friendly alternative to the more formal systems designed for larger libraries. The system runs on any IBM PC compatible with hard disc and has the capability to handle a stock of up to 150,000 items. There are a number of low-cost systems on the market aimed at the small library, including the expanding school-library market.

Mention should be also be made of those packages which are not designed specifically for library use but which can be applied to many library operations, including cataloguing. Major examples are dBase (of which dBase IV is the latest version) and Cardbox-Plus. Evidence of the usefulness of these packages to libraries is supplied by the publication of such works as *101 uses of dBase in libraries*[1] and *Essential guide to dBase IV in libraries*[2] and there are many examples of applications in the professional periodical literature. Lazinger, for instance, describes the use of dBase for producing a Library of Congress subject headings authority list.[3]

It should be noted that a package need not cater for a complete cataloguing system. A variety of packages are available which can perform various of the constituent cataloguing functions. If, for instance, a library wishes to retain a manual card catalogue but wants some assistance in the production of cards, there is a great deal of software available. An example is RLibrary/Cards, which is available for various microcomputers and which was developed by a school librarian and her husband.[4] This will facilitate the printing of catalogue cards using Level 2 of *Anglo-American cataloguing rules*. Packages can also be acquired to download and reformat records from external bases, to produce bibliographies, and to provide subject indexes.

Some systems are designed to interface with other software, e.g. desktop publishing packages. Database Publisher, for example, from GTG Software, allows any DBF format database (many database management systems export files in this format) to be used in conjunction with publishing packages (e.g. Xerox Ventura Publisher or Aldus PageMaker) to produce documents such as catalogues.

The cost of a package will obviously vary enormously. Where the larger systems are concerned, CLSI hardware, for example, might cost anything from £30,000 to over £1,000,000 (c.$55,000 to $1,850,000) and the software £25,000 to over £150,000 (c.$46,000 to $280,000). The Geac Library Information System ranges in price from £50,000 (c.$92,500) to £200,000

---

[1] *101 uses of dBase in libraries* / edited by Lynne Hayman. — London : Meckler, 1990.
[2] *Essential guide to dBase IV in libraries* / Karl Beiser. — London : Meckler, 1990.
[3] Producing an LCSH authority list for special libraries with dBase / Susan S. Lazinger, *Electronic library* 8 (1) Feb 1990 8-14.
[4] Lloyd Konneker, 111 Innsbruck Drive, Clayton, NC 27520, US. Mackintosh version released 1989.

(c.$370,000). Dynix costs £35,000 (c.$65,000) upwards and the software from £12,000 (c.$22,000) for a cataloguing and circulation system to £50,000 (c.$92,500) for all modules on a large system. To these prices must be added maintenance costs which might be anything from $8-14\%$ of the purchase price per annum (for both hardware and software).

Coming down the price scale, the GMC system referred to above costs £879 (c.$1,600) and the TINlib system from £500 to £2,500 (c.$925 to $4,600). A suitable microcomputer for these systems could cost anything from £1,000 (c.$1,850) upwards. RLibrary/Cards cost $139 (c.£75) for the Macintosh microcomputer and there are simpler versions costing only $20-30 (c.£11-16) for both the Macintosh and other machines. Again suitable hardware is necessary.

At the bottom end of the market, a dedicated system designed specifically for use within school libraries is Library Catalogue, from Resource Sheffield L.E.A. This is intended for use with a BBC microcomputer. It will handle up to 950 books on the simpler version, which costs just £25.95 (c.$48).

There are various lists of available software. In general terms there is, for instance, *The software directory*, a comprehensive listing (over 36,000 records) of commercially available packages. This is accessible online via DIALOG. It is produced by the Black Box Corporation and corresponds to the print product of the same name. Also available via DIALOG are the *Business software database*, the *Buyer's guide to micro software (Soft)* and the *Microcomputer software guide*. Probably of more use to libraries are dedicated publications such as, in the UK, *Library systems : a buyer's guide*[1] and *A directory of library and information software for microcomputers.*[2] For those wishing to assess the capabilities, etc., of particular systems in more depth, there are both monographs and relevant articles in the professional periodical press.[3]

Acquiring a package

When considering the acquisition of a package, it is useful, if not essential, for the prospective purchaser to be able to assess its potential by actually seeing it in operation. A demonstration should be requested together with a list of the names of other users so that they may be approached for their views and opinions. More than one possibility should be examined in order to obtain some idea of operational and performance variations.

---

[1] *Library systems : a buyer's guide* / Juliet Leeves. — 2nd ed. — Aldershot : Gower, 1989.
[2] *A directory of library and information software for microcomputers* / Hilary Dyer and Alison Gunson. — 4th ed. — Aldershot : Gower, 1990.
[3] For example: *Dobis/Libis : a guide for librarians and systems managers* / Peter Brophy, *et al.* — Aldershot : Gower, 1990; Cairs-LMS : a library housekeeping system based on Cairs, *Vine* (74) Aug 1989 11-18; Tinlib : two applications / Marion Wilkes, Jim Basker, Carolyn Porter, *Vine* (78) May 1990 4-9.

When deciding which package is right for a particular institution's cataloguing needs, it is also helpful to follow a systematic procedure and to establish criteria by which the suitability of the package may be judged.

Factors which might be considered include: the record format to be used, including the number of fields, the maximum number of characters per field and the number of fields per record; the maximum number of records that the system will need to cater for; the ease with which records can be entered and amended; the way in which retrieval records can be displayed; whether multiple files can be created and interrelated; and the search facilities that will be required.

It is important to ascertain what performance will be like with the amount of data that the institution intends to store (search times, for instance, can increase alarmingly with some systems as files grow in size).

If it is intended to produce hard-copy output such as booklists, facilities for 'report' generation should be examined.

Where the larger, more sophisticated online public-access catalogues are concerned, Hildreth[1] identifies four functional areas which may be used to classify command capability and thus facilitate comparisons between systems. These areas are:

1 Operational control
2 Searching (including access points)
3 Output control
4 User assistance.

(1) includes not only logon and logoff procedures but the availability/non-availability of facilities such as editing (erasure and modification of input), stacking (entry of multiple commands at the one time), the 'saving' of search statements, and the interruption of online output. (2) includes possible search features such as free text, Boolean logic, truncation, etc. Access points could include author, title, author/title combined, subject, control number, ISBN, or other search terms. Where (3) is concerned, examples of possible features are choice of output format, browsing, sorting, and hard-copy printouts. (4) relates to the amount of help that can be obtained by the user, e.g. the listing of commands for review, the examination of index or thesaurus terms, the display of a search history, the explanation of system messages, or the use of 'tutorials' (instructional lessons provided by the system).

Requirements should be discussed with the supplier and an attempt made to ascertain how well the package meets them. Even the simplest of questions may be important.

In general, superfluous embellishments should be ignored; the emphasis should be on finding a package that will do the job efficiently and in a user-

---

[1] *Online public access catalogs : the user interface* / Charles R. Hildreth. — Dublin : OCLC, 1982.

friendly manner. It should be remembered that well written and easy-to-follow documentation is an essential requisite.

Networks

A library which opts to join a network may reap the benefit of advantages in terms of:
    efficiency
    productivity
    currency
    control
    costs.

The possible pitfalls of a lengthy 'go-it-alone' development will be avoided and greater efficiency should also be achieved by the economy of sharing, with communal facilities and files requiring a reduced input from the individual library. This in turn means increased productivity. Currency is more problematic but a cooperative effort should, in theory, mean a more up-to-date and comprehensive central database. Centralized cataloguing should also provide better quality and great consistency and hence control. Shared cataloguing, with input from a number of different agencies can, however, lead to difficulties where quality control is concerned. Whether quality control is affected or not, a further advantage of a cooperative network is the union catalogue which is usually a by-product.

Costs may not, of course, actually be reduced (owing to inflation, etc.) but the aim is to reduce the *rate of increase* in cost. Economies of staff may also be realized but this has not always been proved to be the case in practice and, indeed, it can be advantageous to redeploy staff, whenever possible, to tasks that personnel trained in cataloguing can usefully undertake, such as annotation and analysis, advisory work, guiding and display.

In the five years following the establishment of the OCLC online shared cataloguing system, the overall effect on the Ohio State University Library was considered to be a streamlining of processes, leading to greater efficiency and more bibliographical control.[1] Earlier, it had been concluded that OCLC allowed an increase in OSUL's cataloguing production, though unit costs rose slightly owing to inflation; had inflation not been a factor, there would have been a substantial decrease in unit costs.[2]

---

[1] OCLC at OSU : the effect of the adoption of OCLC on the management of technical services at a large academic library / D. Kaye Gapen and Ichiko T. Morita, *Library resources and technical services* 22 (1) Winter 1978 5-21.

[2] A cost analysis of the Ohio College Library Center on-line shared cataloging system in the Ohio State University Library / Ichiko T. Morita and D. Kaye Gapen, *Library resources and technical services* 21 (3) Summer 1977 286-302.

All of this sounds very attractive but the paramount concern must be the user. The key question to be asked is: 'Will membership of a network provide an improved *local* service?' Apart from the factors mentioned above, the local catalogue should be:

comprehensive in its coverage

simple to use and to understand

always readily accessible

adaptable to local needs.

With regard to comprehensiveness, clearly the larger the central base, the better for the participant, and it must also be possible to create in-house records for material not in this base.

Dobrovitz has suggested that the saving of cataloguing costs by accepting centralized cataloguing without regard to local needs, local emphasis, local terminology and local readers may, in the long run, result in a much higher expenditure of *time* by users.[1] Although he was referring to American systems being used in Australian libraries, the inference has general implications.

The network might reduce the rate of increase in costs but some libraries may prefer to stay independent for the attention to local requirement and flexibility which this provides. Indeed, De Gennaro has maintained that: 'One of the hard lessons we are learning from our experience in the 1970s is that cooperation is a difficult, time-consuming, and expensive way to do something, and results are frequently disappointing.'[2]

The principle of shared cataloguing upon which pioneering networks such as OCLC were originally based has therefore become less sacrosanct in recent years as the competition from other services which attempt to cater more specifically for local needs has increased: 'The interest, energy and resources that went into network building in the 1970's are now going into buying, and installing mini- and microcomputer-based local systems with particular emphasis on the local online catalog and retrospective conversion.[3]

Of course, as De Gennaro points out, these local systems have acquired or will acquire the capability to link with each other (and with other networks) for shared cataloguing and other purposes. Thus the spirit of cooperation will not die; the network will live on, albeit in a different form.

The essentially cooperative nature of membership of a network has been brought out by Pat Capewell in relation to Manchester Polytechnic Library: 'Manchester Polytechnic Library has a more efficient, more accurate, and decidedly faster system than before, in spite of an increased through-put.

---

[1] The future of original cataloguing and the Library of Congress / A. Dobrovitz, *Australian library journal* 20 (4) May 1971 16-19.

[2] Library automation and networking perspectives on three decades / Richard De Gennaro, *Library journal* 108 (7) 1 April 1983 629-35.

The system has demonstrated its flexibility and hospitality, and BLCMP has proved its responsiveness. And we have what was our ultimate in end-products, a union catalogue for all sites, and a better quality product ... What has BLCMP gained from Manchester Polytechnic's involvement? Hopefully we have given, and will continue to give, eager, active, enthusiastic support and participation in projects and groups; and, of course, constructive and thoughtful criticism.'[1]

To sum up, membership of a network can bring with it considerable benefits but it may also pose certain problems with regard to local user needs and the service provided may not live up to local expectations.

Retrospective conversion

A major problem in libraries which automate their catalogues has become the retrospective conversion of existing manual records. This could take many years and prove very costly. In the meantime, multiple catalogues, the 'closed' manual and the new automated, must be maintained. There is no complete, ready-made ideal answer and many libraries have to live with this situation.

There is a range of possible options available, including: keyboarding, either directly to an in-house database or via a bureau service; buying in records from an external source and in a recognized format; or using scanning techniques. The bibliographic utilities and networks (such as OCLC or BLCMP) all provide some form of retrospective conversion service. OCLC, for example, offers five different services. These range from an online customized service performed by OCLC staff, through an offline batch conversion performed partly by the library's own staff and partly by OCLC staff, to the library performing its own conversion using the OCLC cataloguing subsystem and online union catalogue.

The REMARC database (see also p.207) was, as the name suggests, specifically created to assist libraries with retrospective conversion. REMARC is now available on CD-ROM and databases on CD-ROM can, of course, also be of considerable help with conversion.

When translating one's own records more or less as they stand into machine-readable form, automatic scanning and conversion using optical character recognition would clearly offer considerable advantages. Firms such as Optiram/Libpac have made available such scanning facilities with customized format recognition to product output in MARC or any other required format. Incomplete cataloguing information and illegible or handwritten catalogue entries are obstacles but this new technology continues to evolve.

---

[1] The customer and the network : a customer's view of BLCMP / Pat Capewell, *Catalogue & index* (45) Summer 1977 5-7.

Ralls has provided an insight into retrospective conversion in a university library using BLAISE, SCOLCAP, OCLC, REMARC and Optiram/Libpac within a Geac-based system.[1]

---

[1] The evolution of a retroconversion / Marion Ralls, *Vine* (58) Mar 1985 31-8.

Chapter 20

Evaluating the index and cataloguing research

Catalogues, indexes and index languages need to be evaluated; such evaluation is an important part of the management process. It is necessary to examine such qualities as ease of use, cost, browsing facilities, whether the system is too time-consuming for the indexer and/or searcher, and how up to date it is. The importance of some of these qualities may vary in different in-house situations; browsing, for example, may be particularly important in a public library but irrelevant in some special libraries. Other factors, such as cost, are nearly always highly critical.

A further criterion that has become more important with the development of online access, is whether the user can interact with the system, modifying the search strategy continuously as he/she progresses according to the results obtained. Such an approach may be described as *heuristic*, as compared with the more time-consuming *iterative* method where the librarian performs the search in accordance with user requirement. The librarian then passes the results to the user who examines them and either accepts them or returns later with a modified query. The iterative approach is still used in many instances; for example, where the librarian/information officer performs an online search for a client in a database or databases which are available via a service such as DIALOG. The heuristic approach is, however, becoming more common as the number of OPACs increases.

One very interesting point in relation to online public-access catalogues is that it now becomes possible to examine the way in which the user makes use of the catalogue without the user being aware that he/she is being observed; i.e. by utilizing the inbuilt capabilities of the machine. Clearly this makes for a more realistic and unbiased analysis. It could be ascertained, for instance, how many searches had been made for a known item and how many for a subject.

Where computerized systems are concerned, *user-friendliness* (the ability of the automated system to allow interaction with a user without difficulty) is also very important.

When assessing the all-important quality of *efficiency*, it is usual to consider the information system's specificity, exhaustivity, recall and precision. These terms are defined and explained below.

Specificity is the degree to which an information system allows the exact subject to be specified. For example, an information system may cater for only the indexing of the general concept 'university education' without subdivision. It is impossible, therefore, to specify a subject such as 'the use of audio-visual aids in the teaching of mathematics in universities'. The system lacks *specificity*.

Exhaustivity is the extent to which the subject content of a document is analysed by the indexer. For example, a document dealing with different breeds of dogs could simply be indexed under 'dogs', but the indexing could be made more *exhaustive* if each individual breed, 'alsatian', 'boxer', 'dalmation', etc., were also indexed. This is known as *depth indexing*.

Recall is the amount of material or number of documents produced in answer to an enquiry which meet, that is, are relevant to, the requirements of the user. It could be considered that *recall* relates to the *total number* of documents retrieved, *whether relevant or irrelevant*. However, as explained here, recall relates only to those retrieved documents which are *relevant*. This would appear to agree with the general consensus of opinion amongst the major textbooks and also with the British Standard Institution's *Glossary of documentation terms* (BS5408:1976).[1] In this glossary, recall is defined as 'the retrieval of *required* documents of their records from an information store' (the italics are the present author's).

The *recall ratio* is the ratio between the total number of documents present in the collection that are relevant to an enquiry and the number of these actually retrieved by a search. For example, there may be 20 documents relevant to an enquiry in an information system of which 15 are retrieved by a search. The *recall ratio* is therefore 75%.

Precision is a measure of the relative efficiency of a system by a comparison of the number of *relevant* documents retrieved with the *total* number of documents, relevant or irrelevant, produced by the search. For example, referring to the example for recall, if there were, in fact, a further ten documents retrieved that were not relevant to the enquiry then the *precision ratio* would be:

$$\frac{15}{15 + 10} = 60\%$$

---

[1] A new edition of this standard is to be published in 1991. Apparently, 'recall' will no longer be defined but the 'recall ratio' will be defined as follows: 'In a retrieval system, the ratio of the number of relevant documents retrieved to the total number of relevant documents in the system database'.

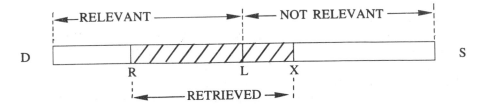

DS = Total number of documents in collection
DL = Total number of documents relevant to enquiry
RL = Total number of *relevant* documents retrieved by the search
RX = Total number of *all* documents retrieved by the search

The RECALL RATIO therefore $= \dfrac{RL}{DL}$

and the PRECISION RATIO $= \dfrac{RL}{RX}$

The terms are interrelated in that 'specificity' increases 'relevance' at the cost of 'recall' but 'exhaustivity' increases 'recall' and decreases 'relevance' (although each index term could be 'weighted', that is, allocated a number which would indicate *degree* of relevance).

Although these terms have been introduced only comparatively recently as a guide for testing the efficiency of systems, the underlying principles are far from new. It has long been apparent that 'specificity' increases 'relevance' but reduces 'recall', as the following example illustrates. If an enquirer asks for information on budgerigars and a search is made under that specific term, few documents will be produced but they will all be highly relevant. A search under the broader term 'cage birds' would obviously produce more items but these would not be so relevant and a search under the even wider term 'pets' would produce a great number of items but many of these would obviously not be relevant at all.

In recent times, especially since the advent of the computer, librarians and information workers have become more and more inclined to question whether existing information systems are the best that could be designed and to consider which of the existing systems, if any, best meet prescribed needs.

Various institutions, organizations, services and individuals have carried out important evaluations and tests, promoted investigation and research into various aspects of cataloguing and indexing systems, and looked at new, innovative ways in which cataloguing and indexing could be improved. There have been many examples of such work, some of which are described briefly below.

Cranfield Projects[1]

IN 1957 Aslib set up the first Cranfield Project, an investigation into the comparative efficiency of four subject-indexing systems, carried out at the College of Aeronautics, Cranfield (now Cranfield Institute of Technology). The four systems tested were an alphabetical subject catalogue using an authority list of subject headings; classified catalogues using the Universal decimal classification; a specially compiled faceted classification, and a post-coordinate system. The Project found that none of the indexing systems was significantly superior to the others. One interesting subsidiary finding was the fact that faulty indexing caused 60% of the failures to retrieve source documents!

The second Aslib-Cranfield Project was primarily intended to study the *methods* which might be employed to test the efficiency of various retrieval systems. Some of the results of this project were, to say the least, surprising. The most efficient system was found to be that using natural language single terms; the least effective system used concepts expressed in natural language terms. Control of synonyms and confounding of word endings improved the performance of natural language single terms, but any other method of vocabulary control did not.

Aberystwyth Projects

The College of Librarianship Wales began an investigation into indexing systems, supported by a grant from the Office for Scientific and Technical Information (now the British Library Research and Development Department) in 1968. Various types of indexing languages, including post-coordinate and faceted classification schemes were tested, using a collection of items in the fields of library science and documentation.[2] The conclusion reached was that the languages tested did not often exhibit significant differences in retrieval performance, effectiveness and efficiency, and no really large differences were observed. The uncontrolled languages tested performed overall just as well as the controlled languages. The basic result was, therefore, similar to the Cranfield Project in that no one system was found to be markedly better than any other.

One of the incidental discoveries of the above Project was that where single terms are concerned, it can be helpful to know the context in which the term is being used. This led to a further investigation, EPSILON, or the Evaluation

---

[1] The reports of the projects were published between 1960 and 1966; see also The Cranfield tests on index-language devices / Cyril W Cleverdon, *Aslib proceedings*, 19 (6), June 1967. 173-94.

[2] *Report of an information science index languages text* / E. Michael Keen and Jeremy A. Digger. – Aberystwyth : College of Librarianship Wales, 1972 – Part 1, Text – Part 2, Tables.

of Printed Subject Indexes by Laboratory investigatiON.[1] This study set out to construct, compare and evaluate a number of different kinds of printed subject indexes covering documents on library and information science. The types of indexes included chain procedure (as used in *British technology index*), articulated indexing (as used in *World textile abstracts*) and shunted indexing (as used in PRECIS).

EPSILON failed to separate, as far as performance was concerned, methods such as articulated indexing, PRECIS and KWAC (KeyWord and Context) but found that, in most of the measures used, chain procedure fell below the efficiency standard of other methods; although it could be brought up to the same standard if more time were spent upon it.

As an offshoot of the EPSILON project, the College of Librarianship Wales prepared a manual of practice on the production of subject indexes (MOPSI, see p.89).

MEDLARS

The MEDLARS evaluation study undertaken between 1966 and 1967 was the first major study of an operational rather than an experimental system.[2] This investigation, which was carried out in the United States at the National Library of Medicine, the National Institute of Health and three universities, looked at the needs of users as well as attempting to identify the factors which might affect the performance of an information system. There were a number of important practical developments arising from this study. Not least of these was MEDLINE, which arose from the conclusion that there was a need for improved user-system reaction and response time, thus pointing the way to an online system. Another example of a practical development is the modifications which have been made to MeSH (Medical Subject Headings), the controlled vocabulary used in the system, which was found to be the root cause of much inefficiency.

Centre for Bibliographic Management

The Centre for Bibliographic Management, which has been funded by the British Library Research and Development Department since 1977, evolved from early computer cataloguing activity at the University of Bath which led to particular concern with experimental catalogue research. It was established as the Bath University Programme of Catalogue Research, later became the Centre for Catalogue Research, and adopted its present name in November 1987: the word 'catalogue' had become too narrow to describe the breadth

---

[1] *On the performance of nine printed subject index entry types : a selective report of EPSILON* / E. Michael Keen. — Aberystwyth : College of Librarianship Wales, 1978.
[2] See: Medlars : report on the evaluation of its operating efficiency / F.W. Lancaster, *American documentation* 20 (2) April 1969 119-42; Medlars : a summary review and evaluation of three reports / Sidney L. Jackson, *Library resources and technical services* 14 (1) Winter 1970 109-21.

of activity with which the Centre has become involved. The advent of the OPAC has seen more and more of the related catalogue research and development work being done elsewhere and the Centre has always been concerned with the 'design' and 'management' of the data rather than with the technical development of systems.[1]

Matters that have been investigated by the Centre include the content and sources of catalogue data for local use, the impact of cataloguing-in-publication, the size and content of catalogue entries and the provision of subject access through keyword indexes. One example of an important research report issued by the Centre is *Full and short entry catalogues* in which it is claimed that 'short entry catalogues can satisfy the vast majority of users' present needs while providing substantial cost savings for the library'.[2] Publications consisting of papers presented at seminars and conferences organized by the Centre have included: *Keyword catalogues and the free language approach*[3] and a series of proceedings of conferences on 'Online public access to library files'.[4]

The Centre has monitored the 'hit rate' for UKMARC (i.e. the currency of records for cataloguing purposes) since 1980. Results are published in the Centre's *Newsletter*. During 1988, it was noted that the hit rate had risen significantly following the implementation by the British Library Bibliographic Services of the AACR 2 Level 1 (see p.34) and LC subject data omission proposals. CIP performance has made a considerable contribution to the steady increase in the hit rate over the past ten years. In 1990, academic libraries could expect a hit rate of over 80%, with the public library rate slightly lower.

BEDIS (Book Trade Electronic Data Interchange Standards Committee)
In the United Kingdom, as a consequence of a conference on electronic transfer standards in the book world organized by BNB Research in 1986, the MARC Users Group set up the Book Trade Electronic Data Interchange Standards Committee (BEDIS). In recent years the work of this Committee has continued under the umbrella of BTECC, the Book Trade Electronic Communications Committee.

BEDIS has produced certain recommendations which attempt to define the means by which 'the various players within the book community can

---

[1] *Newsletter* / Centre for Bibliographic Management (15) Mar 1988 1.

[2] *Full and short entry catalogues* / Alan Seal, Philip Bryant, Carolyn Hall. — Bath : University Library. Centre for Catalogue Research, 1982. iii.

[3] *Keyword catalogues and the free language approach* / edited by Philip Bryant. — Bath : University Library. Centre for Catalogue Research, 1985.

[4] *Online public access to library files: conference proceedings.* — Oxford : Elsevier, 1985, 1986 and 1988 (the latter entitled: *Influencing the system designer*).

communicate bibliographic and commercial information freely and effectively amongst one another.'[1] These recommendations include:

1 the identification of a range of data elements, 58 in all, that publishers are to be asked to make available to other users of bibliographic information. These elements have been prioritized into 'mandatory', 'highly desirable' and 'optional'. Mandatory elements have been defined as those elements necessary to make a meaningful identification of an item'

2 that software houses should be encouraged to provide UKMARC conversion packages and that the British Library should expand the UKMARC format to include those few bibliographic elements required by publishers but absent from the format.

'It remains to be seen, however, [whether the spirit of cooperation already engendered] can be translated into action'.[2]

OCLC Office of Research

OCLC research is 'focused on discovering practical solutions to the challenges that face the producers, providers and users of the world's information'.[3]
The OCLC Office of Research supports a wide range of projects, some of which are internal and others external and collaborative. The results are published in the OCLC *Research report series*.

The following titles are indicative of cataloguing-related research topics:
Bibliographic control and document architecture in hypermedia databases
Enhanced bibliographic retrieval
MARC UP : a prototype for improving retrospective conversion
Design principles for third-generation online public access catalogues : taking account of users and library use
Increasing the accessibility of the Library of Congress subject headings in online bibliographic systems.

User surveys − catalogues

There have been a number of surveys of catalogue use, both within specific library systems and nationally. The American Library Association's Cataloging and Classification Section commissioned a nationwide survey in 1958[4] and the UK Library Association Cataloguing and Indexing Group organized a survey of the use in catalogues in British libraries, which was carried out

---

[1] Book Trade Electronic Data Interchange Standards : the work of the BEDIS Committee, *Select : National Bibliographic Service newsletter* (1) Jun/Jul 1990 5-6.

[2] ibid.

[3] *Annual review of OCLC research, July 1988−June 1989.* — Dublin : OCLC, 1989.

[4] *Catalog use study : directors report* / Sidney L. Jackson ; edited by Vaclav Mostecky. — Chicago : American Library Association, 1958.

by the schools of librarianship between 1969 and 1971.[1] The latter was followed by regional studies, each of which concentrated on a specific aspect; for example, description and annotation, physical forms, guiding and classification.

Although now somewhat dated because of the major advances that catalogues have made in the intervening period, some of the results of these surveys are still of interest. For example, of the 3,252 library users participating in the British survey only 1,914 actually made use of the catalogue. Many of the respondents did not know that there *was* a catalogue, or, if they were aware of its existence, did not know how to use it. Quite a number of non-users stated that they could manage without the catalogue and some preferred to ask the staff. Little use was made of conventional bibliographical description but many users would have liked more contents notes and annotation, particularly indicating the content, scope and standard of the document. Subject catalogues were found to be particularly difficult for the uninitiated user to handle with confidence and there were suggestions that the class mark is not always a quick key to the location of an item in large libraries.

In 1981, the Council on Library Resources provided the funding to enable five organizations in the United States (J. Matthews & Associates, Library of Congress, OCLC, the Research Libraries Group (RLG) and the University of California's Division of Library Automation) to conduct a study of library users and online public-access catalogues. The major objectives were to produce comparable data on existing systems and to provide information for use in guiding the development of future online catalogues. Two types of data were collected:

a   information about the requirements of those who use online catalogues
b   information about the performance of existing OPACs in relation to user expectations.

Results began to flow from this massive study in mid-1982[2] and the full report was published in mid-1983.[3] One of the major findings was that there is great user satisfaction with this form of catalogue; 94% of all users in the survey preferred the online catalogue to the card catalogue. (The main transition in the US has been from card to online, the microform catalogue being largely bypassed. This contrasts sharply with the position in the UK.) One feature of other physical forms of catalogue that users apparently like to see in the online form is browsability (i.e. a facility for scanning a number of entries at once) and another major finding of the survey was that there is a need for a subject-access facility, something which not all OPACs provide.

---

[1] *UK catalogue use survey : a report* / A. Maltby. — London : Library Association, 1973.
[2] See, for example, The CLR public online catalog study: an overview / Douglas Ferguson *et al. Information technology and libraries* 1 (2) Jun 1982 84-97.
[3] *Using online catalogs : a nationwide survey* / edited by Joseph R. Matthews, Gary S. Lawrence and Douglas Ferguson. — New York : Neal-Schuman, 1983.

Follow-up studies have tended to confirm the above findings. For example, the University of Wyoming conducted a survey of online catalogue users in 1986. This was an adaptation of the Council on Library Resources study and the results were consistent with national findings, with very few exceptions.[1]

User surveys – PRECIS indexes

Liverpool Polytechnic has undertaken two surveys relating to PRECIS:
   a survey of reactions of indexers in all kinds of libraries[2]
   a study of user reactions.[3]

Of the 377 organizations responding to the first survey, 255 (67%) had given no thought to its adoption, and of the remaining 122, only 25 were actually using the system for indexing. The reasons quoted most often for rejecting PRECIS were its complexity and labour-intensiveness and it is interesting to note that the British Library is now simplifying the methodology (see below). Some indexers regarded the document-specificity of PRECIS and the open-endedness of its vocabulary as advantages, and others saw them as disadvantages.

The small number of organizations using PRECIS in their own systems is not, of course, an indication of the total number of users. Anyone who makes use of the British National Bibliography or of UKMARC (1971–90) for subject access (including those who access British Library files online) can be considered a PRECIS user.

In the PRECIS user study (a survey of users in 91 organizations), the main conclusion was that users generally reacted favourably; the document specificity was considered very useful. Users found the full subject statements more helpful than a string of terms, as in chain indexing, or broad subject headings, as in the Library of Congress subject headings. Some non-librarian users found this aspect of PRECIS particularly impressive. The ability of PRECIS to show relationships between terms was also appreciated.

The British Library is replacing PRECIS with a new subject system, COMPASS, as from 1991 (see p.63).

Automatic indexing

By removing the human intellectual element from indexing and allowing a machine, that is a computer, to select terms for index entries, a form of automatic indexing is obtained. Computerized 'keyword from title' indexes

[1] The University of Wyoming catalog survey / David A. Baldwin, Anne T. Ostrye, Diane W. Shelton, *Technical services quarterly* 5 (4) 1988 15-26.
[2] *A study of indexers' reactions to the PRECIS indexing system* / K.G.B. Bakewell with the assistance of J.M. Bibby, E.J. Hunter, V. de P. Roper. — Liverpool : Liverpool Polytechnic, Department of Library and Information Studies, 1978.
[3] *User reactions to PRECIS indexes* / Helen Jane Peters. — Liverpool : Liverpool Polytechnic, School of Librarianship and Information Studies, 1981.

are automatic to a degree, but is there any way in which a computer can be programmed to identify appropriate terms from the text of an item?

Initial attempts at automatic indexing were based upon determining, by statistical methods, the words which occur most frequently in a document (excluding common words). This method can be improved by comparing the number of times a particular word appears with the number of items it might be *expected* to appear. The advantage gained is immediately obvious; with the earlier technique a word occuring only a few times would be ignored but, using the latter method, the word might be proved to be very significant. Other experiments have concentrated upon the discovery that if words are 'paired' together in a document upon a number of occasions then this has an added significance.

In addition to the simple descriptors (words or word stems) which are normally used in automatic indexing systems, it has also been shown that it may be possible to improve the quality of such systems by the addition of more complex descriptors, for example phrases, and other techniques evolve around the selection of sentences. Sentences can be weighted according to predetermined measures of significance. Sentences with the highest weights are likely to be those which best summarize the subject content of an item. Examples of 'measures' are 'word frequency', as described above, and the *position* of a sentence — for example, the first sentence of a paragraph might be an important indication of the paragraph's subject content.

An automatic indexing system can be linked with a machine-based thesaurus to provide controlled language indexing.

Research into techniques such as those described above has continued over many years and operational systems have been devised. Some of these systems have been shown to possess a number of defects and inadequacies; others have been put to practical use and are claimed to be successful. For example, Thonssen describes an automatic indexing system (PRIMUS-IDX) which interfaces with an automatic thesaurus management program (INDEX) to enable large quantities of texts to be indexed quickly, consistently and cheaply.[1] The recent application of expert system technology (see below) should also be noted.

The overall objectives of research into automatic indexing can be said to be rather more than simply to represent the subject content of a document by index terms; it is possible to produce an automatic extract ('autoextract') which 'compares reasonably well with an abstract prepared by a skilled abstractor'.[2]

---

[1] Automatische Indexerierung und Schnittstellen zu Thesauri = Interfaces between automatic indexing and thesauri / Barbara Thonseen, *Nachrichten für Dokumentation* 39 (4) Aug 1988 227-30.

[2] *The subject approach to information* / A.C. Foskett. — 4th ed. — London : Bingley, 1982. 50.

The SMART project, which was developed in the United States by Salton, and which is sometimes referred to as Salton's Magical Automatic Retrieval of Text, is concerned with the effectiveness of computer-based retrieval systems relying entirely or almost entirely on machine processing of text.[1] Out of the early experiments evolved new techniques for the construction of computer-generated thesauri. The system could be used online and a comparison with MEDLARS proved that the SMART procedures worked well.[2] A detailed discussion is outside the scope of this work but it is, perhaps, worth recording that Salton came to the sweeping conclusion that there is little justification for maintaining controlled manual indexes.

Automatic classification

Allied to automatic indexing, although somewhat outside the scope of this present work, is automatic classification. At the Cambridge Language Research Unit, for instance, investigations spanning a number of years from the early 1960s were involved with the machine analysis of documents for the discovery of 'keywords' for indexing purposes. Attempts were made to construct automatically a classification of keywords based upon the way in which terms 'co-occur' in documents. Terms thus related are grouped together into 'clumps'; terms inside each clump have a stronger affinity with each other than with terms 'outside'. Using clumps alone did not lead to very satisfactory results and later experiments utilized four different kinds of group, the original 'clumps', together with 'strings', 'stars' and 'cliques'. A 'string', for example, is a set of terms in which each term is found to be most strongly associated with the one next to it.

This is 'clearly and indisputably a newer form of classification'[3] which may have far-reaching effects in the future. At present such work is still mainly at a theoretical level but there is a possibility that it could well improve the search capability in computerized databases to a marked degree.

Sparck Jones 'considers that the immediate prospects for operational automatic classification are "not bright", because of the failure to fully establish appropriate methods and applications, and the high cost of experiments'.[4] Yet she believes that large files need more sophisticated tools, such

---

[1] *Automatic information organization and retrieval* / Gerard Salton. — New York : London : McGraw-Hill, 1968; see also The evaluation of automatic retrieval procedures : selected test results using the SMART system / Gerard Salton, *American documentation* 16 (3) Jul 1965 209-22.

[2] *The subject approach to information* / A.C. Foskett. — 4th ed. — London : Bingley, 1982. 543.

[3] *Sayer's manual of classification for librarians* / Arthur Maltby. — 5th ed. — London : Deutsch, 1975. 324.

[4] Indexing languages : classification schemes and thesauri / J. Aitchison, *In Handbook of special librarianship and information work*. — 5th ed. / editor L.J. Anthony. — London : Aslib, 1982. 207-61.

as classification, and since automatic classification has not been conclusively shown to be unhelpful compared with human classification, its longer term prospects should be of interest to all concerned with information systems.

It is certainly possible that some form of classification, whether 'automatic' or not, 'built-in' to computerized databases could improve the search capability to a marked degree. It might, for instance, be feasible that a search on one term could be translated automatically into a search for other related coordinate or subordinate terms indicated by the classification. This could greatly improve the efficiency of the system. If, to take a simple example, an item dealing with the 'use of parachutes to stop ocean-going tankers' was searched for under 'parachutes' and 'ships', the automatic classification facility would reveal that 'tankers' was closely related to 'ships' and the relevant document would be retrieved.

Expert systems

Part of the British Computer Society's approved definition states that 'an expert system is regarded as the embodiment within a computer of a knowledge-based component from an expert skill in such a form that the system can offer intelligent advice or take an intelligent decision about a processing decision'.[1] In other words, an expert system is a computer program which can take the place of a human expert in some particular area of knowledge. As such, clearly there are possible applications within the cataloguing and indexing field.

For example, expert system techniques might be successfuly applied to the task of selecting index terms. One such system is that operated by the Central Abstracting and Indexing Service of the American Petroleum Institute (API-CAIS), which selects index terms from abstracts of articles appearing in the technical literature. A rule-based system has been created, using the API thesaurus as a base, which has been operational since 1985. The index terms selected by the computer are reviewed by a human index editor (as are the terms selected by CAIS's human indexers). After editing, the terms are used for printed indexes and for online computer searching.[2]

Other examples include L-IDIA (L-Intelligent Document Information Analyser), which is the central part of an expert system designed to analyse automatically the content of documents in natural language (relevant to well defined domains of knowledge)[3] and an expert system described by Gauch

---

[1] *Build your own expert system* / Chris Naylor. — 2nd ed. — Wilmslow : Sigma, 1987. 1.
[2] An expert system for machine-aided searching / Clara Martinez, John Lucey, Elliott Linder, *Journal of chemical information and computer sciences* 27 (4) Nov 1987 158-62.
[3] Rappresentazione della conoscenza e processi cognitivi in L-IDIA = Representation of knowledge and cognitive processes in L-IDIA / Gilberto Marzano, *L'Indicizzazione* 3 (w2) Jul-Dec 1988 30-45.

and Smith for searching in full-text.[1] Where the latter is concerned, an intelligent search intermediary helps end-users to locate relevant passages.

An obvious possibility is automatic cataloguing based upon a set of rules as embodied in a code such as AACR 2, and there have been several pieces of research aimed at achieving this. One example is the research carried out by James at the University of Exeter,[2] another is the work of Hjerppe at Linkoping University,[3] and an investigation into automated title-page cataloguing has been carried out under the direction of Weibel at OCLC.[4] However, 'for an expert system to generate the required conditions for a specifically designed goal, the logic in the knowledge base must be consistent. There have been problems in every attempt to convert AACR 2 into the highly structured rules necessary to run an expert system'.[5] Meador and Wittig conclude that this may well lead to further changes in the rules becuse the impact of technology will demand greater consistency. Apart from this, Weibel cites other unsolved problems as the incorporation of the cataloguer's general knowledge into the system, the complexity of the rules, and a lack of reliable data capture techniques.[6]

Switching languages

One of the problems that has exercised the minds of librarians over the years has been that of switching from one indexing language to another. Apart from direct one-to-one translation, there is the possibility of the use of having an intermediate neutral language designed to switch indexing decisions recorded in one indexing language into equivalent decisions in other languages. The intermediary should have the same coverage and specificity as the languages with which it is to be used and should be hospitable to index languages with different structures; that is, faceted or enumerative classification, thesauri or alphabetical word lists.

---

[1] An expert system for search in full-text / Susan Gauch, John B.B. Smith, *Information processing and management* 25 (30) 1989 253-63.

[2] Towards an expert system for cataloguing : some experiments based on AACR 2 / Roy Davies and Brian James, *Program* 18 (4) Oct 1984 283-97.

[3] *Artificial intelligence and cataloguing : building expert systems for simple choice of access points : results and revelations* / Roland Hjerppe and Birgitta Olander. — Linkoping : Linkoping University, Dept of Computer and Information Science, 1985.

[4] Automated title-page cataloging : a feasibility study / Stuart Weibel, *Information processing and management* 25 (2) 1989 187-203.

[5] Expert systems for automatic cataloging based on AACR 2 : a survey of research / Roy Meador III, Glenn R. Wittig, *Information technology and libraries* 7 (2) Jun 1988 166-72.

[6] Automated title-page cataloging / Stuart Weibel. *op. cit.*

Horsnell investigated the feasibility of a switching language in the field of information science. She reported that switching is possible and that overall recall and precision values for normal indexes and indexing obtained by switching are similar.[1]

Other developments in this area include work conducted under the auspices of UNISIST to provide an international switching language which could be applied to all publications to indicate the subject fields covered. The original intention was that this would be an intermediate language between two established languages,[2] for example:

German natural language – switching language – French natural language

but the eventual product was the *Broad system of ordering*.[3] This is a general classification scheme, with a fairly low level of specificity (as the title suggests). Although the scheme, which was the work of an FID (International Federation for Documentation)/BSO Panel, is intended for information exchange and switching, it is not a true switching language in the context of the criteria explained above.

Conclusion

It is right that we should investigate and attempt to evaluate indexing systems rather than take their performance for granted, but we should not be too surprised if the results of these investigations are sometimes inconclusive. Cleverdon wrote, when reporting on the second Cranfield investigations: 'As with Cranfield I, the outcome of this test is to raise more questions than it answers. It would be absurd for any organization to abandon conventional indexing and controlled index languages, whether thesauri or classification, on the basis of these test results. It would, to the author, seem equally absurd to aver that any system is operating at maximum efficiency unless a careful evaluation of the operational and economic characteristics of the system has been made'.[4] The final sentence is particularly important.

---

[1] *Intermediate lexicon for information science : final report* / Verina Horsnell. — London : Polytechnic of North London. School of Librarianship, 1974, and *Intermediate lexicon research project : phase 2* / Verina Horsnell and A. Merrett. — London : Polytechnic of North London. School of Librarianship, 1978.

[2] *Organising knowledge : an introduction to information retrieval* / Jennifer E. Rowley. — Aldershot : Gower, 1987. 201.

[3] *BSO : Broad System of Ordering : schedule and index.* — 3rd revision / prepared by the FID/BSO Panel (Eric Coates, Geoffrey Lloyd, Dusan Sumandl). — The Hague : FID, 1978.

[4] The Cranfield test on index language devices / Cyril Cleverdon, *Aslib proceedings* 19 (6) Jun 1967 173-94.

Chapter 21
Book indexing

Why study book indexing?

It is important for a librarian to know something about book indexing. He/she may one day have to compile an index — perhaps to a library guide or to some local publication — and will certainly have to use indexes when carrying out any form of reference or readers' advisory work.

But there is perhaps an even more important reason for cataloguers to be interested in book indexes. The Subject Access Project of Pauline Atherton and her colleagues at the School of Information Studies, Syracuse University, USA, carried out some years ago with the financial support of the Council on Library Resources, compared retrieval of books via keywords selected from contents tables or indexes with retrieval via MARC records.[1] The much higher success rate of the keywords was perhaps not surprising, in view of the greater depth of indexing made possible by using text words compared with conventional subject headings, and the potential of book indexes as the basis of online searches is obviously considerable, *provided the indexes are good enough*. The significant point is made in the report of the project that, as subject descriptions are merely *extracts* from each book, some effort must be made to improve the contents pages and indexes in books so that these extracts will be more content-bearing.

Other advantages claimed for BOOKS (the name given to the database generated from keywords) included less costly online searching than MARC searching and the ability to answer some queries which could not be answered using 'today's catalogue information'.

---

[1] *Books are for use : final report* / of the Subject Access Project to the Council on Library Resources. — Syracuse, N.Y. : Syracuse University, School of Information Studies, 1978 — Pauline Atherton, Director.

Some principles of book indexing

Just as a library catalogue is the key to a library's stock, so a book index unlocks the contents of a book. Without an index, a particular piece of information may be very difficult to find again. Many of the principles of cataloguing are equally relevant to book indexing — for example, how to establish headings for persons, corporate bodies and places, and how to arrange entries. Similar methods may also be used to establish subject headings. Chain indexing may, for example, be used either consciously or unconsciously: if pages 52 – 75 of a book deal with transport, pages 60 – 64 with rail transport and pages 65 – 69 with air transport, the following entries will suffice:

air transport 65 – 69
railways 60 – 64
transport 52 – 75

As with chain indexing, there is no need to subdivide 'transport' since the person who wants information about railways or air transport will find it when he reads 52 – 75 and may well find some of the other information there relevant to his needs.

Unlike in cataloguing, the indexer may not always be consistent in his use of spelling and terminology when indexing several books, because he will use the term or spelling preferred in the book; for example, he may use 'esthetics' and 'sidewalks' in the index to an American book but 'aesthetics' and 'pavements' in the index to a British book. He will, of course, use one term consistently in one book — regardless of what the author has done — and should always provide references from unused terms. As in alphabetical subject cataloguing, *see also* references should also be used to link related subjects.

See references should, however, be replaced by additional entries if it is just as economic to do so. For example, it is just as quick, more economical, and obviously more helpful to the reader to provide two entries

EEC 251
European Economic Community 251

rather than a cross-reference

EEC *see* European Economic Community

though many experienced indexers overlook this elementary fact. Obviously a cross-reference would be preferred if it avoided a great deal of unnecessary repetition:

EEC *see* European Economic Community
European Economic Community
  agricultural policy 252
  harmonization of qualifications 175
  prices 184

The indexes should always subdivide entries, on the lines of the 'European Economic Community' entry above, rather than make strings of page references. Most indexers agree that subdivision should be considered as soon as there are six page references.

It must be remembered that an index is not a concordance: it is just as bad to over-index as to under-index, because such a practice leads to a proliferation of unnecessary and unhelpful entries, and a term should not be indexed simply because it is *mentioned*. For example, chapter 13 of Randolph S. Churchill's *The young Churchill* (Sphere Books, 1972) begins: 'On his arrival in London from Cairo at the end of April Churchill decided to get on with the battle of life as quickly as possible'. This tells us nothing about London (except that Churchill had arrived there) or Cairo (except that Churchill had left there) and we would not index either place. The indexer of the book agreed with us in the case of Cairo but not in the case of London. Correctly, he/she provided index entries under Cairo to pages 228, 232 and 256 − 7, all of which contained information about Churchill's activities in Cairo. Clearly there should be no index entries under 'Battle of life' or 'Life, battle of', though we have known books which have provided this kind of entry.

Guiding the index

Just as a catalogue needs to be guided, so a book index usually needs a prefatory note (however short) to explain the arrangement, inclusions and omissions, and any special features. Many indexes do not, unfortunately have such a note: an analysis of 113 indexes, as part of the Subject Access Project referred to above, showed that 91% of the indexes lacked an introductory note and one of the recommendations was that such 'scope' notes should always be provided.[1]

The computer and book indexing

A number of computer programs are now available which aim to assist in the compilation of indexes to books and periodicals. The indexer can work through a manuscript, a printed proof or an already completed book, selecting appropriate terms from the text for inclusion in the index but, instead of entering these on cards or slips ready for editing, sorting, etc., the terms are input directly to the computer. The computer will then automatically carry out the necessary manipulation, merging and sorting of the entries to produce the final index.

---

[1] Characteristics of book indexes for subject retrieval in the humanities and social sciences / Bonnie Gratch, Barbara Settel and Pauline Atherton, *The indexer*, 11 (1), April 1978. 14-23.

Manipulations which will be necessary include 'flipping', 'half-flipping', 'yanking' and 'rotating'. For example, the entry:

hopscotch, marathons 188

could be 'flipped' to give the additional entry:

marathons, hopscotch 188

The 'half-flip' makes a new entry from the subheading of an entry, e.g.:

United States, networks 68

could be 'half-flipped' to give the entry:

networks 68

A 'yank' feature permits any heading or subheading to be 'yanked' into another entry. Take, for example, the following entry:

grasshoppers, feeding habits 25

The heading 'grasshoppers' could be 'yanked' from this entry and the subheading 'jumping records 36' added to give the new entry:

grasshoppers, jumping records 36

'Rotating' allows headings and subheadings within an entry to be rotated, for example, the entry:

peeling, records, onions 190

could be rotated by the computer to give the additional entries:

records, onions, peeling 190

and:

onions, peeling, records 190

Different programs may refer to the above operations by different names; those used here are taken from the instructions for the computer indexing program MACREX (Version 3.1).[1] In this instance, the indexer indicates which type of manipulation is required by the use of particular function keys.

Examples of other facilities which must be provided are those for the production of see and see also references, for the ignoring of articles or other character strings when sorting, for distinguishing between subheadings and inversions (e.g. between 'salmon, spawning' and 'Salmon, John'). Such facilities are provided for by inputting entries in specified formats.

---

[1] *MACREX : a computer program to assist in the compilation of large and small indexes to books and periodicals* / written by Hilary and Drusilla Calvert. — PC/MSDOS version 3.1. — London : Calvert, 1987.

For example, the entry:

{The }War of the worlds 86-7

would, with MACREX, print as 'The War of the worlds' but file under 'War
. . . .'.

Entries can be displayed on the screen at any time for editing (deletion, amendment, etc.) The index may be alphabetized in either letter-by-letter or word-by-word order. MACREX allows a choice to be made. When the indexing is complete, the index will be printed out in page form.

If the indexing is done before page proofs are ready, the page numbers of the manuscript can be used initially and later converted to the page numbers of the printed text.

It may be possible to use a word processor or text editor for the inputting of the entries and then to transfer these entries to the indexing program for formatting, editing and sorting. Some word processing systems provide automatic index generators. An example is Wordstar, which allows the user to mark words and/or phrases in a document for use as index entries and to add descriptive text to these entries if required.[1] A separate index file is subsequently created and this file can then be loaded into Wordstar for perusal and amendment if necessary.

Guides for indexers

The British Standards Institution has published a very useful guide to the preparation of book indexes, *British Standard recommendations for preparing indexes to books, periodicals and other documents*, which is now in its third edition.[2] In the United States there is the USA standard *Basic criteria for indexes.*[3]

A body which has done a great deal to raise the standard of indexes and the status of indexers is the Society of Indexers, which was formally constituted, in the UK, in 1957. The first edition of the British Standard on indexing was produced largely on the initiative of the Society and one of the Society's other major achievements has been the regular publication, since 1958, of a twice-yearly journal, *The indexer*. The Society has actively encouraged the use of new technology for the production of indexes and its newsletter *Microindexer* provides appropriate practical advice. The production of a series of Open Learning units is in process of which five have been published to date (*Training in indexing* Units 1−5).

---

[1] *Using Wordstar Versions 5, 5.5 and 6* / Alan Balfe. — 2nd ed. — Heinemann Newtech, 1990. 218-21.

[2] *British Standard recommendations for preparing indexes to books, periodicals and other documents*. — [Rev. ed.]. — London : British Standards Institution, 1988. — (BS 3700 : 1988).

[3] *Basic criteria for indexes*. — Rev. ed. — New York : American National Standards Institute, 1974. — (USAS Z39.4-1974). Consideration is apparently being given to the preparation of a new edition of this standard.

The indexer is now the official journal of four societies, viz: the Society of Indexers; the American Society of Indexers (formed in 1968 and affiliated to the British Society in 1971); the Australian Society of Indexers (formed in 1976); and the Indexing and Abstracting Society of Canada/Société canadiènne pour l'analyse de documents (formed in 1971).

There are several good textbooks on book indexing. Two authoritative works presently in process of publication are those by Mulvany and Wellisch.[1] *Indexing, The art of*, by Knight[2] and *Book indexing*, by Anderson,[3] can also be recommended.

---

[1] The book by Nancy Mulvany is to be published by Chicago University Press and that by Hans Wellisch, *Indexing from A to Z*, by H.W. Wilson.

[2] *Indexing, The art of* / G. Norman Knight. — London : Allen & Unwin, 1979.

[3] *Book indexing* / M.D. Anderson. — Cambridge : University Press, 1971.

Final note — towards the year 2000

The reader will have perceived that, even as this book was being written, important local, national and international initiatives were being planned and implemented. Events are happening at such speed that it is becoming more and more difficult for the librarian to keep up with the pace of technical and organizational developments.

What can be said with some certainty is that more and more libraries across the world will implement online public-access catalogues. The OPAC, supplemented by remote online access to other services for the location and downloading of information and records, is a very powerful tool. Further, the catalogue must no longer be viewed as a separate entity but as an essential component of an integrated system. It should be linked to circulation control and acquisitions so that the user can be provided with current personal and general loan-status information, be informed of the latest additions to stock, and ascertain not only whether an item is available but when it will become available. As an extension, it should also be possible for the user to transmit automatically a request for an item onwards to other libraries and information centres, or even to publishers and booksellers. Electronic messaging and facsimile transmission are already in use for interlending and other purposes. Electronic order transmission is available to some extent and is expanding rapidly.

The user will also expect that the terminal that provides him/her with catalogue access will also provide access to other services. Such services may be provided by in-house or remote hosts. 'Catalogues will be the bibliographic component of a complex of interacting systems linked and presented to their users by sophisticated interface programs which will appear to the user of the systems to constitute one system'.[1]

It is already possible to access many OPACs remotely, even, if appropriate equipment and telecommunications links are available, from the comfort of one's own fireside. This will become more common and such access can be non-stop 24-hour access, seven days a week.

Further technical improvements to OPACs can be expected; for example, more effective search facilities and enhancements to the user interface and display screens, perhaps with the help of hypertext systems. At an 'OPAC 2000' seminar in November, 1990, it was felt that emphasis has not always been given to what *users* want, with interfaces remaining librarian orientated.[2]

---

[1] Technical services, 1984–2001 (and before) / Michael Gorman, *Technical services quarterly* 1 (1/2) Fall/Winter 1983 65-71.
[2] *Vine* (81) Dec 1990 3.

The use of CD-ROM will also expand. Suppliers of turnkey cataloguing systems are now able to provide interfaces with CD-ROM services such as the *BNB* on CD-ROM. Complete system supply has already partially replaced centralized record supply. CD-ROM, with its vast storage capacity, is facilitating online full-text retrieval and advancements in optical disc technology will continue to improve the medium. It is already possible to integrate text, graphics and sound on a CD-ROM and output it through a personal computer and 'the same principal and technique used to add audio to CD-ROM is now being further extended to incorporate video as well'.[1] CD-I (CD-ROM Interactive) is already with us. Thus CD-ROM is becoming a multimedia facility. Where telecommunication links are a problem, CD-ROM has particular advantages and the medium therefore offers considerable potential in less-developed countries.

One of the major disadvantages of CD-ROM is that the user cannot add information to the disc. WORM (Write Once Read Many times) and eraseable/rewriteable discs are available but, currently, CD-ROM is the predominant optical-disc format used for catalogues. WORM discs have been used for document filing systems and some organizations have experimented with eraseable-rewriteable discs. The Home Office, UK, for example, has used rewriteable-disc technology for the 'backing-up' of large databases.[2] As rewriteable discs become less expensive and more readily available they will certainly have an effect on catalogues and cataloguing.

Where record supply is concerned, it may well be that, in the future, publishers will generate basic records which will include not only fields the publishers themselves require but additional data elements. These records will then be made available to other users of bibliographic information.

The computer will continue to decrease in size; it will become faster and more powerful as the design of circuitry gets ever more sophisticated; it will become more user-friendly. Links between computers will be more efficient and data will be passed from point to point at higher speeds. All of this will have an effect on library catalogues.

There is no doubt that this is an exciting, changing, challenging time to be a cataloguer. If we want quality systems meeting exacting standards, we have to take a more active role. 'We should not be satisfied with anything less than the best.'[3]

---

[1] CD-ROM publishing, *Business systems and equipment* Nov 1989 60.
[2] Rewriteable optical disks trial at the Home Office, Bootle / Bernard Williams, *Information media and technology* 23 (3) May 1990 107-8.
[3] *Vine* (81) Dec 1990 3.

Index

This index is arranged according to the *BLAISE filing rules*.

The abbreviation 'def.' preceding a page number refers to a definition of the term indexed.

The abbreviation 'e', 'p' or 'r' following a page number indicates an extract, a photographic illustration or a reproduction, except for reproductions of computer screens which are indexed as 'sample screens'. Other illustrations and diagrams are treated as part of the text and no specific reference is made.

The abbreviation 'b' following a page number indicates an entry for a work referred to in the text. These are normally entered under the responsible person or body, except where AACR 2 specifies main entry under title.

287

punched cards: catalogue production
123
punctuation pattern of AACR 2 35
punctuation symbols: filing 115
Putnam, Herbert 8−9

query languages: def. xxv
quick searches: OPACs 176, 178
Quinly, William J. 26

Ralls, Marion 259
Ranganathan, S. R. 10−11,
  12−13, 88
  Colon classification 56
Rather, John C. 113b
Ray, Pam 251b
real time: def. xxv
realia: examples (AACR 2) 51
recall ratio 261−2
recall: def. xxvi, 261−2
records: def. xxvi, 132−57
references
  AACR 2 36, 42−3
  alphabetical subject catalogues
    71−8
  book-indexing 275
  Current technology index 89
  def. xxvi
  filing 119
  in lieu of added entries 43
  PRECIS 60
related works: def. xxvi, 38
relational databases: def. xxvi
relational operators: def. xxvi, 168
relative indexes 56, 81
relevance 261−2
REMARC 207, 211, 258−9
remote access: def. xxvi
report formats *see* display formats
Research Libraries Group 205, 267
Research Libraries Information
  Network 205−6
response time: def. xxvi
responsibility, statements of: def.
  xxvi, 33, 35
  examples 44−52
retrospective conversion 207,
  258−9
Reyes, Caroline 76b

Richmond, Phyllis A. 61b
RLG 205, 267
RLibrary Cards 253, 254
RLIN 205−6
Roberts, Winston D. 141b
role operators (PRECIS) 59−60
roles (post-coordinate indexing) 95
Root thesaurus 18−19, 101
Roper, Vincent de P. 268b
Rosenthal, Joseph A. 238b
rotated indexing 85−6
  book indexing 277
Rovira, Carmen 76b
Rowbottom, Mary 155b
Rowley, Jennifer E. 273b
Royal Library (Netherlands) 225
Royal Library (Sweden) 227
RTECS 214

sacred scriptures 38
Saffady, William 204b
Salton, Gerard 270
Sayers, W. C. Berwick 270b
'scatter' 107
Scofield, J. L. 234b
Science citation index 90
SCOLCAP 219−20
SCONUL 220
scope notes
  book indexes 276
  def. xxvi
  LCSH 73−4
  thesauri 100
SCORPIO 208
Scottish Libraries Cooperative
  Automation Project 219−20
SCSS 252
SDC 210
Seal, Alan 131b, 208b
searching
  Boolean logic 95−8, 167−8
  CD-ROM 156−7
  classified catalogues 55
  DIALOG 212−3
  dictionary catalogues 78
  keyboard-free terminals 130
  offline systems 158−60
  online systems 145, 161−9
  OPACs 170−89

302

VINE xi
Virginia Tech Library System 219
VISCOUNT 218
visible indexes 121, 127
visual display units: def. xxvii
vocabulary control 149−50
voluminous authors: filing 109−10
VTLS 219

WADEX 69
Wales. College of Librarianship
  87, 263−4
Wales. University College *see*
  University College, Wales
Walker, Stephen 108b
Washington Library Network *see*
  WLN
Wath, Nancy V. de 233b
Wayne State University 207
Weibel, Stuart 272b
weighting: automatic indexing 262
Weihs, Jean Riddle 26, 238b
Wellisch, Hans B. 279b
Western Library Network *see* WLN
Wheatley, Alan 89
Whitaker (J. and Sons) 241
  database 215
Wild card characters 167

Wilkes, Marian 254b
Williams, Bernard 281
Wilson library bulletin xi
windows 195
Winkler, Paul W. 29b
Witten, Anita 29b
Wittig, Glenn R. 272b
WLN 155−7, 204−5, 224
Word and Author Index 69
word by word filing 114−15
word frequency 269
word processors
  def. xxvii
  incorporated in database manage-
    ment system 144
  uses in book indexing 277
workflow 235−6
Wordstar 278
World textile abstracts 264
WORM: optical discs 281

Xerography: catalogue production
  123
Xerox Ventura 253

yanking entries: book indexing
  277
York Monastic Library 5